Larry Dierker

MY TEAM

Choosing My Dream Team from My Forty Years in Baseball

SIMON & SCHUSTER PAPERBACKS

New York   London   Toronto   Sydney

SIMON & SCHUSTER PAPERBACKS
Rockefeller Center
1230 Avenue of the Americas
New York, NY 10020

First Simon & Schuster paperback edition 2007

SIMON & SCHUSTER PAPERBACKS and colophon are registered trademarks of
Simon & Schuster, Inc.

For information about special discounts for bulk purchases,
please contact Simon & Schuster Special Sales at
1-800-456-6798 or business@simonandschuster.com.

Designed by Karolina Harris

Manufactured in the United States of America

10   9   8   7   6   5   4   3   2

Library of Congress Cataloging-in-Publication Data

Dierker, Larry.
    My team : choosing my dream team from my forty years in baseball / Larry Dierker.
        p.   cm.
    Includes index.
        1. Baseball players—United States—Biography. 2. Baseball players—United
    States—Statistics. 3. Baseball players—Rating of—United States. I. Title.
    GV865.A1.D54 2006
    796.357092'2—dc22   200644292
    [B]

ISBN 978-0-7432-7514-9

*To the best coach in our family, my mother,
Marilynn, who had me reading, writing, and
tying shoes before I got into kindergarten. She
also won city high school championships in girls'
swimming and gymnastics in Los Angeles.*

Contents

Introduction   *Twenty-Five Good Men*   *1*

1   *Catcher*   *25*

2   *First Base*   *41*

3   *Second Base*   *61*

4   *Third Base*   *71*

5   *Shortstop*   *85*

6   *Left Field*   *101*

7   *Center Field*   *117*

8   *Right Field*   *129*

9   *Starting Pitcher*   *143*

10   *Relief Pitcher*   *183*

11   *The Underdogs*   *201*

12   *Lineups*   *227*

Acknowledgments   *263*

Index   *265*

Introduction

Twenty-Five Good Men

 FOR MANY YEARS, avid baseball fans engaged in what were called "hot-stove league" sessions. These meetings were nothing more than informal fan forums. Each fan would express an opinion on such topics as which players were the most valuable, which league was the best, which pitcher had the best fastball or curve, and anything else that might come up. Is Pedro Martinez as good as Bob Gibson was? These meetings still happen, but sometimes there is no meeting place except a website. SABR (The Society for American Baseball Research) meetings are sometimes held without a human voice. Each member (known as a *sabermetrician*) participates on the web whenever it is convenient. It's a far cry from sitting around a hot stove during the winter.

Sometimes, a group of friends or fans would start what is called a Rotisserie League under an agreed-upon set of rules for drafting players and allotting points for each player's accomplishments. This became popular and, as you might expect, a lot of folks started gambling on the outcome. Now, it isn't necessary to organize anything. You can sign up for a league and its website will put you on a team and keep score. The broadcasters and writers for almost every team form a league each year and put a bob or two on the outcome, so the badinage continues throughout the summer in the press box.

When I was an eighteen-year-old rookie, I participated in what amounted to a traveling hot-stove league with the Astros. It was called a press caravan, but it was more like a medicine show. Several of us Astros players traveled through Texas and Louisiana in January to get the outer-market cities primed for the upcoming season. Our goal was to get a bunch of somnolent Lions Club members to come to a few ball games in Houston. So what if we were a last place team, an expansion team with no real chance to win a pennant? We still needed fans. One time, in Tyler, Texas, I spotted a guy snoozing through our speeches. I couldn't blame him. We were not the best players and we were even worse speakers.

But even a middling, cellar-dwelling player was important to a few of the attendees. Real baseball fans are everywhere, even in the remote Piney Woods of East Texas. We always took questions from these folks at the end of our spiel. Oftentimes I was asked what it was like to face Willie McCovey or Pete Rose. Sometimes, we were asked to predict who would win the pennant or offer an opinion on who was the best hitter, Willie Mays or Hank Aaron. On the bus, between cities, we talked about these things ourselves. Each year there was another caravan, offering more hot-stove-type sessions. I loved them.

About halfway through my thirteen-year pitching career, we stopped going on these PR trips. I was tired of them at that point anyway. When we cranked them up again in the 1980s, I was halfway through my broadcasting career. As a broadcaster I was the MC of these events, then became the featured speaker when I took over as manager in 1997. I managed the Astros from '97 to 2001 and we won our division in four of those five years, which made it a lot easier to promote the team.

After a few years in the broadcast booth, I started writing a column for the *Houston Chronicle*. Many fans told me they enjoyed reading it, and a few asked when I was going to write a book. "When I retire," I said. Well, I retired in 2001 and wrote *This Ain't Brain Surgery* about things I had done during my baseball career in Houston. Now, I am back in the booth, and have done just about everything you can do in professional baseball. I have pitched, sold tickets, broadcast, and managed. I have been involved in the building of the team, working with the general manager on free agent signing and trade opportunities. This was no hot-stove baloney. This was the real thing.

So I got to thinking about my own all-time team. I wondered if I could come up with twenty-five guys who would be practically unbeatable. I jotted down a few names. Then I compared them.

During the off-season, I usually do a few radio shows for the Astros. They have a weekly show called *Astroline*. And, of course, the local sports talk shows always want a guest when something big happens in the off-season. One thing that almost always comes up is an analysis of who are the best players at each position in the history of the sport. As much as I know, I don't feel comfortable comparing Ty Cobb to Ken Griffey Jr. or Alex Rodriguez to Honus Wagner. I do think I can compare Griffey with Willie Mays, however. And those two guys span more than fifty years of the sport. I started thinking about the best ballplayers I have ever seen and decided to pick my all-time team—that's how this ball got rolling. Before it stopped, I had to consider how many players and pitchers to select and how to arrange them. I thought it would be easy to write about the guys I have seen. All I'd have to do is look at the hitting statistics and consider the fielding, running, and throwing, based

on firsthand knowledge. I knew this would lead to some de-
bate, but I thought I could select a team that would be almost
impossible to beat. This was my first mistake.

In reality, there is always another team that can beat you.
Put the American League All-Stars of the sixties up against
Sandy Koufax in his prime and they might not be able to score
a run. No matter which pitchers I choose, there will be many
whom I do not choose who could beat my guys on any given
day! Who was the best pitcher, Juan Marichal or Jim Palmer? If I
choose Barry Bonds and Frank Robinson as my left fielders,
Billy Williams or Rickey Henderson could be the star of the
game for the other team. I am living proof that any good
pitcher can beat any team on a given day. Though I didn't even
come close to posting Hall of Fame numbers, I did beat Koufax,
Juan Marichal, Gaylord Perry, Phil Niekro, Tom Seaver, Bob
Gibson, Steve Carlton, Don Sutton, Nolan Ryan, Fergie Jenkins
—Hall of Famers all—and a few other good pitchers who did
not make it to Cooperstown. I supposed, starting out, that I
could field a team that would win maybe 80 percent of the
time. Now that I have looked at the stats, I think My Team
would be lucky to play .600 ball. But I still think I can pick a
team that is better than any you could pick from my leftovers,
even though my leftovers are mostly Hall of Fame players, or
will be soon. As I worked through the list, trying to separate the
wheat from the chaff, I realized that there wasn't any chaff. For
that reason, I have constructed an opposing team that I call the
Dogs, short for Underdogs. This team is filled with players I
could easily have chosen for My Team. To make it a little
tougher for myself, I have even selected a manager for that
team, a guy who foiled me more than once when I was managing. Once I selected the Dogs, I *still* had Hall of Fame players
left over. This process was much more difficult than I thought it
would be.

One of the biggest challenges I faced was evaluating
American League players. Because I have been in the National

League throughout my career, there are some American League players whom I have seen only on television. Players like Robin Yount, who spent his entire career in the American League and went to Arizona for spring training, are not as familiar to me as those who trained in Florida or played in a lot of postseason games. When I felt the need to get another perspective on a player, I consulted players, managers, and scouts who saw him more often. Limiting the field and consulting other experts made it easier for me to defend my choices. Now that I have finished my research, I feel that I can truly say that I know what I'm talking about. That doesn't mean I'm right. Someone else who has seen the same players will have a different opinion. That's what kept the hot stove burning in the winters of my youth, and keeps the rotisserie turning in the age of computers and sabermetricians.

Criteria for My Team

Oftentimes, a player needs a couple of years in the major leagues to reach his potential, but the great ones usually last a long time. Eligibility for My Team will arbitrarily require every position player and starting pitcher to have at least ten good years. Because relief pitchers generally have a shorter shelf life than starting pitchers, I am only requiring them to have eight good years. Most great players have very high totals in such categories as home runs and RBI in their prime years, but their batting stats will show a great decline in the last few years. They are household names and fan favorites and, even when their production drops, they are still good enough to make the starting lineup. The same thing often applies to a pitcher's ERA. The best are still good enough to win games even after they lose the zip on their fastballs.

Some of the greatest players of all time, like Sandy Koufax, Dizzy Dean, and Don Mattingly, have had short careers, which can work against them if they had a few average seasons. In forming My Team, I will concentrate on each player's prime years and not discredit him if he has several lackluster seasons at the beginning and end. A few players, like Carlton Fisk, have long but checkered careers. They end up with ten good years, but don't show the kind of consistency that you find in the truly great hitters and pitchers. Most of the guys I am considering have at least eight good years back to back.

I have included a player from the past at each position to provide a historical perspective. In my opinion, it is impossible to accurately evaluate a player you have never seen. Sure, you can look at his numbers, but numbers are comparable only among players of the same era. Before 1920, the game was played with a relatively dead ball. For this reason, none of the players hit many home runs. This is why you can't compare Ty Cobb to Willie Mays or Christy Mathewson to Tom Seaver. I do believe, however, that direct comparisons of players from 1920 on are relevant to some extent. These guys might be lumped into a category of modern, or *live-ball,* players. I believe it is possible to make a general comparison using the statistics from 1920 on, which is why I have included some statistics from the best of that era.

The Numbers Game

My Team and the Dogs will have two players at each position and a nine-man pitching staff, five starters and four relievers. With the starting pitchers I select, I am confident that I will need only four relief pitchers. Two of them will be guys who can pitch three innings or more in the rare, but always possible, case of one of the starting pitchers getting hurt or simply having a bad day. The typical benchmarks for starting pitchers are wins, winning percentage, and ERA in relation to the rest of the league. For relief pitchers, the emphasis is on saves, save percentage, and, of course, durability. The two short relievers I pick will have to be able to pitch in a lot of games per season.

Inherited runners scoring is a good measure but is a relatively recent statistic and not available for the relievers who pitched in the first half of my study, so I will be unable to use it.

More than any other player, the pitcher depends on the performance of his teammates. In 1987, Nolan Ryan led the National League with a 2.76 ERA but got little support from his teammates and went 8-16. Conversely, Roger Clemens went 17-9 with the 2003 Yankees with an ERA of 3.91. The Rocket won the Cy Young Award in 2004, his first year in the National League, and the ERA title in 2005. I will look at the typical standards when I pick my staff, but I will also look at two other indicators: base runners per inning and home-run frequency. (The league's on-base average and slugging percentage against each pitcher would be better tools than runners per inning and home runs per inning, but these statistics are also relatively new.)

Hall of Fame pitcher Robin Roberts didn't allow many base runners but he did give up a lot of home runs. I will be looking for five starters and four relievers who don't allow many runners per inning and don't give up many extra-base hits either. By examining runners per inning and home-run frequencies, I can level the playing field so that a pitcher is not punished as much for playing on a weak hitting or poor fielding team. This is not the perfect way to evaluate a pitcher because the range factor on defense has a significant impact on runners per inning and cannot be quantified. John Tudor took full advantage of the great defensive coverage of the Cardinals in the 1980s. Conversely, Burt Hooton toiled for a Dodgers team that didn't cover much ground. Once I cut the staff to say, fifteen pitchers, I will have to consider what I have seen with my own eyes to make the last cuts.

For the position players, I will use a variety of offensive statistics. The numbers that I consider to be most important are each hitter's on-base average (OBA), his slugging average (SLG), and his combined OBA and SLG or (OBS), which is baseball's $E=MC^2$. To put the numbers in context, I have compared them with the league average.

Each player's OBS number will be of primary importance in my evaluation of his offensive ability. Still, the bottom line is runs. For this reason, I have included runs scored per plate appearance and RBI per at-bat. Since you can score after drawing a walk, I use runs per plate appearance instead of runs per at-bat. There are several ways a batter can drive in a run without an at-bat, like a sacrifice fly, a squeeze bunt, or by walking or getting hit by a pitch with the bases loaded. These events account for such a small portion of RBI that they are almost insignificant. That's why I have used RBI per at-bat. Runs scored and RBI are strongly influenced by the batters that come before and after any player in the batting order. A player's OBS is not dependent on the rest of the lineup, which is why I don't consider runs scored and driven in to be as good a measure as OBS. Still, the name of the game is how many runs you score and how many you allow. Some guys have the knack for delivering big hits or walking, stealing, and scoring. I think it is useful to look at these numbers but I will not build my team on them.

I am also presenting base-stealing statistics for each position player. From a statistical perspective, stolen bases don't have much impact on total offense. But there are some players whose base-stealing numbers are important, like Rickey Henderson, who stole a lot of bases and didn't get thrown out often, or Harmon Killebrew, who attempted very few steals. The impact of stolen bases is small for most players, but when a player tries to steal often, his success rate is worthy of consideration. If a player hardly ever attempts a steal, it follows that he is not very fast, and from that you can infer that he is a station-to-station runner who could clog the bases and prevent runners behind him from moving up another 90 feet. You might also infer that he doesn't cover much ground in the field, but that can be misleading. Anyone who watched Brooks Robinson can tell you that.

Several players I have considered for My Team have not played ten years at one position. I have had to make a judgment call with Ernie Banks, Robin Yount, and Craig Biggio because they switched positions. Banks will be considered a shortstop because that is the position he played during his most productive seasons at the plate. I have included Biggio as a second baseman for the same reason, and also because he won four Gold Gloves playing second and none at catcher or in the outfield. I have not considered Pete Rose at all, even though he made the All-Star team at all five positions he played. He did not produce nearly as much offense as the players I have chosen for the corner positions. If he had stayed at second base and been a great fielder, I would have included him as a second sacker. However, during most of his career he played average defense at the corners and didn't hit well enough to even be considered for My Team. Rose was known more for his batting average and determination than his slugging, as you can see:

ROSE	AB	PA	BA	OBA	SLG	R/PA	RBI/AB	SB	CS
	14053	15861	.303	.375	.409	1/7.3	1/12.1	198	149

AB: at-bats; PA: plate appearances; BA: batting average; OBA: on-base average; SLG: slugging percentage; R/PA: runs per plate appearance; RBI/AB: runs batted in per at-bat; SB: stolen bases; CS: caught stealing

These statistics are impressive more for the length of Rose's career than for his run production. In terms of quantity he has no peers; in terms of quality he doesn't measure up. To express this another way, I submit the 1970 numbers on my Astros' teammate Jesus Alou. Jesus usually hit for a high average but, because his swing path was slightly downward, he hit more ground balls than fly balls. Since most of his hits were singles and because he didn't walk much, or steal many bases, his production was not what you would expect of a .300 hitter:

1970

ALOU	AB	PA	BA	OBA	SLG	OBS	R/PA	RBI/AB	SB	CS
	491	519	.306	.335	.384	.719	1/8.8	1/10.3	3	2

Jesus was a corner outfielder. In 1970, he scored 59 runs and drove in 44 runners. Take a look at the outfielders who made My Team and you will see why a .300 batting average can be misleading. This is the last time I will list a player's batting average, because it is almost irrelevant.

The statistics I will use are designed to give a clear picture of a hitter's value. These numbers can be further refined to account for the characteristics of the home ballparks in which he played most of his games. The hitters who came up before and behind him in the lineup are important, too, as they created his opportunities to score runs and drive runners home. One thing that jumped out at me, as I looked at the possible candidates, was the symbiotic relationship of the Cincinnati Reds hitters of the 1970s, when they were called the Big Red Machine. Joe Morgan and Johnny Bench benefited from the quality of the rest of the lineup—Morgan more in terms of runs scored and Bench in RBI. Tony Perez, George Foster, Dave Concepcion, Dan Driessen, Ken Griffey Sr., and Rose all scored a lot of runs and drove in a lot of runners, but not as many as you might expect. When you look at their contemporaries on other teams, you can't help but notice that the horsepower of the Red Machine came from an eight-cylinder engine. This was a machine that hit on all eight.

For full statistical charts, visit www.SimonSays.com and search for *My Team* by Larry Dierker.

Once I select the players, I will have to line them up in the batting order. This may be difficult, as most of them batted in the middle of the lineup, but someone has to hit second and eighth. Hypothetically, this could spoil the togetherness of the guys on the team but, in this case, I don't think it would. If Hank Aaron were hitting sixth on this team instead of third, it would be because of the quality of the players in front of him. On My Team, he might be able to accept this position in the batting order because he would have numerous RBI opportunities. Similarly, someone who is used to hitting away may hit second and be asked to bunt occasionally. Ordinarily, great players don't like to make outs, even if an out advances a runner. I don't like it either, and I wouldn't give many bunt signs, anyway. But if an advance could lead to a decisive run late in the game, the player would probably accept a sacrificial role for the good of the team.

Lineup Theory

The ability to get on base (OBA) is especially valuable at the top of the batting order. The power number (SLG) refers to a batter's total bases and is most important in the middle of the order, where RBI are of utmost importance. Ideally, a leadoff man should get on base at least 40% of the time. An RBI hitter should have a slugging average in the .500 to .600 range or higher. If you have an on-base average of .400 and a slugging average of .600, your OBS is 1.00, which means that your average at-bat is as good as a walk. Many of the players on My Team will exceed this number several times during their careers.

One good way to organize a lineup is to stagger left-handed and right-handed batters. This makes it hard for the other manager to use his bullpen. If he brings in a lefty to face a lefty and the next hitter is right-handed, he has to let the lefty face him or use another pitcher. Oftentimes it is better to go left, right, left even if the numbers suggest going left, left, right. Very few teams have enough good players to do this. The Big Red Machine was an exception.

Those Reds of the seventies had a characteristic that I will consider important in choosing My Team—versatility. Like most pitchers, I had trouble pitching a good game against them. If I was throwing well, I could handle all the right-handed hitters. But even then, the left-handed hitters could beat me. Rose was good at getting on base. Morgan was good at pulling the ball through the right side of the infield with a man on first. He could also hit home runs and steal bases. Dan Driessen and Ken Griffey Sr. were good left-handed hitters with midrange power, who could bunt for a hit or steal a base. The Reds left-handed spray hitters hurt me more than their right-handed power hitters. If I prevented the Machine from getting into high gear, it shifted itself into a low gear, working for walks, bunting, and stealing bases. Several times, I pitched as well as I could and still gave up three or four runs and didn't finish the game. I did manage to beat them a few times and that was especially rewarding. It put a feather in my cap but, in the end, it was only a hat with a couple of feathers, not a full-feathered head-dress.

All That Glitters Is Not Gold

I faced many of the guys I have selected (whether I wanted to or not) during my thirteen years on the mound. I also had to come up with a plan for pitching to a lot of them during my five years as the Astros' manager. I can't help but look at the diamond through the eyes of a pitcher, which is what makes it difficult to pick a team. I consider fielding and base running to be very important, much more important than a lot of bona fide experts do. If I had a choice between two guys with similar offensive numbers, I would pick the better fielder. In some cases, I would even take a lesser hitter, especially at the key positions up the middle of the diamond.

When I compare the best fielders, I will not total the Gold Glove awards each player has received. I will consider Gold Gloves as a yardstick, but I will also use what I have seen with my own eyes. Sometimes Gold Gloves are only gold leafed. Steve Garvey, for example, won four of them and I consider him to have been below average in the field. I know he was great at digging low throws out of the dirt (he had to because he was only five-foot-ten and the other infielders had to throw the ball low or risk throwing it over his head). He didn't make many errors, but never threw to second or third on force plays like the better first basemen. When we played the Dodgers, our scouting report stated that we should bunt the ball to Garvey because, even if we bunted it too hard, he still wouldn't go for the force play. Rafael Palmeiro won a Gold Glove at first base in 1999 and he was mostly a DH that year. Some managers and coaches probably didn't even see him play first base in '99, as he played only 28 games in the field.

The Gold Glove winners are selected by major league managers and coaches. I still remember getting a ballot in Phoenix one September, just before batting practice. We were told that the ballots would be collected after batting practice. It was like voting for the president of Yugoslavia. Since we didn't get any fielding stats, we had to do it based on what we remembered, having seen each player only fifteen times or so. Usually memory serves well, but not always. Bob Gibson used to win the Gold Glove every year, but I'm sure there were seasons when another pitcher had a career year with the glove and Gibby didn't. The same is true of Greg Maddux. I know Bill Doran should have won the award over Ryne Sandberg at least once because I watched him every day. But Sandberg was the incumbent, and that counts for a lot when the voters don't have any information and little time to vote. As a result, the guy who wins it every year often keeps winning it every year until he gets too old and it's obvious that another fielder is better. My eyes tell me that Derek Jeter is a better shortstop than Alex Rodriguez even though A-Rod had already won two Gold Gloves when he went to the Yankees and Jeter had not yet won one. Joe Torre decided to play Jeter at short and A-Rod at third (and A-Rod won another Gold Glove at third). I would have made the same decision. "Bodywise, I thought Alex would make a smoother transition to third than Derek," Torre said. "Plus, I was already comfortable with Derek at short. He ran the infield and I didn't want to change that. A-Rod was a great shortstop, too. He has a little more arm strength than Derek. I was sure of what I wanted to do, but I didn't know how Alex would take it. To my relief, I found that he was a team player and he was happy to make the switch.

"The other thing I have to say about Jeter is that he does so many things that help you win a game that don't show up in the box score. He makes the big plays and gets the big hits. He may not have the power of A-Rod and Tejada, but you can almost always count on him in the clutch." Range usually equates with footspeed. It is a big part of defense and, in my mind, it is almost impossible to quantify. If you look in the notations at the front of the *Baseball Encyclopedia* by Pete Palmer and Gary Gillette, you will find formulas that are designed to measure a fielder's range and throwing ability. I am skeptical about the value of these numbers. Offensive production is one thing; fielding is another. One shortstop may get 600 assists during a season while another, who seems better, may only get 550. If you look carefully at the two shortstops you may find that the guy with 600 was playing behind a pitching staff with a lot of sinkerball pitchers. Because this pitching staff may allow more assist opportunities than a staff with a lot of fly ball and strike-out pitchers, you cannot immediately assume that assists will equate with range. You can't blame Larry Bowa for lack of as-sists at shortstop because Mike Schmidt was playing third, cut-ting off some ground balls that Bowa could have played.

I would also consider the psychological offensive implica-tions of where to play A-Rod and Jeter. A-Rod is a power hitter, and can easily hit enough homers to fit the third base stereo-type. Jeter is a very good hitter as it is. If he were playing third base, he might try to hit more home runs and I don't think that would be a good idea. If it's not broke, don't fix it! I agree with Joe. Someone else's eyes might not see it the same way as Torre's and mine do. For this reason, it is almost impossible for me to evaluate Babe Ruth or Ted Williams. I'd have to see them to really understand them.

In the late 1980s, the Braves had a great double-play com-bination in Rafael Ramirez and Glenn Hubbard. They led the league in twin killings for several years in a row. However, the Braves had woeful pitching back then and it is likely that the duo turned so many double plays not only because they were good at it, but also because there were so many double play oppor-tunities. Again, you can't trust the statistics completely. You have to review the numbers *and* use your own eyes to make up your mind.

One thing that everyone knows is that it is important to have good defensive players up the middle. The positions where managers are usually willing to sacrifice offense for de-fense are, and always have been, catcher, shortstop, and center field. In choosing the players for these positions I will consider fielding to be even more important. That said, I will not ignore hitting. Ozzie Smith is the best fielding shortstop I have ever seen, but I could not pick him over Alex Rodriguez at short. Ozzie was a little better with the glove, but A-Rod is a very good fielder and a much better hitter.

The corner players on defense—third base, first base, left

field, and right field are in the lineup for their offensive talent. I will not have any bad fielders on the team, but may lean toward the better hitters at these positions. I will also consider a platoon situation or two. The platoon strategy ensures extra playing time for a player who might come in to pinch-hit in a game he doesn't start. Using a platoon arrangement allows a manager to have a game-ready pinch hitter on the bench at all times. Earl Weaver's Orioles made good use of this tactic with John Lowenstein and Gary Roenicke in left field, and the Astros got a lot of mileage out of the Phil Garner/Denny Walling tandem at third base in 1986.

Margin for Error

It is obvious that there are subtle factors that influence a player's statistics. (Where does he play half his games? Who hits in front of or behind him?) These must be considered when a general manager makes a trade or signs a free agent. Most of the time, they even out over the course of a career and for that reason I will consider them but will not try to quantify them. If I did, this book wouldn't be much fun to read—it would be like a math textbook.

Baseball isn't like most sports. It is always played in a quadrant but the outfield fences vary. Some parks have tall fences; some have low ones. Some outfield fences have odd angles, which makes it difficult for outfielders to play the carom. Some parks favor the pitchers; some parks favor the hitters. Mike Piazza has played for the Dodgers and Mets. Both teams have large, pitcher-friendly ballparks, so Mike has had to play half his games where it is relatively difficult to hit home runs. Conversely, when Roger Maris was chasing Babe Ruth's single-season home-run mark, he played half his games at Yankee Stadium where it is easy for a left-handed hitter to pull a pitch over the right-field fence. In fact, it is no coincidence that Babe Ruth was a left-handed hitter who played in the same stadium as Maris. Joe DiMaggio got the opposite effect out of the same ballpark because he was a right-handed hitter and Yankee Stadium is deep from right-center field to the left-field foul pole. These days, most players play for several clubs, some good, some not so good. Over a long career, many of the things that influence production balance out. What helps him in one ballpark, hurts him in another.

Another thing that skews the averages is the designated hitter. Since 1973, American League hitters have had the slight advantage of no pitcher in the batting order. When you play 162 games in a season, having nine hitters instead of 8.5 makes a difference—not a big difference, but enough to consider. In addition, the depth of high-quality starting pitchers was greater in the sixties and early seventies, so you have to give the hitters of that era a little extra credit. The pitchers of the subsequent decades deserve extra credit because they pitched in a harder-hitting environment.

Intangibles

Ultimately, I will make judgments that are based on aspects of a player that cannot be quantified, such as fielding, base running, durability, poise, and personality. Generally, I favor a team that makes it hard to score over a team that scores a lot of runs. I'd rather have good pitching and defense and only average hitting, than poor pitching and fielding and great power hitting. For several years in the eighties, the Cubs had many slow players who were good power hitters. They played well at Wrigley Field but did not do so well in the larger parks on the road, especially the Astroturf fields where speed is more important. A few years later, the Tigers had the same type of team. Neither team won. Yet the speedy Dodgers of the sixties and Cardinals of the eighties won a lot, even without much power. A fast team with good pitchers and fielders can win on grass or Astroturf, in a big park or a small one.

One SABR-based statistic that I used as a rule of thumb as a manager regards stealing bases. Almost all advanced baseball statisticians agree that a runner who successfully steals two bases for every time he is caught stealing is breaking even in terms of the runs his team scores. When he succeeds, he ignites the offense and generates more RBI opportunities for the hitters who come after him in the order. He also takes the double-play possibility away from the opponent. When he is thrown out, he most often kills a rally.

Statistically speaking, simply stealing bases isn't worth much unless your success rate is very high. But, even then, there are subtleties. The SABR guys may know what the math says, but they don't know how a pitcher *feels* when a base stealer is dancing off the bag. As a manager, I preferred a team that attempted to steal a lot of bases. We ran often when we had a break-even 67 percent success rate—or even a little lower—because I *know* how I felt when a fast runner was taking a big lead and juking around trying to get a good jump. As a manager, I figured that if we could put more pressure on the opposing pitcher he wouldn't perform as well. In my mind, stealing, or even the threat of stealing, is important because it creates opportunities for hitters. There is no way to quantify the effect of this pressure. The only way to get a feel for it is to watch thousands of games and consider the value of a speedy base runner while you are watching. In other words, use your own eyes and brain.

There are also situations in which you might want to steal a base even if it is a low-percentage play. Let's say you have a good hitter in the batter's box with two outs and an average runner at first base, and the count is 0-2—not too promising a situation. If you try to steal and fail, the good hitter leads off the next inning with a fresh count. If you are safe, the hitter has a 1-2 count and a chance to drive in a run with a single. In my mind, the risk, though great, is worth the potential reward. If it doesn't work, you're in good shape to start the next inning.

I favor a team with at least three left-handed hitters. Players who hit right-handed usually do better against right-handed pitchers than lefty hitters do against left-handed pitchers. Since there are more right-handed pitchers and hitters it is not necessarily an advantage to have too many left-handed hitters in the lineup, especially if your opponent has a few left-handed starters and a few lefty relievers. My Team will have more right-handed hitters than lefties, but the left-handed hitters I do choose, like Barry Bonds, will be able to hit left-handed pitching.

Going beyond the numbers, you start dealing with what is often referred to as a team's *chemistry*. Chemistry is the sum of the intangible qualities each player brings to the team. Teams with good chemistry play with great energy all the time. They don't make excuses for poor play. The players get along well with one another, and each player accepts his role on the team. All hitters have streaks and slumps. When you have a confident team, the guy in the slump doesn't worry if he fails to get a runner home from third base with no outs. He depends on the guy behind him to score the runner. And he really believes it will work out that way. When a fielder makes an error that threatens to open the floodgates, he depends on his pitcher to pitch out of the trouble without giving up a run.

It will be impossible for me, or anyone else, to select a twenty-five man team full of guys who are content to play the backup roles. Almost all the guys I pick are, or will be, Hall of Fame players and none of them would be satisfied sitting on the bench. But there are two intangible qualities that I will consider in choosing My Team. One of them gurgles like a brook and the other is a raging inferno.

It is always helpful to have a gurgling guy or two who can keep things loose. A practical joke or impromptu comic line helps when a team is struggling. A guy who not only wants to beat the other team, but wants to *kill* them, can be an asset, too, even without a sense of humor. In the last fifteen years, the Astros have had a few guys whose presence on the team meant more than the numbers they posted. Casey Candaele could have made a living as a stand-up comedian. Luis Gonzalez is the best practical joker I have ever seen. Being around them was exhilarating, like running the rapids. It will be hard to find guys like that for My Team because oftentimes the guys who fill these roles are not the star players. I do know of at least one player who will make the team on talent and can improve the chemistry, too. As Branch Rickey once said, "His secret weapon is the frivolity in his bloodstream. Willie Mays has doubled his strength with laughter."

Carl Everett is not a comedian—he is a flame eater. In 1998, his competitive fire helped us maintain a sharp edge throughout the season. Carl had one of his best years in '98 and, because of his burning desire, I felt like we were always on the precipice of a brawl. Craig Biggio isn't likely to start a fight (or crack a joke), but he does play like a demon and expects no less of his teammates. Pete Rose was the same way. If you have guys who can keep things loose and other guys who can draw the bowstring tight, you have a chance at good chemistry.

Putting It in Perspective

Most old ballplayers (with the exception of WWII era players) feel that the golden age of the sport was when they played. A lot of the old guys think the modern players aren't as well-schooled as the guys they played with and against. The guys who are playing now think the old-time players were inferior athletes who couldn't even make the majors these days. I am not inclined toward either argument. I think there are more good players in the game now, but I also think the best of the past would still be big fish, even in the bigger talent pool of this generation. As I reviewed the field of old-timers, I found that they were only slightly smaller in stature than the current crop. You cannot say the same thing about basketball or football, where size has become much more important. I think Cobb and Mathewson would have been stars in any era.

Still, I am inclined to think the universe of players is deeper in talent now than ever before. Sure, there are fourteen more teams now than there were when Cobb roamed the outfield, but there are more athletes to choose from these days. After Jackie Robinson broke the color line in 1947, many black athletes chose to play baseball and became stars. In recent years, the percentage of black players in the major leagues has declined to 1 in 10. The percentage of black players in the major leagues was more than 1 in 4 in 1970. One reason is that many of the great black athletes have chosen football or basketball careers. It stands to reason. Football and basketball are the primary spectator sports in high school and college. A lot of inner-city kids, who may have the ability to become professional baseball players will never know it because they don't have a ballpark nearby, let alone all the equipment it takes to play. There are still a lot of good black ballplayers today—players that could not have displayed their talents prior to 1947. Players from the Caribbean countries have made great inroads in the last forty years. They have, in effect, replaced the black players. And now, some fine players from Asian countries and Australia are showing that they can stand up against the best in America. Ten years from now, My Team may have more of an international flavor.

In baseball, the size of the player is not very important. Great size and strength isn't an advantage in swimming or track, either. Yet records in these sports continue to fall, which suggests that improved nutrition, conditioning methods, and medical advances have helped the modern athletes maximize their potential. The runners and swimmers aren't getting much bigger but they are getting a little bit faster. Still, no amount of conditioning could make Shaquille O'Neal a faster bike rider than

Lance Armstrong. If you argued that the baseball players of today are better athletes than those of the early days of the sport, I would have to agree. But I could also say that Mickey Mantle and Willie Stargell have hit monster home runs in some of the ballparks where Barry Bonds and Sammy Sosa still play. In some of these parks, the old guys hit home runs to the outer reaches beyond where anyone has hit one recently. I can also mention that some of the fastest old-time players were timed with a stopwatch, and that it appears that they could run about as fast as the fastest players today. I'm sure that is what Red Smith had in mind when he said that 90 feet between bases is the closest mankind has come to perfection.

Baseball rewards players with skills that you can't improve upon just by being bigger and stronger, like quick, soft hands, good hand–eye coordination and throwing accuracy. In the National League, where real baseball is played (with no DH), everyone has to be able to play offense and defense. There is a little more specialization now, however, especially with regard to relief pitching. In my day, a good starting pitcher could complete a lot of games. Now the closers finish most games. I will have to keep these things in mind as I select My Team.

Because starting pitchers will have to have ten good years to qualify for My Team, I cannot select the most dominant pitcher I have ever seen, Sandy Koufax. Because I require My Team's players to play in the field, I can't consider Paul Molitor, because he was a DH more often than he played a position. Since relief pitchers normally have a shorter career, I will require them to have only eight good years and will not include winning percentage because it is not a good indicator of a reliever's value. When you come out of the bullpen, the most important quality is consistency. If you have nine good outings and then give up three runs in one-third of an inning in the next outing, your ERA may not look so good, but your manager will send you right back out there because he knows you have been successful 90 percent of the time.

I have not attempted to adjust a pitcher's statistics to include the quality of the teams he pitched for or the effect various ballparks may have had on his ERA. I have, however, thought about some factors that influence performance. I have given some extra ERA credit to pitchers in the American League since 1973, when the designated hitter rule put the extra hitter in the lineup. I have considered the quality of each pitcher's teammates and the nature of his home ballpark. I have not attempted to quantify these things. As Toby Harrah once said, "Statistics are like a girl in a bikini. They show a lot, but not everything." For instance, Steve Carlton won 27 games with a good ERA in 1972 for a last-place Phillies team in a relatively small ballpark. He certainly had more obstacles to overcome that year than Jim Palmer, who won 21 games for a great Orioles ball club that year. Tom Seaver won a lot more games than he lost despite playing for a weak-hitting team in his early days with the Mets. He did, however, pitch a lot of games at Shea Stadium, one of the best pitcher's ballparks in the league, which had to help his ERA.

Comparing the accomplishments of the pitchers of my generation with those who came along later is difficult because of the prominence of the closer in today's game. The best starting pitchers of the sixties and seventies went the distance at least one-third of the time. If they had had Mariano Rivera to pitch the ninth instead, they would likely have won more games and posted lower ERAs. When I look at Bob Gibson and Pedro Martinez, I will have to consider the quality of the teams they pitched for and their place among their contemporaries. Perhaps someone could come up with a formula to make these comparisons, but because you would have to make arbitrary judgments to come up with the formula, I will make arbitrary judgments without it.

• • •

If I do nothing else in selecting My Team than make you try to think of a better one, I will have accomplished my goal. If I help you understand the intangible qualities certain types of players bring to the ballpark, I will make you a more informed fan. Either way or both, choosing My Team should be thought provoking. I scratched my head as I considered the ability of each individual player as a piece of the puzzle. Choosing My Team made me decide which pieces would fit together best to form the most beautiful team picture.

As a reminder, you can find the full statistical charts by visiting www.SimonSays.com and searching for *My Team* by Larry Dierker.

1

Catcher

 IF I WERE GOING to start a team, I would look for a catcher first. I suppose Jeff Torborg was just trying to be funny when he said, "There must be some reason we're the only ones in foul territory, facing the other direction." But he had a point. No player sees the field quite like the catcher. This unique vantage point is one of the reasons so many managers are former catchers. In order to do their job well, catchers have to work closely with the pitching staff and also participate in the offense. Catchers are the only players who are deeply involved with both the process of scoring runs and also preventing the other team from scoring. Every position player can help prevent runs by making good defensive plays, but only the catcher is involved in the pitcher's thinking process. Most teams look for a catcher who can handle the defensive part of the job first and consider any offense he can add a bonus.

A catcher's defensive requirements are physical, mental,

and psychological. First and foremost, you have to be tough. They don't call the catcher's gear "the tools of ignorance" for nothing. In fact, "the tools of stupidity" might be a better description because most catchers, even in Little League, know they are going to get banged up. By the time their careers are over, most professional catchers have a mangled right hand. So many pitches are fouled off or skip in the dirt in front of the plate that it is impossible to catch them all cleanly with the mitt. Invariably, the catcher's bare hand takes a few direct hits during the course of the season. If he has to catch a knuckleball pitcher it's even worse. Only a masochist could enjoy the physical punishment a catcher has to endure on a daily basis. Catching is, however, the easiest way to make it to the major leagues because catchers are always in demand. It's still not easy, especially when you consider how many chances there are to make a mistake. Still, if you are not a pitcher, there is only one position you can play without being a good hitter or a fast runner. If you have a good memory, soft hands, a decent arm, and a hard head you can become a major league catcher.

Back in the early part of the last century, catchers didn't have any ignorance tools except a crude wire mask. They squatted back behind the plate with no equipment to protect their legs. In 1907, Giants' catcher Roger Bresnahan started wearing a pair of cricket leg pads. Opposing players mocked him at first, but the other catchers around the league weren't so critical. In fact, within a year, they all wore them. Having invented shin guards, Bresnahan set about to improve the face mask by padding the outer edge to cushion the blows. Before that, few catchers could stay healthy long enough to catch 100 games in a season. After the shin guards and improved mask, it was not uncommon for a receiver to work 120 or 130 games. These days, catchers have more and better protective gear than ever before, but they still get hurt a lot. To be honest, the catcher's gear isn't worth much when a big, fast runner hits you like a linebacker while you're protecting home plate. Sometimes it takes a moment or two to recover from such a hit, but the catchers I've seen always do. They may not come back out the next inning after a major collision, but they won't give the opposing runner the satisfaction of taking them out of the game until the third out is made. That's the physical part.

The mental part has to do with calling the game. A good catcher can help a pitcher by recognizing and remembering a hitter's weaknesses. Ultimately, the pitcher calls the game because he has veto power over the catcher's signals, but the catcher sees the hitters every day while the starting pitchers only see them once in each series, at most. Some pitchers are obstinate about throwing the pitch they want to throw in cases when the catcher calls for another pitch. I was—but some pitchers depend on their catchers to do all the thinking.

Even though he's remembered more for his quirky sayings than for his catching, Yogi Berra claims that he could remember every pitch, all season long, and for more than a season on some guys. That statement would be greeted with by many raised eyebrows, but I don't think he was exaggerating very much. Yogi has an odd way of expressing himself sometimes, but there is a lot going on under that bald dome. He can remember the box scores of both leagues, every day. Ask him what this or that hitter did the day before and he can say, "two for five with a double." He always knows the standings and he can also tell you what the various pitchers did the day before. I was greatly impressed because I couldn't always remember everything that happened in our own game the day before—even the ones I pitched. But Yogi isn't like you and me.

A catcher who has caught the same pitcher for a few years can develop a sixth sense about what pitches should *not* be thrown to a power hitter and what pitches *should* be thrown to a contact hitter. With instinctive knowledge and a good scouting report, this type of battery can hold a charge well enough that the pitcher seldom has to shake off a sign. Most catchers can't remember things as well as Yogi, but many of them can retain more than you might imagine. The best defensive catcher I ever pitched to was Johnny Edwards. Johnny had a good memory and the ability to change the game plan based on how his pitcher was throwing on a given day. I'll never forget what he told me one night in San Diego. It was the third inning and I was struggling. I still hadn't given up much, maybe a run, but I was in trouble the first two innings and it seemed like I was shaking off the fastball about half the time. When I got to the bench, Johnny came over and sat next to me. He asked me why I wasn't throwing more fastballs. I told him that it was because I didn't feel like I had a very good fastball. "Bullshit!" he said. "How many fastballs have they hit hard so far?" I thought about it for a moment and said, "None." "Well," he said, "you may not feel like you're throwing it well, but it looks pretty good from my angle." I started throwing more fastballs after that and breezed through the rest of the game.

The best catchers learn to work with each pitcher on the staff individually. They understand his unique mannerisms and tendencies and learn how to use them to the best advantage. They also have to learn to get along with the arbiters. Once a catcher is in the big leagues for a few seasons, the umpires form an impression of him. If he doesn't argue very often and blocks every ball that could get through and hit the umpire, he can gain some respect. And the word gets around, believe me. I'm not suggesting that a good catcher can get all the borderline pitches called strikes for his pitcher. That's not going to happen, but he may get more than half of them. At the other extreme is the catcher who argues all the time and doesn't block pitches in the dirt very well. That gets around, too, and it keeps coming around.

The first time Brad Ausmus was the Astros' regular catcher, he developed a good relationship with the pitching staff. He got down low, gave a good target and threw a lot of would-be base stealers out. He didn't hit very well and, after he was with the team a couple of years, nobody noticed him. Even though the team kept winning and the pitching staff was effective, Brad was taken for granted. In 1998, the Astros had a switch-hitting catcher named Mitch Meluskey at Triple-A in New Orleans. Mitch was knocking the cover off the ball and his manager thought Mitch was ready to play in the big leagues. The Astros also had two other major league catchers, Tony Eusebio and Paul Bako. The team thought it could get by with Eusebio and Bako until Mitch was ready to take the job so they traded Ausmus. Eusebio and Bako did a good job in 1999 and we won the Central Division. In 2000, Meluskey was our opening day catcher.

A lot of people questioned the Ausmus trade. They thought it was done to save money. That was part of it, but not the biggest part. A few reporters told me that no team had ever won a championship with a rookie catcher. I couldn't think of an exception to that rule but I suspected there was one, maybe more than one. I honestly thought we would be a better team with Meluskey. I told the writers that I thought Mitch was adequate in terms of catching the ball, framing it in the strike zone, blocking pitches in the dirt, and throwing to the bases. "That's all I care about," I said. "The pitchers should call their own games anyway."

That's when I learned the importance of the psychological aspect of catching. Most of the pitchers didn't want to call their own games. That baffled me. How could they expect Mitch to call the game when he had never seen the hitters? He could probably remember the scouting report as well as most guys, but scouting reports are only a place to start. You also have to get a feel for the game as it moves along. Mitch wasn't too good at that and he didn't care to learn. He also complained every time he thought the umpire missed a call. The pitchers used him as a scapegoat when they didn't pitch well. It wasn't his fault alone, but his personality made things worse. He didn't try to talk to them; he didn't really want to work with them. Instead, he got mad at them. He was obviously much more concerned with his hitting than with his catching.

We finished fourth that year, after three straight division championships. I still think there must be teams that have won with rookie catchers, but I was ready to concede that Mitch wasn't the guy we needed in such an important defensive position. I was upset with him but I was also upset with the pitchers. I don't think I would have minded pitching to him if he did the mechanical things well. I could call my own game and would benefit from his hitting. But I also learned that most pitchers didn't look at it the same way I did. We ended up trading Mitch to Detroit and getting Ausmus back. We lost hitting in the deal but gained pitching. We won the division again in 2001.

Today, I think catching is even more important than I did before. As an outsider, it is difficult to learn which catchers can call a good game and keep the pitchers and umpires in a good frame of mind. For that reason, my catching choices for this team may be based more on offensive numbers than they should be, but I won't make a determination without talking to someone who has seen each of them more than I have.

As far as the offense goes, here is a look at the field: Lance Parrish, Mike Piazza, Johnny Bench, Ivan Rodriguez, Gary Carter, Tim McCarver, and Carlton Fisk. Because Yogi Berra finished catching before I came to the big leagues, his stats are provided for the purpose of comparison. (See table on opposite page.)

Two catchers jump off this chart waving semaphores. Mike Piazza wins by a mile when it comes to offense; Tim McCarver can't stand in the batter's box with the rest. I never realized just how good a hitter Piazza was until I looked closely at his numbers. Mike is from Tommy Lasorda's home town, Norristown, Pennsylvania, and Tommy was a friend of Mike's father and is

THE CANDIDATES

PLAYERS	OBA	SLG	OBS	R/PA	RBI/AB	SB	CS
PARRISH	.318	.450	.768	1/8.9	1/6.4	23	31
PIAZZA	.388	.569	.957	1/6.9	1/5.0	16	17
BENCH	.347	.493	.839	1/7.5	1/5.3	46	31
RODRIGUEZ	.351	.496	.847	1/6.9	1/6.6	86	41
CARTER	.344	.468	.811	1/8.0	1/6.0	28	24
MCCARVER	.330	.388	.718	1/10.8	1/8.6	49	38
FISK	.354	.474	.827	1/7.1	1/6.5	93	43
BERRA	.356	.491	.847	1/6.8	1/5.2	20	22

Mike's godfather. Tommy arranged a tryout for Mike and he hit a lot of pitches over the fence at Dodger Stadium. The scouts were unimpressed. They didn't think he could hit very well at game speed. And they didn't think he was a good defensive player, partly because he was not a fast runner. "What would you say if he were a catcher?" Lasorda asked. They agreed that that would be a different story. "Okay, he's a catcher," Lasorda said. The Dodgers' scouts weren't the only ones who were unimpressed with Mike. But they did sign him in 1988—in the 62nd round—as a catcher.

As it turned out, he could hit the ball over the fence at game speed, but he never became the type of catcher that you didn't notice. Anyone could see that his throwing was below average. His hands were adequate but not great. Because so many of his seasons were shortened by injuries, the Mets started playing him at first base from time to time. Who could blame them? They wanted him to get as many at-bats as possible. But Piazza wasn't better as a first baseman than as a catcher, so the Mets abandoned that experiment. Frankly, I think the Dodgers would have moved him early in his career if they had the foresight to see how good a hitter he would become and that catching would limit his playing time. I'm sure they were hoping he would become a good defensive player. A great hitter who can play catcher is a precious commodity. In fact, the Big Red Machine with Johnny Bench and the Tigers of the 1980s with Lance Parrish were built on the foundation of a hard-hitting catcher.

I heard a lot of people say that Piazza was not a good receiver but I can't say that he was glaringly inadequate. He didn't have a strong, accurate arm, but there aren't many catchers who gun down more than 30 percent of the base stealers anyway. Allowing a few more steals is clearly acceptable if you are one of the top hitters in the league.

Calling the game is another story—a story that has to be told by the pitchers, who are often motivated to shift the blame if they don't pitch well. Plenty of pitchers had good years pitching to Piazza. He isn't the best catcher, and good pitching is more important than having one deadly hitter in the lineup every day. Still, I have heard a lot of nonsense about pitch selection. The pitchers should select the pitches, not the catcher. When the catcher can help with the thinking, that is the best possible situation. I would have been delighted to pitch to Piazza. I would also be happy to have him on My Team. He may not be the captain type because he is a quiet guy who values his privacy. So were some of the back-up catchers who caught Greg Maddux. If I were to select Mike, he would be the back-up catcher and perhaps a pinch hitter when he didn't start. In this position, he wouldn't have to be a team leader.

Gary Carter was like Bench, a good fielder and a good power hitter. He usually hit clean-up or fifth in the batting order. He had power, was a good RBI man, and was a little faster runner than Bench. While Bench came from salt-of-the-earth Oklahoma stock, Carter was, or at least appeared to be, a California hot dog. He was always smiling, always in front of the camera. When I needed an interview, I invariably turned to Gary because he could talk as well as he could play and he was a terrific player.

Carter was only twenty years old when he arrived in Montreal; Steve Rogers was a few years older and just starting his long and successful pitching career when Carter joined the team. They grew up together in Montreal, learning the hard way, by trial and error. Carter was a shortstop in high school and passed up a football scholarship to UCLA to play professional baseball. Because of his size and arm strength, the Expos immediately made him a catcher. Rogers remembers how hard Gary had to work to learn the position at age twenty. "He really studied the scouting reports and tried to learn the hitter's weaknesses. It was a challenge for him, at first, but it didn't take us long to get on the same page. My sixth best pitch was a split-fingered fast ball. Sometimes I never threw it in a game and if I used it three or four times, that was a lot. One day I had everything working and a couple of times I was thinking split when he flashed the sign. I only threw three splits that day and I was expecting to have to shake off a lot of signs to get to it. Every time the thought crossed my mind it crossed his, too, and he called for the pitch. It was amazing."

Carter had a strong arm when he arrived in the National League, but his throwing mechanics weren't the best at first and some teams took advantage of that. "Norm Sherry worked with him on the footwork part of it," Rogers said. "Once he got it down, it was hard to run on him. Then, later in his career, he injured his elbow and lost some arm strength. Once Gary learned the position, I thought he was as good as Bench."

What a lot of people don't know is that behind the flashy smile, there was one tough ballplayer. "One time, Kid [Carter's nickname] hurt his thumb on a tag play and had to come out of the game," Rogers said. "The next day, he got the thumb taped and went out to take batting practice—just before the team doctor arrived at the stadium. The doctor said, 'He's not going to hit until I examine him,' so they brought him back into the training room. As it turned out, he had completely severed the ligament and had to have surgery the next day. And he was ready to go out and play with it that way."

Later in his career, Tony Scott slid into home plate and tore the calf muscle away from Carter's shin bone. This time he did play. "He played five or six games that way and he could hardly run to first base," Rogers said. "He was a real gamer. A lot of people only saw what was on the outside. The big smile, his self-promoting, talkative nature. But, believe me, there was a lot more to him than that. I'm glad they finally had the good sense to vote him into the Hall of Fame."

When I started considering catchers, I was sure that Johnny Bench would win the job easily. His eminence has not turned out to be quite that obvious. Lance Parrish was just about as good a hitter and both of them benefited by being in a lineup with a lot of other good hitters. Jack Billingham pitched to both of them. "Lance was a young catcher when I went to the Tigers," Billingham said. "He was a good receiver and he studied the hitters and improved a lot in just the few years I was there. He had a good arm and a lot of power. I thought he was solid, all the way around, but I still couldn't rate him above Bench."

Pudge Rodriguez hasn't been quite as good an RBI man as Bench, but his teammates haven't been on base for him as much either. There is no question he can outrun the rest of them and it shows in the runs scored column. And there is no doubt he can throw as well as anyone, even Bench. However, he has had the reputation for caring more about hitting and throwing than about calling the game. His mechanics behind the plate are good. But I never got the feeling that the pitchers were happy with the way he called the game. I have heard that about Bench, too; bad pitchers are good at making excuses.

I suspect that some of the smoke in Pudge's image relates to a fire somewhere within him. His ability is off the charts, but his attitude could probably be better. He isn't a take-charge guy. He just quietly does his own job. Still, his coach and then-manager with the Rangers in Arlington was a former catcher, Jerry Narron. Narron paints a different picture of Pudge. "He didn't speak English very well his first few years," Jerry said. "I think that's why he got the reputation for not calling a good game. Actually, he didn't call a bad game, but he did have a communication problem at first." Narron was more eager to talk about Pudge's strengths. "He is such a great athlete that he can do almost anything on the field. Sometimes he would turn around and hit left-handed during batting practice. He could hit the ball in the upper deck from that side. In fact, he might have been even better as a switch hitter."

And then there is the throwing. "Pudge flat out changed the game," Narron said. "He threw so well that he completely shut down the running game. Our pitchers could concentrate on the hitter because they didn't have to worry about stolen bases. The runners couldn't even get a good secondary lead because he would pick them off. I don't know how many runs he saved us with his arm but it was a bunch." It is tempting to select Pudge as my number-one catcher because he has become as good a hitter as all the other catchers, except Piazza. When I consider the first few years, however, when he had communication problems and was not as productive a hitter, he comes up just short. I wouldn't consider an inability to call a good game a big liability because the pitchers I will have don't need a lot of help in that area. I would, however, rate him down a notch or two offensively because he has played in an era of great offense and, when he was with the Rangers, he played his home games in a hitter-friendly ballpark.

Carlton Fisk has good numbers, too, but he posted them over so many seasons that he wasn't as consistent as Bench, Piazza, or some of the other candidates. He was a better receiver than Piazza, and, like Mike, was often sidelined with injuries. His breakthrough season was 1972 when he won the American League Rookie of the Year award. (He fell one-half game short of being a rookie catcher on a division-winning team.) The last year I used to evaluate him was 1990 and he played on until 1993. It took me eighteen seasons to come up with ten good ones. Fisk made the All-Star team eleven times, and was elected to the Hall of Fame in 2000, but he won only one Gold Glove. By the time he was finished he had caught more games than any catcher in history and he took the defensive part of the job seriously. Perhaps *too* seriously. When I was a pitcher, he would have driven me crazy running out to the mound all the time. But no one can say that he didn't work hard on the mental part of the game.

I was watching a discussion show on ESPN one time when they were honoring Yogi Berra. Fisk was one of the guests along with Yogi, Johnny Bench, and Gary Carter. I can't remember what everyone said, but I do recall Fisk coming on strong about leadership. He said that he took pride in calling a good game and that he controlled the pitching strategy. He didn't appreciate pitchers shaking him off because he knew the hitters better than they did. I wouldn't have liked that at all. He might know the hitters, but he could not possibly have known how the pitcher felt. Sometimes you have a feeling that you can throw a certain pitch and you want to throw *that* pitch. Every pitcher will tell you that if you throw a pitch without conviction, the hitter will hit it hard. It happens all the time. You are thinking curveball and the catcher signals for a slider. You think, "Well, a slider is a breaking ball, too. Maybe I should just throw a slider." When you do, you throw it in the dirt and the runners advance or you hang it and the hitter rips it. Even after twelve years and over two thousand innings, I still did it occasionally, even though I knew I shouldn't. I can't explain why, but virtually every pitcher I've talked to has had the same experience. This is not to say that you will always succeed when you go with your own idea. I just think you have a better chance when you follow your own instincts.

The Astros once had a slugging catcher named Cliff Johnson. Cliff was always trying to shed the notion that he was not a good defensive catcher. He couldn't shed it because he wasn't very good. One day, I was getting shelled and Cliff came out to the mound to talk to me. When he got there, I said, "Clifford, what the hell can you possibly tell me that I don't already know?" "Ah, man," he replied, and trotted back to his position. Most pitchers don't like company on the mound. As old-timer Rube Bressler told Lawrence Ritter in *The Glory of Their Times:*

> Those conferences out there on the mound really get me. The pitcher *knows* he's in a jam. What can they say to him? They just remind him of it, that's all. Having pitched and played first base both, I know what they do. The catcher and the infielders run over to you and pick up your rosin bag, like they never saw one in their life before, and all they say is, 'Bear down, buddy, you'll get out of this. Just bear down and work hard. You can do it.' Then they give you a quick pat on the rear end and run back as far as they can get out of the line of fire.
>
> Now just what do you learn from that? You already had a vague feeling that things weren't going just right. To tell the truth, you knew darned well that you were in a heck of a jam. And you've *been* bearing down, and you've *been* working hard. All it does is make you even more worried than you already were, which was plenty. There are mighty few pitchers who can survive those conferences on the mound, take it from me.

Fisk probably didn't read Ritter's book and, if he had, he likely would have ignored it.

When I get to the final decision, I come back to Bench. Even though he didn't run as well as Rodriguez or hit as well as Piazza, he was a solid RBI man throughout his career and the absolute model of catching mechanics. His hands are so big and strong, he can put you in a vise grip you can't get out of. And, more important, his hands are soft. He could pick up pitches in the dirt as well as anyone and was terrific coming out of his stance to go after foul pop-ups. His arm was legendary and he was consistent. Pete Rose and Joe Morgan may have started the Big Red Machine, but Bench kept it going. I only needed eleven years to come up with ten good seasons for him. He was named Rookie of the Year in 1968 and made the All-Star team fourteen times. "He was a little cocky," former Reds pitcher Jack Billingham told me. "But he never took his hitting back behind the plate like some catchers do when they're in a slump. In terms of catching, he could do it all."

Of all the catchers in this comparison, only Bench and Tim Mc-Carver played most of their careers when major league pitching was at its zenith. In the end, I am right back where I was in the beginning. I think we all tend to glamorize players from our own era and I'm trying to be objective, but I can't pick anyone over Bench. Oddly, I didn't have much trouble getting him out. In fact, McCarver was a tougher hitter for me. But I can't pick the hitters on this team based on how they did against me. I got Bench out, but Steve Carlton didn't. Strangely enough, Carlton is the only reason McCarver is even in the mix. If I needed an everyday catcher, I would not pick Tim. If I needed a good player with a personality, a sense of humor, and the ability to get the most out of a great pitcher once every five days, he would make the team as Carlton's personal catcher. But if Greg Maddux makes the starting rotation and Carlton doesn't, I'll go with Piazza as my backup. Maddux has always pitched to his team's back-up catcher anyway. Some say these guys have been his valets, and most of them have been weak hitters, like Charlie O'Brien, Eddie Perez, and Paul Bako. This strategy certainly worked well for Bobby Cox. I used it, too, assigning one of my starting pitchers to the back-up catcher. This tactic gives the everyday catcher a rest once a week or so, and it gives the back-up catcher an important job. Since Greg does most of his own thinking anyway, and doesn't throw many pitches that are hard to catch, I think he would be delighted to work with Mike Piazza.

Looking at the catchers of the past, I come up with Bill Dickey, Mickey Cochrane, Roy Campanella, Yogi Berra, and, from the Negro Leagues, Josh Gibson. Dickey was solid; some say he was the foundation of the Yankees Dynasty, 1930s edition. He was smart and hard nosed and an excellent hitter. Cochrane was another leader type. He became a player/manager for the Tigers at age 31 and he led them to 101 wins his first season, 1934, before losing to the Gashouse Gang Cardinals in the World Series. He hit for average and walked a lot but was not a home-run hitter. By the numbers, Cochrane was the best of the bunch, but he suffered a near-fatal beaning midcareer and was never the same afterward. Campanella had already served in the Negro Leagues for several years before the color line was broken and he joined Jackie Robinson with the Dodgers. He was a little old to be a rookie, but not too old to win three league MVP awards before his career abruptly ended when he was paralyzed in a car wreck. Of all of them, Yogi Berra had the most at-bats and posted comparable offensive numbers. And he was, by all accounts, the most fun. I have posted his statistics, but the statistics for Josh Gibson, who played only in the Negro Leagues, are sketchy. Old-timers can still point to the spot in Yankee Stadium where he hit a home run in a Negro League game. No one, including Babe Ruth and Mickey Mantle, hit one farther. Perhaps the best way to explain him is to quote Campanella. "When I broke in," Campy said, "there were already a hundred legends about him. Once you saw him play, you knew they were all true. I couldn't carry his bat or glove." All of these old-time catchers are in the Hall of Fame.

In my field of choices, Bench made it to Cooperstown on the first ballot. Fisk made it on his third try, as did Carter. Piazza and Rodriguez will likely make it, too. Despite his longevity, McCarver will not make the Cooperstown squad. And he may not make mine. Bench will start most of the games but, every fifth game, either Maddux or Carlton will take the mound and will not throw to Bench. If it's Carlton, it's McCarver, who also has the slight advantage of being a left-handed hitter. If Maddux makes it, I will go with Piazza.

CATCHER: BENCH AND PIAZZA OR MCCARVER.

2

First Base

I CAN SEE IT NOW. It's try-out day for first-year Little Leaguers and a big, fat kid trundles out on the field. The coaches stifle their laughter and put the kids through their paces. Fatso doesn't do too well in the running and fielding drills, but when he swings the bat, the ball travels faster and farther than when the other kids hit it. One thought immediately crosses all the parents' minds: first base.

There are some people who think first base is a slugger's position and that the fielding is so easy that anyone, even a slow, fat guy, like Cecil Fielder, could learn to do it. I am not among them. Several great athletes, including Hank Aaron and Mickey Mantle, have stumbled into all kinds of traps around the first-base bag. There is a lot more to the position than catching throws from infielders and learning to pick up ground balls and feed them to the pitcher covering the bag.

Many good hitters play first base because it doesn't require great foot speed. It does, however, require split-second decisions. The most common mistake a new first baseman makes is deciding to cover the bag instead of going for the ball when it is hit to his right. As a rule of thumb, a first baseman should go for every ground ball he can get, and let the pitcher cover the bag. There are some choppers that both the first and second basemen can get to; these plays are easier if the first baseman covers the bag. The best first basemen make split-second decisions and break one way or the other immediately. Instinctive reactions, by definition, are those that cannot be learned. I don't know of another way to describe how the best first basemen decide which way to go before they really have time to think about it. Perhaps it's muscle memory. It helps a lot to know where the second baseman is playing and how much ground he can cover. It also helps a lot if you know you can make a good throw to the pitcher because you can be more aggressive in fielding the ground balls. If you go to the bag when you *know* you can get to the ball but think that the second baseman *might* also be able to get it, you will allow some base hits when you are wrong. It's a much easier play when the second baseman throws to the first baseman, but it is still possible for the second baseman to make the play and throw to the pitcher for the out. If there is any doubt, the first baseman should go for the ball, but there are a lot of first basemen in the major leagues who are not aggressive on grounders to their right.

In addition, there are plays that require more than just standing near the bag. For instance, on a double down the left-field line with a man on first base, the first baseman has to trail the batter to second base in case there is a play there, because the shortstop and second baseman have other coverage responsibilities. The first baseman becomes the cut-off man on a hit to right field with a man on second base, and it helps to have an accurate arm and a quick transfer after you cut the ball off. The first baseman also has responsibilities on bunt plays and pick-off throws.

First Base

• • •

Most teams grudgingly tolerate a lackluster fielder at this position if he is a good run producer. If you watch the game like most fans, you don't notice the aggressiveness of the first baseman. He seems to be the least important infielder and, even though this is generally true, he is not an *unimportant* infielder. Since the first baseman handles the ball more than anyone but the pitcher and the catcher, it takes a lot of concentration to play the position well. Daydreamers need not apply. Still, many famous first basemen have been uninspired fielders. They made their money with their bats, not their mitts.

The players I am considering for this position are all adequate, but some of them are sluggers first and fielders as an afterthought. Some are not aggressive on balls to their right. Some seldom throw to other bases for force-outs or tag plays. Like all managers, I would tolerate an average fielder to get his booming bat in the lineup, but I will give extra credit to those first basemen who are good fielders.

The candidates for My Team are Harmon Killebrew, Willie McCovey, Willie Stargell, Orlando Cepeda, Eddie Murray, Andres Galarraga, Jeff Bagwell, Keith Hernandez, Don Mattingly, Jim Thome, and Frank Thomas. I imagine some fans will wonder why I have not included Fred McGriff or Ernie Banks. McGriff was perhaps a better hitter than Cepeda but he was well below average as a fielder and base runner. Banks split his career between shortstop and first base. He did his best hitting in the late fifties when he won two MVP awards as a shortstop. He did not play ten full years at either position, but since he was better when he was younger, I will include him as a shortstop. Killebrew played third base, left field, and was a DH at the end of his career. I am considering him a first baseman because he played there more than anywhere else.

For a historical perspective, I am including Lou Gehrig. Gehrig's hitting exceeded that of all of the moderns, but he played in the most bountiful offensive era in the history of the game. He also played half his games in a ballpark that favored left-handed power hitters—Yankee Stadium. His biography is also clear about one weakness: At the start of his career, he was not a good fielder. Let's take a look at the whole field.

THE CANDIDATES

PLAYERS	OBA	SLG	OBS	R/PA	RBI/AB	SB	CS
BAGWELL	.418	.572	.990	1/6.0	1/4.8	166	61
F. THOMAS	.438	.594	1.032	1/6.3	1/4.5	26	17
GALARRAGA	.359	.526	.886	1/7.0	1/5.2	99	53
HERNANDEZ	.393	.446	.839	1/7.3	1/6.5	80	51
MATTINGLY	.360	.484	.844	1/7.5	1/6.1	13	9
MURRAY	.383	.505	.888	1/7.3	1/5.6	66	23
STARGELL	.373	.550	.923	1/7.0	1/5.0	6	8
MCCOVEY	.391	.554	.945	1/7.4	1/5.0	15	11
CEPEDA	.357	.526	.882	1/7.1	1/5.5	121	57
KILLEBREW	.387	.546	.933	1/7.2	1/4.7	17	15
THOME	.419	.586	1.005	1/6.1	1/4.7	10	14
GEHRIG	.458	.659	1.117	1/4.9	1/3.8	80	89

I hate to eliminate Mark McGwire because he admitted to using androstenedione, a muscle-building substance that he could buy at a health-food store. Some people think he was using illegal steroids as well, even though there is no hard evidence. If you go by the numbers, though, you might guess that he was doing something different from 1996 through 1998. If we eliminate those seasons, he has only eight good seasons to go on and doesn't qualify for My Team.

I know Tony La Russa, McGwire's manager throughout most of his career, would object. He clearly thinks Big Mac didn't break the law. But Tony knows enough to know he doesn't know everything. It is common for players to confide in coaches. It happened on every team I ever played with. When the avuncular coach becomes the manager, the players always find another confidante. La Russa's belief is shaped not only out of respect for McGwire, but also for his first base coach. "I based my judgment on Dave McKay," he said. "He has as much integrity as anyone I know and I've known him for a long time. He was with me in Oakland when McGwire came up. Mac was always big but, in the beginning, he had some baby fat. I saw him grow stronger, but not from one year to the next. Dave has been into fitness and nutrition along with weight training for a long time. He put Mac on a program and slowly the fat turned into muscle. Dave would tell you that what Mark did was based on working his ass off, not steroids." But even Dave might not know. The only one who knows for sure is McGwire, and he has not admitted to taking steroids— or denied taking them.

I am surprised how upset people get about this issue. In my mind this is not the same as taking illegal recreational drugs. I would have taken steroids in self-defense if I thought my opponents were taking them. Almost all the players of my generation could say, "There, but for the grace of God, go I." I know because I asked a lot of them.

(A shadowy aspect of this issue is that it can take many forms. I have spoken with some of the medical people who work with athletes and have learned that it is possible to use steroids and get stronger without really getting bigger. I had assumed that you could pick the culprits by measuring their biceps.)

I did all the research and analysis on Rafael Palmeiro before he failed his steroid test in 2005. Now I have to eliminate him, too. This makes my selection process easier, but it also turns my stomach. Any manager in his right mind would be happy to have McCovey, Thome, Murray, Thomas, or Killebrew on his team, despite the fact that they were not great fielders. They were all decent with the mitt, and made up for their fielding shortcomings with their power hitting. At first, I didn't have Frank Thomas on my list of candidates because I thought of him mostly as a DH, and there is no DH in my league. When I reviewed his record during his best ten years, I found that he played first base more often than he was a DH. Big Frank wasn't the best first baseman in the world but Thome and Killebrew weren't too nimble either. All three of them have better hitting numbers than most of the other candidates. Tom Paciorek, who broadcast White Sox games during the first half of Thomas's career, said of him, "The one thing that stands out for me is the way he hit the good pitchers." One time the White Sox were playing the Blue Jays and Juan Guzman was just plain nasty. Frank got our first hit in about the fifth inning. He hit a perfect slider, down and away, off the right center field fence for a double. He ended up scoring in that inning. Then late in the game it was 1–1 and we had a man on first. Guzman threw him a 96 mph fastball right in on the hands and Frank hit it off the left center field fence and we won the game. In terms of having good at-bats against the best pitchers, he's the best I've ever seen. He was okay at first base before he got so big. He couldn't throw well at all, but he had pretty good hands. He was faster than you would think, too—not a bad base runner."

Stargell was a little better in the field. He had good hands and a good arm. He would throw to second or third base for outs without hesitation, but he did not have good range. Cepeda was a little faster and he had a pretty good arm. He was a lot like Galarraga in the field but he didn't have quite as good an arm and wasn't quite as fast. If you consider defense only, Hernandez and Mattingly are the best, followed closely by Galarraga and Bagwell. Hernandez won 11 Gold Gloves and is the best defensive first baseman I have ever seen. Mattingly won nine Gold Gloves and many experts who saw him more often than I did believe that he was as good as Hernandez.

Before he had shoulder surgery, Bagwell was as aggressive as any of them. He is the only guy I have seen play shallow on a left-handed hitter with a man on second and nobody out, and throw the runner out at third on a tag play. He may have missed a few outs on ground balls that he could have gotten if he were playing back. I don't remember this happening, but the rally-killing throws to third are unforgettable plays. And there were at least eight or ten of them. I have also seen Jeff charge so hard that he actually fielded bunts on the third-base side of the infield and was able to get the force at third on what looked like a good bunt. He also had an uncanny knack for knowing when the second baseman could get to a ball and when he couldn't. When he went to his right, he went quickly and without hesitation. Before his shoulder surgery, he made firm throws to the pitchers so that they didn't have to break stride approaching the bag.

In recent years, Jeff has used the underhand lob more often. This is understandable, because no first baseman wants to throw the ball hard and throw it away, allowing the runner to advance. He didn't worry about this when his arm was sound. Almost every first baseman except Hernandez and Mattingly lobbed the ball more often than he should have. Sometimes, the lob throw forces the pitcher to decide between looking at the bag and trying to catch the lob or looking at the ball and trying to touch the bag. You can't look two places at the same time and, most of the time, the lob toss comes when the first baseman is close to the bag and should run over and touch it himself. Still, I don't recall many misplays on lob tosses. I do, however, remember making an error on one myself. On that play, the first baseman started running to the bag, then decided he wasn't going to make it in time and lobbed it to me. I looked at it, stuck my glove out, then looked for the bag. I got the bag but the ball bounced off my glove. All of the first basemen on the list, including the uninspired fielders, were good at digging the low throws out of the dirt. That's the aspect of the position that attracts the most attention and, though it isn't easy, you don't need to be a gifted athlete to learn how to do it.

Galarraga was a lot like Bagwell. I have not seen him throw to third for a tag play, but Andres had real soft hands and a good strong arm. He was nicknamed the "Cat," which is an unusual moniker for a big guy, but his athleticism made him worthy of the name. He almost never boxed a ground ball. Like Bagwell and Hernandez, he ranged far to his right to make plays. I believe he was faster than Jeff and Keith. In fact, I think he had more range than Bagwell and as much as Hernandez.

Keith Hernandez and Don Mattingly did all of these things as well or better than anyone, and had the advantage of throwing left-handed. Though *I* haven't seen either of them throw a runner out at third base on a tag play, I suspect they did. They both had strong, accurate arms and were willing to take the risk of an aggressive throw on a play that was bound to be close. Like Bagwell, they have fielded bunts on the third-base side of the infield and gotten the force at third. In fact, Hernandez's arm was so good that the Cardinals made him the relay man instead of the cut-off man on hits down the right-field line. He had a better chance to throw out an advancing runner than Cardinal's second baseman Tommy Herr. He was the cut-off man on balls straight away to right field and right center as one would expect. I have seen Keith throw runners out on a relay from the outfield and cut balls off and throw runners out at second or third, even when it seemed like there was no possibility of making the play. The only other first baseman I have seen who compares to Hernandez and Mattingly is Wes Parker, but Wes didn't hit well enough to make My Team or the Dogs. Bagwell won one Gold Glove, but recently the honor has deservedly gone to Mark Grace and J. T. Snow. Gold Gloves are often given to guys who don't have great range but also don't make many errors. You can't tolerate too many errors at any position but, generally speaking, range is more important than fielding percentage, even at first base. Very few first baseman have a strong arm and the willingness to use it.

Killebrew, Murray, McCovey, Stargell, Thome, Thomas, Mattingly, and Cepeda were station-to-station base runners. Bagwell, Galarraga, and Hernandez weren't jackrabbits, but they did have enough speed to go from first to third on a lot of singles and score from first on most doubles. This ability helps the offense in ways that are incalculable unless you watch all the games and keep track of what happens to the trailing runners. When a base runner is a base-clogger he prevents the runners behind him from moving up. If the first runner advances, many times the trail runner advances, too. This takes the double-play option away from the defense and puts another runner in scoring position. I have seen more of Bagwell than the rest of the first basemen and have often commented on his instincts. Except for Willie Mays, Jeff is the best instinctive runner I have ever seen. Mays could go from first to third on a hit to right and run full speed while looking backward. Bagwell never looked back, but he did take the extra base most of the time and, though a lot of the plays were close, he slid feet first and almost never got thrown out. He never took the big belly-flop slide like Pete Rose, but he didn't get thrown out nearly as often either.

The way this discussion is heading, with my predilection for good fielders, you might assume that I am going to go with Hernandez or Mattingly and Bagwell or Galarraga as a platoon at first base and you might be right. But first, let's look at the hitting.

In terms of OBS, Frank Thomas is the best hitter in the group. His runs scored per plate appearance and his RBI per at-bat are slightly lower than Jim Thome's, but he didn't have as many good hitters in front of and behind him. Thome got some help at Jacobs Field because it is a hitter's ballpark. He also got some help from his teammates. With Robby Alomar and Kenny Lofton getting on base in front of him there were a lot of RBI opportunities. He also scored more often than you might expect because he had Manny Ramirez, Albert Belle, and a few other sluggers like David Justice and Matt Williams hitting behind him. Most of the teams Thomas played for were mediocre at best, which makes his OBS even more impressive. If he had played for the Tribe, as Thome did, he probably would have scored more runs and his RBI numbers would have been better, too. The best thing a pitcher can do against hitters like Thomas and Thome is to get them to hit the ball on the ground. I would pitch both of them low and away with sinkers and breaking balls and come inside of the inside corner occasionally. I'd probably walk them a lot, just like the pitchers of their own generation.

Bagwell slots in just behind Thome. Jeff played his first nine years in the Astrodome, one of the best pitcher's ballparks in the league, which makes his production even more impressive. It offsets the fact that he played when the pitching wasn't as good as it was in the sixties and seventies. Bagwell was a mistake hitter. He seldom hit a good pitch out of the ballpark but he almost always hit a mistake pitch hard during his prime years. I would pitch him like any other power hitter, high and tight and low and away. He walked almost as much as Thome, but he ran a lot better. He could steal a base and, for that reason, he could make you pay double for a walk. One thing I have to consider is that the opportunities to score and drive in runs in the era of the DH helps the modern American League hitters. I have to keep reminding myself of this. From this perspective, Thome had a significant advantage over Bagwell in terms of opportunities.

First Base

As a pitcher I would rather face all the right-handed hitters than any of the left-handed hitters. I could retire them with a good fastball up and in, or a slider low and away most of the time. However, if I got the fastball out over the plate or the slider to the middle of the plate, up or down, they would punish me.

Until 1969, when McCovey won the MVP award, I could pound him up and in without fear. He didn't really learn to hit the up and in fastball *in* '69, but he did stop swinging at it. Since it is hard to get a called strike up and in, I started having trouble with him, either walking him or getting behind in the count and giving him a pitch out over the plate that he could handle. It's hard to believe, but McCovey used a short, light bat, just like the players of this era. With his long arms, he didn't need a long bat. Most of the hitters used heavy bats back then. Most of the power hitters swung from the knob of the bat then, too. Now, because Barry Bonds has hit with so much power while choking up on the bat, more hitters are choking up, which makes the light bats seem even lighter.

I was more fearful of throwing McCovey a sinker away than I was with Stargell. McCovey hit the ball up the middle and to left center a lot. Stargell usually pulled the ball against me. I had some success throwing McCovey sliders, but it seemed like every time I threw one to Stargell, he would get an extra-base hit.

Both of these sluggers hit just about as well as the players of recent vintage. I'm sure their numbers would be better if they had played in the eighties and nineties and the first decade of this new century. But they wouldn't run any faster or field any better and, for that reason, I have left all but one of them off My Team.

Willie Stargell was tough on me. It seemed like every hit he got went for extra bases. In one game at Forbes Field, he hit a grand slam off me before I got an out! Willie used a heavy piece of timber. He twirled it around like a baton as he waited for the pitch. He had great plate coverage and was a good off-speed hitter. About the only way I could get him out was with fastballs up and in. I did strike him out a lot that way, but he more than made up for it when I failed to get it all the way in there. Stargell most often played left field during the first part of his career and played more games in the outfield than he did in the infield. He did play 848 games at first base and I think there are others who would be better in left field because they could run faster and cover more ground. Willie was pretty good at first and very good in the clubhouse. "I don't know who said he was a bad first baseman but they were wrong," said team-mate Phil Garner. "He may not have had as much range as some of them but he had soft hands and a very good arm."

Harmon Killebrew was the prototypical home-run hitter. He was short and hit out of a wide-legged squat, similar to Bagwell. When he hit a high pitch with his uppercut swing, it seldom came down in the field of play. He hit home runs in wholesale lots and drove in more than 100 runs nine times, even though he played in a low-scoring era. I would try to keep the ball down on him with sinkers and sliders. It's hard to uppercut a knee-high pitch. I faced him a few times in spring training and don't remember any long homers. Of course, I don't remember striking him out either. I am pretty sure, however, that I would rather face "Killer" than McCovey or Stargell. They all would have posted better numbers if they had come along a little later.

Unlike Killebrew, Orlando Cepeda was a low-ball hitter. He swung a heavy bat, like Stargell, and generated his power more with his arms and torso than with his wrists. He hit a two-run homer off me in my first big-league game and I lost the game 2–0. Cepeda hit over .300 ten times, but his production fell short of some of the other first basemen because he didn't walk very much. I usually threw him riding four-seam fastballs rather than sinkers at the knees because he liked the low pitch.

In May 1968, I faced Bob Gibson in St. Louis and we were

ahead 3–2 when Cepeda came up in the ninth with two outs and a man on second base. Getting three runs off Gibson that year was practically a miracle and I was determined to take advantage of it. Since I had already thrown Cepeda a lot of four-seamers that day, I had the brilliant idea of throwing him a two-seamer down around the knees. The Baby Bull took a mighty swing at it and hit it straight up in the air. It seemed to stay up there forever but, when it finally came down, our shortstop caught it to end the game. That's the last time I threw him that pitch. It was designed to get a ground ball and when he popped it up I got the win due to pure luck.

I never faced Eddie Murray, but I did watch him in the postseason and also when he was with the Dodgers and Mets near the end of his venerable career. He was a switch-hitter and was a little bit better against right-handed pitchers. I'm not sure how I would pitch to him because I've seen him hit good pitches on the corners and miss pitches right down the middle. That, in itself, would not tempt me to pitch him down the middle. I did learn, however, that there was more to hitting all those tough pitches than luck. "He was such a great clutch hitter," his long-time teammate Rick Dempsey said. "And it was no accident. Eddie would swing at pitches low and away and up and in during batting practice. He actually practiced hitting tough pitches, trying to flare them over the infield. You won't see many hitters doing that." Murray scored more and drove in more runs than any of them. His ratios aren't as good as those of many of the others, but his longevity is very impressive.

Andres Galarraga has good ratios, but I had to do a little interpolating to judge him. One thing that hurt him is that he inexplicably had a two-year slump in 1991 and 1992, during the prime of his career. On the other hand, he did reap the benefits of playing half his games in Denver for five seasons, where he had a slugging percentage close to .600. The Big Cat struck out a lot. I would have pitched him just like I pitched Johnny Bench, Roberto Clemente, Cepeda, Bagwell, or almost all right-handed power hitters—up and in with the fastball and low and away with the fastball and slider, with an occasional off-speed pitch in the dirt. I don't think he would have hit for much average against me but I know he would have hit a few home runs.

In 1979, Willie Stargell and Keith Hernandez tied for the N.L. MVP award. Hernandez led the league in hitting that season and also scored the most runs. That year he reached his career high with 105 RBI. Stargell was hurt in the early part of the '79 season and didn't produce as many runs as Hernandez. Hernandez was not a typical hitter at his position. He hit for high average but did not hit a lot of home runs. His RBI ratio is last among this elite group of players and his OBS is also last. He is, however, the only first baseman who walked more often than he struck out, and I feel safe in saying that he advanced more runners just by making contact than any of the others. When a runner advances on an out, it can be a positive event for the team, but until quite recently it has not been considered a statistic.

Hernandez's RBI production was good, even in the midst of these slugging first sackers, and his runs scored ratio is excellent. I was traded to the Cardinals in 1976 and Keith and I lived in the same apartment complex. We occasionally rode to and from the ballpark together and I got to know him pretty well. One time, I asked him if he remembered how I pitched to him the year before. He told me that I pounded him inside and that he was frustrated that he didn't hit me harder. I told him that though I hoped to get him out on an inside fastball, I tried to set it up by throwing sinkers off the outside corner of the plate. This is one of the principles of good pitching: Show the hitter some pitches almost where he likes them and then go back to his area of weakness. He liked the fastball away, so I threw it too far away, trying to give him the impression that I would make a mistake in his happy zone. I wouldn't purposefully throw a strike out there. If I did, he would hit it hard. One day, when we were riding to the ballpark, he told me that the pitcher who was going for the other team that night (I think it was Larry Christenson) had pitched him like I had and he was determined to change that. "I'm going to sit on the inside fastball," he told me. "When he comes in there I'm going to hit it hard, even if I hit it foul. I'm going to show him I can hit that pitch. Then maybe I'll get a fastball away." Sure enough, he hit an inside fastball into the right-field corner for a double. If I had pitched to him after he became an experienced hitter, he likely would have done the same thing to me.

In terms of team chemistry, Bagwell, McCovey, and Killebrew were similar—silent types who had great strength and sharp focus. "We called McCovey 'Easy'" his Giants teammate Jack Hiatt said. "because he was so easygoing. He was quiet. I don't think he ever got thrown out of a game. And in a world of superstars (Mays, Marichal, Perry, Cepeda) he was never the least bit jealous. He was one of the guys and even though he didn't talk a lot, he always listened and laughed. Most people don't know how hard it was for him to play with two bad knees. They didn't know because he never talked about it. But we all saw him getting them taped before every game, even when he was young." The Big Cat, Galarraga, laughed a lot, but he was more of a go-along-and-get-along guy than a leader. All these guys were chemistry neutral—they wouldn't do anything to upset the chemical balance.

Jim Kaat played with Killebrew and described him as the cornerstone of the franchise. "He wasn't an emotional guy, but he was a gentleman and he was rock solid," Kaat said. "One time a writer told me he was not going to vote for Killer for the Hall of Fame. 'He's nothing but a home-run hitter,' the guy told me, and I said, 'Yeah, but he hit 573 of them.'" Killebrew was eventually voted into the Hall of Fame, four years later. "I think a lot of people saw him as one-dimensional and he was," Kaat said. "But that one dimension won us a lot of games. If he were playing today, he would probably be a DH."

Like Stan Musial, Jim Thome is a happy warrior. He led more by what he did than by what he said. "He will speak his mind," Phils manager Charlie Manuel said. "But he doesn't yell at people or anything like that. He just goes out there and takes his ground balls every day and shows his teammates how a major leaguer is supposed to act. I was his hitting coach when he was a kid and I've never had a more coachable player. And he's honest, almost to a fault. He's never been a fast runner, but he used to go first to third easily. Now, it's a little harder. In fact, the only thing that sometimes hurts him is when the team is going bad and he starts trying *too hard*. But that doesn't happen very often. Mostly, he is just a real happy guy. He loves just being at the ballpark."

Bagwell led the Astros by example throughout his career but seldom spoke about it. In fact, he is so quiet that I can't really say I know him very well even after associating with him for 11 years. But, like Thome, he takes his ground balls, doesn't ask for favors or make excuses. He had a tremendous effect on all the young players that came to the Astros during and after he became a star, more than ten years ago.

Stargell was not neutral. He was a positive influence on the Pirates, especially late in his career. His observation that the umpire says, "Play ball" instead of "Work ball," says a lot about his personality. He loved the game and had a good time on the field, often smiling and shooting the breeze. In 1979, he came on strong at the end of the year, leading the "We Are Family" Pirates to a World Championship. His Pirates teammates called him "Pops."

"He was a team builder," Phil Garner said. "In the first game of the World Series that year, I made an error with the bases loaded and it cost us two runs and the game. After the game I was disconsolate. I felt awful. Willie came up to me on the bus and said. 'Look, I made an error, too.' When I looked up, he had his index finger tucked into his palm and his hand pushed up against his nose so it looked like he didn't have an index finger.

'I cut off my finger,' he said. I couldn't help laughing. It really helped me feel better. But, that's the way he was. He always noticed things like that and always said just the right thing."

Another teammate, Dave Giusti, had the same experience. "I gave up that opposite-field home run to Johnny Bench in the playoffs," he said. "After the game, Willie came up to me and said, 'Don't worry about it. He never hits to the opposite field. He just got lucky. And besides, it's not that important. Think about your family. You have a great family and that's what's really important.'"

For Garner, the stars on the hats were as memorable as anything. "He started the gold stars we wore on our hats," Phil said. "It seems so juvenile, but it became a morale builder on our club. You remember those stovepipe hats we used to wear. He decided who got a star. There were no criteria except that you did something exceptional to help us win a game. After a while, guys started stealing stars from other guys. Kent Tekulve was only awarded two or three, but all of a sudden he had twelve on his hat. We all got a laugh out of that." It's one thing when a zany player like Casey Candaele makes you laugh, keeps you loose, consoles you. But it's another when the best player on the team does it.

Stargell was a leader in both words and deeds. "One time when we were playing in St. Louis, Darold Knowles struck him out with a big sidearm curve," Garner recalled. "Willie came back to the dugout and said, 'If he throws that pitch again, I'm going to hit it out of the stadium.' Well, the next time he came up Knowles got him down in the count 0-2. Then he threw that curve and Willie hit in into the upper deck. It wasn't just what he said that helped the team. It was also what he did.

"And the other thing he did that everyone on the team had to notice was keep his head in the game. He didn't slam helmets or bats; didn't yell at pitchers or charge the mound. He was as competitive as anyone else but he kept his fire burning on the inside."

Murray was another quiet man, but he did say enough to spark some fires with the media. He sometimes seemed aloof, was often moody, and some people thought he was a negative influence in the clubhouse. It would be hard to verify this by talking to his teammates. Orioles catcher Rick Dempsey scoffed at the notion. "Eddie was a great guy on the team. On the field and in the clubhouse and on the bench between innings." Dempsey claims that Murray set the bar high for the younger players by being so persistent and consistent. His understated hostility toward opponents gave the teams he played for a little more grit.

Cepeda had a more complicated personality. He was moody at times but, when he was with the Cardinals, he was a great teammate and a very smart player. When he was playing well, he was a positive influence on the team. But he didn't play well for as many years as some of the other candidates. From the standpoint of team chemistry, I would say that the "Baby Bull" was average.

Keith Hernandez was a complicated guy, too. He is one of the few guys who got crosswise with Whitey Herzog. One day, when I was with the Cardinals in 1977, we had a doubleheader and it was a hot, steamy, windless day in St. Louis. Suffocating heat waves rose from the Astroturf and you couldn't wear metal spikes because the rivets would burn your feet. Keith played the first game and the lineup was posted for the second game about five minutes before we had to go back to the field. When his name wasn't on the card, he threw a tantrum, cussing and throwing things around the clubhouse. I'm not sure I know of another player—including Ernie Banks—who would have reacted so violently to not playing two games on that particular day.

In addition to having that competitive fire burning all the time, Keith was one of the smartest players I have known. He was the infielder who took the signs and called the bunt defense plays for both the Cardinals and Mets. During the 1986

LCS, he was the only player on the Mets who didn't accuse Mike Scott of scuffing the baseball. "We're big-league hitters," he said. "If he throws it in the strike zone, we're supposed to be able to hit it." That statement says a lot, too. He expected to succeed, no matter what. Even though he went only 1 for 7 against Scott in that series, he was not intimidated or psyched out when he faced him. Although he sometimes seemed immature and could be disruptive, I would say that, on balance, he was a positive force on a team. I am tempted to select him because his fielding would save runs, and because My Team will have plenty of home-run power in the lineup anyway. Keith would be a good table setter, score a lot of runs, and help the pitchers with his fielding.

The best right-handed hitters in the bunch are Thomas and Bagwell. Jeff's hitting numbers aren't quite as impressive as Thomas's, but the Astrodome effect and the DH largely offset that margin. They were both a little better than Stargell and McCovey, and a lot better than Hernandez. I prefer Bagwell to Thomas because of his fielding and base running. I would not go with a straight platoon arrangement. I would start Bagwell against some of the right-handed pitchers and all of the lefties. I could use pitcher vs. hitter matchups and left vs. right comparisons in filling out the lineup card. Chances are, Bagwell would play more than half the time. Considering everything, I am taking Willie Stargell as my second first baseman. His tangible qualities are excellent and his intangibles are over the top.

FIRST BASE: BAGWELL, STARGELL.

3

Second Base

WHEN I WAS YOUNG and just getting started in the game, there seemed to be an unwritten rule that the kid who could run sort of fast but had a weak arm always played second base. And it was almost inevitable that this kid could make contact with the ball, but didn't have any power. As I continued in the game, and the distance between bases stretched out to 90 feet, speed and quickness on the infield became even more important. The kid that played second usually hit at the top or the bottom of the lineup where he had to learn to bunt and steal bases. Second basemen were usually spray hitters who could put the ball in play on the hit-and-run. It seems like there were, and always have been, plenty of second basemen who can do just about everything except throw hard and hit home runs

In the big leagues, things changed. Some second baseman at the highest level have good arm strength and a few can hit the ball out of the ballpark. This is nothing new. Starting with Larry "Nap" Lajoie, the guy whose team, the Cleveland Naps, was named after him, there has been a steady procession of hard-hitting second sackers. Eddie "Cocky" Collins, came along just behind Lajoie. Then came Rogers Hornsby; "The Fordham Flash", Frankie Frisch; Tony "Poosh 'em up" Lazzeri; "The Mechanical Man," Charlie Gehringer; and Bobby Doerr. I'm sure there are others, but I know these guys could really hit.

Another player who could provide All-Star caliber play at second base is Martin Dihigo. Dihigo played in the Negro Leagues, the Mexican League, and in his native country, Cuba. He could play virtually every position on the field and was also an excellent pitcher. He is the only player to make the Hall of Fame in three countries, the United States, Mexico, and Cuba. I suppose I could mention Dihigo in just about every chapter, since he played all the positions, but my impression is that he did not have the home-run bat to play the corner positions on My Team. I doubt he could pitch for My Team either, but I think he should be mentioned in any discussion of the greatest all-around players in the history of the sport. In fact, he might have been the most versatile player of all time, but he was not as good a power hitter as Babe Ruth and probably not as good on the mound, either.

As I build My Team, I have no shortage of choices for second base. Since many of the players are similar offensively, I will still be looking for the best fielders, and I will also be looking for guys with good intangible qualities. All but two of my candidates are good at getting on base, which would enable me to use them at the top of the lineup. Jeff Kent and Ryne Sandberg hit with more power than most of the others, but would probably fit better toward the back half of the lineup, in an RBI slot. Since I will have power hitters at many of the other positions, I may choose the players who can hit at the top of the lineup.

Because it is an up-the-middle position, quickness, speed, good hands, and good balance are more important than they are at the corner fielding positions (first base, third base, left field, and right field). The ability to turn the double play (which requires more than a little bit of courage, because runners come at you from behind) is critical. It is easier to turn the double play if you have quick feet, quick hands on the transfer from glove to hand, and a strong arm. But it is possible to play second base well without arm strength. Joe Morgan won five Gold Gloves with a weak arm, and Craig Biggio won four. Still, arm strength is important on several plays. One is the double play when the throw from shortstop or third base is high and wide on the outfield side. With a feed like this, the only way you have to avoid the collision is to back up toward left field. Without arm strength this type of double play is almost impossible. A strong arm also helps a lot on relays from the outfield. Additionally, arm strength determines how close any infielder has to play when the infield is drawn in to stop a runner from scoring from third on a ground ball.

Many second basemen are former shortstops who were not quite good enough in the field to play short. In some cases, they didn't have soft enough hands; in others, they lacked arm strength or speed. At second, you can drop the ball and still pick it up in time to get the runner at first. Joe Morgan couldn't have played shortstop for lack of soft hands and a strong arm. Jeff Kent is a pretty good second baseman with a strong arm but isn't fast enough to play short. On the other hand, Roberto Alomar could have played shortstop or any other position.

Second base is a good place to hide an average fielder who is a good hitter. There is no place on the field to hide a poor fielder. For this discussion, I will have the luxury of selecting only players who are good in the field, at the plate, and on the bases. My Team will be playing on natural grass, where speed is not quite as important and soft hands are even more important. This shouldn't rule anyone out, but it may be a tie-breaker in my mind if everything else seems even.

I don't know who the old-timers would have picked to

play this position. I imagine Lajoie, Collins, Frisch, Gehringer, Lazzeri, and Doerr would all have their advocates, but Hornsby was clearly the best hitter. I can argue for or against almost any of these fine players. For comparison, I used Hornsby's stats, as many historians consider him to be the best right-handed hitter of all time. But even Hornsby had an Achilles heel. He had trouble going into the outfield to catch pop flies.

I had to leave a lot of good players off this list. Lou Whitaker, Willie Randolph, Frank White, and Chuck Knoblauch were probably in the same class with Bobby Grich, who is on my list, but I couldn't quite convince myself to list them among the candidates for various reasons.

The players I am considering for the position are Rod Carew, Joe Morgan, Ryne Sandberg, Bobby Grich, Craig Biggio, Roberto Alomar, and Jeff Kent. Biggio started his career as a catcher, but wasn't a great fielder at that position. He did win four Gold Gloves at second base and none as a catcher or in his short career as an outfielder. Because he has played several positions, he would give My Team more versatility. This is how it shakes out: see table on next page.

The hitting totals favor Kent, who is arguably the best power-hitting second baseman in the last forty years, and who is not too far behind Rogers Hornsby on the all-time list. In fact, he now leads Hornsby in home runs, making him the all-time home-run leader among second basemen. Even if he keeps it up for a few more years, I am inclined to look for a fielder who can cover more ground and hit at the top of the lineup. If I select the best run producer at every position I will end up with a slower team with average range on defense and average base running.

After Kent, it becomes a matter of splitting hairs. Roberto Alomar appears to be a slightly better hitter than Joe Morgan, but he has played in an era of great offense. If you factor the era into the analysis, Morgan comes out ahead of all of them, but not by a wide margin. Bobby Grich comes up short in OBS

Second Base

THE CANDIDATES

PLAYERS	OBA	SLG	OBS	R/PA	RBI/AB	SB	CS
MORGAN	.405	.458	.862	1/6.2	1/7.8	510	117
CAREW	.404	.449	.853	1/7.2	1/8.6	264	128
GRICH	.369	.414	.784	1/8.0	1/8.4	89	60
SANDBERG	.352	.472	.824	1/6.9	1/7.7	277	79
ALOMAR	.386	.469	.855	1/6.5	1/7.2	355	83
KENT	.357	.519	.875	1/7.0	1/5.3	74	41
BIGGIO	.382	.450	.832	1/6.3	1/9.0	269	91
HORNSBY	.441	.601	1.042	1/5.6	1/5.0	100	?

and runs scored per plate appearance, but was a good RBI man. He is very highly regarded by scouts, who sometimes see things that aren't in the numbers.

Grich came up to the big leagues with his minor league roommate, Don Baylor, in 1970. Baylor has a vivid memory of the first few days with the Orioles under manager Earl Weaver: "He told us that the team was 16 games in front of the pack and that he wanted to win it by 20 games so we could just sit and watch." Luckily, there were two Robinsons, Frank in the outfield and Brooks at third base, who helped with the transition. It was a good cop/bad cop situation. "Brooks was really nice to us," Baylor said. "He made us feel comfortable and treated us like teammates right from the start." The bad cop, Frank, made them earn their keep. "He wasn't mean, but he was tough. We had to prove we could play before he would accept us."

Both Baylor and Grich spent the next year in the minor leagues and got called up again in September. In 1972, both started playing a lot. "He was a quarterback and was going to go to UCLA, and I was going to play football at UT under Darrell Royal," Baylor said. "We ended up signing to play baseball instead and have been friends ever since. I went from the Orioles to the A's and then to the Angels in 1977. That same year, he went from the Orioles to the Angels. I know I'm prejudiced but, for me, Bobby was the best. He could hit anywhere in the lineup and was a Gold Glove fielder. He only made about five or ten errors a year and he could stand in there with the best of them on the double play. They say Mazeroski was the best, but I'd have to see it to believe anyone could turn it better than Bobby."

(Although this doesn't have anything to do with My Team, I can't resist telling one story. Baylor told me that Grich's favorite player when he was growing up in Long Beach, California, was Angels shortstop Jim Fregosi. When Bobby went to the Angels, Fregosi was the manager. Bobby was single and he had an eye for the ladies. One night he spotted a pretty girl in the box seats and sent one of the clubhouse kids up to her with a note asking if she would join him for a drink after the game. She sent the note back. "I would love to, but there is this one problem," she wrote. "My husband is your manager, and I don't think he would like it.")

Ryne Sandberg, a recent inductee into the Hall of Fame, could hit a home run and steal a base. He was also the most spectacularly understated fielder I have ever seen at the position. He was not, however, a patient hitter. For that reason, he would be better suited to an RBI slot, further back in the batting order. A free-swinging power hitter who can steal a base would be an asset in the 8-hole. He would fit nicely in that spot in the lineup because his base stealing would obviate the need for a sacrifice bunt with the pitcher batting. If he took off right away and made it, the pitcher could bunt him to third or the manager could employ a pinch hitter. (There is no DH in My Team's league.)

Second Base

Rod Carew was an outstanding hitter and a good base stealer, too. (He was especially good at stealing home.) His numbers are lower than you might expect because, like Morgan, he played when the pitching was better than it is now. Carew also played on natural grass throughout his career, which made it more difficult to steal a base and to get a triple.

Craig Biggio slots in just behind Morgan. He had the advantage of spending most of his career in a high-scoring era but had the offsetting disadvantage of playing in the Astrodome during his prime seasons. Biggio is like Pete Rose, with more speed and more power. He won't last as long as Rose, but I would say that he was one of the top-ten offensive players in the league during the late 1990s. He can also serve as an emergency catcher, which is about as important as a hood ornament. It's still a nice accessory, though, because it gives the manager the ability to use his second catcher as a pinch hitter. For example, let's say it's the bottom of the ninth and I had a hitter like Willie Stargell due with the tying run on second base. If my second catcher were Mike Piazza, and a lefty with a wicked slider like Sparky Lyle were on the mound, I might use Piazza to pinch-hit for Stargell. If Piazza tied the game and it went into extra innings and Bench got hurt, I could put Biggio behind the plate, because he is a legitimate catcher. (No manager would want to be caught without a real catcher in an extra-inning game.)

Biggio and Morgan were destined to play second base because they didn't have strong arms or soft hands. They both plucked ground balls instead of gathering them in like Alomar and Sandberg. Morgan and Biggio overcame their shortcomings with desire. They had first-step quickness, raw speed, and unwavering determination. Neither of them made as many clean plays on ground balls as Sandberg and Alomar, but they still got the outs even when they had to knock a ball down and quickly pick it up and throw it. Because they were fast enough to get in front of most ground balls, the bobbling assist was almost always possible. Both of them played a little further up the middle and faced slightly toward the first base dugout to compensate for their lack of arm strength. No, they couldn't turn the double play like Bill Mazeroski, and didn't look graceful fielding ground balls, but they found a way to do a good job. If they had been third basemen, they wouldn't have had enough arm strength to knock a ball down and throw a runner out like they could at second base. Biggio and Morgan were born to play second, but, unlike the Little League kid who was a weak hitter, they could generate a lot of firepower. Pitcher Jack Billingham, who went to Cincinnati with Morgan in the deal that became famous in Cincy and infamous in Houston, summarized Morgan in just a few words. He said, "In Houston, Joe was an All-Star; in Cincinnati, he became a Hall of Famer. He's the best hitter I ever played with."

Before I started analyzing the statistics, I thought that the switch-hitting Alomar would rise to the top because he was blessed with more natural ability than the rest of the candidates. His offense was excellent, as were his defensive range and his arm strength. He was fearless at the plate. In fact, he hit a home run off Nolan Ryan the first time he ever faced him and he was only 20 years old at the time. In the field he was so smoooooth—almost to the point of insouciance. What worries me is that he has changed teams so often. The fact that he moved around so much sends up a red flag. I'm not reactionary enough to kill an Alomar entry on circumstances. But I still have to ask myself, "Why would a gifted player like Robbie or like Richie (Dick) Allen get traded so much?" In Allen's case, I tend to think that management (not teammates) thought he would spoil the chemistry of the team. Dick used to show up late for batting practice, a behavior that wouldn't be acceptable in any ordinary business. Most managers declare that they have one set of rules that apply to everyone on the team, but I have never found this to be true. There are always exceptions to the rules, and, almost every time, they involve concessions to star players, like Allen. I think the players on a team can accept two sets of rules, one for the rank and file and another for the stars, as long as those stars keep shining. Management is less liable to be tolerant. Allen had extraordinary ability, but most people thought he could have been even better. Perhaps it was the same way with Alomar. Still, one thing is clear: Roberto could make some plays that Morgan and Biggio could not make. He was such a gifted athlete that he made difficult plays look easy and could steal a base without raising much dust. And he could hit the ball out of the ballpark, too.

Of course, Morgan and Biggio were also great base stealers with home-run power. They accomplished the same things as Alomar, but didn't look as good doing them. In the final analysis, I lean toward a combination of Morgan and Biggio. What Alomar performs with sleight of hand, Biggio and Morgan trump with relentless will. In my scheme of things, Morgan would start most of the games and Biggio would start once or twice a week, pinch-hit, and pinch-run. Both of them would hit in the lead-off spot, which would allow me to change one name on the lineup card without changing the whole card. The intangibles favor Morgan and Biggio, too. Though both of them are so fiercely competitive that they can sometimes create friction, they are also so determined to win that they give a team an edge. The luxury of having a third catcher on the squad is the deciding factor for me between Biggio and Alomar.

I know there are experts who would favor Kent for his power, Alomar for his athleticism, and Grich for his toughness. Some might favor Carew for his ability to hit virtually any kind of pitch in the strike zone, and hit it hard in any direction. Had Rod played on Astroturf, he would have stolen more bases and scored more runs. He would never have hit as many home runs as the others, but his numbers would be better if he had played for the Big Red Machine. Cubs fans will be indignant at the snubbing of Ryne Sandberg, and with good reason. Except for

Alomar, Sandberg probably had the best combination of talents. But on My Team, he would have to hit eighth, which is the spot I have reserved for my catcher.

I have a feeling that another team could be formed of the players I have rejected that could beat my team 40 percent of the time. (In fact, I've chosen that team, the Underdogs.) Forty percent seems like a big number until you realize that the last place team each year plays about .400 baseball or a little less, while the best team plays about .600, sometimes a little better. At the second base position, I don't think it is possible to get a 60-40 advantage. I feel good about my choices, but I would be happy with a 55-45 split. I also think I can get better than a 60-40 advantage at some of the other positions.

SECOND BASE: MORGAN, BIGGIO.

4

Third Base

LOOKING BACK through the archives, I find that the pantheon at third base is almost empty. My guess is that, during the early days of the sport, when the dead ball was in play, fielding at this position was deemed more important than hitting, especially power hitting. As a result, Pie Traynor is the only player I have found to give a historical perspective. Traynor's numbers are pretty good but not as impressive as many of the recent defenders of the hot corner. Another player who might have been as good as any of them is Judy Johnson, who played only in the Negro Leagues and was one of the best third baseman of his time.

From a fielding standpoint, third base is all reactions. You don't have a lot of time to think about whether you should stay back on a ground ball or charge it. Lateral range is not as big a factor as it is at shortstop and second base, but a strong arm is an asset because it allows you to play deep on right-handed power hitters, thus improving your range. It also allows you to block a ball and pick it up in time to throw a runner out. If you play back, you need a high caliber, accurate gun. If you don't have the strong arm, however, you can overcome that disadvantage with a quick release and accurate throws. To play third well, you have to be able to throw on the run from different angles, from cutting in front of the shortstop on a chopper to charging a swinging bunt, from making a bare-handed play to throwing across your body. Still, the talent that is most important at third is quickness. You have to decide how to play the ball before you have a chance to think about it, and you have to get out of the blocks immediately. During the last forty years or so, there have been many third basemen who have hit hard and fielded well enough to play every day.

Take Brooks Robinson, for example. He won sixteen consecutive Gold Gloves and is still considered by many scouts to have been the best fielding third baseman ever—and he didn't have a strong arm at all. "But Brooks was smart," said his teammate Don Baylor. "He knew where to play and where to throw the ball when he got it. If it was first and third, he knew when to throw home and when to go for the double play."

During the early 1990s, the Astros utility infielder was Casey Candaele. When Casey filled in at short, he did just fine. He played second base about as well as anyone. I had no doubt he could play third base well, too. At one point, when Ken Caminiti was injured, Casey had to play third for about a month. He started slowly, making a few errors, and never got much better. I asked him what was so tough about it and he said it was the angle. "When I play short," he said, "I see the pitch and the hitter's reaction to it. It seems like I have a lot of time to decide how to play a ground ball. It's the same thing at second base. But when I play third, I don't get a good look at the pitch because I'm standing off to the side of it. It's all reactions and I don't always make the right decision. I never thought it would be that hard to play third, but it has been."

Gary Gaetti, another great third baseman, that didn't quite make the list of candidates, probably could have helped Casey by telling him what he told me. "You really can't watch the pitch at third," he said. "You have to watch the hitting zone, right in front of the plate. If you watch the pitch, it'll throw you off and you won't get a good jump."

When I think about the best third basemen, I am reminded of a passage from Lawrence Ritter's classic baseball book, *The Glory of Their Times*. When Tommy Leach was a twenty-year-old third baseman for Auburn (of the New York State League), his manager told him that his contract was either going to be sold to Washington or to Louisville, both major league teams at that time. "Which one do you want to go to?" his manager asked. Leach told him that he would like to go to the team where he would have the best chance of playing. His manager said the Washington team had a great third baseman by the name of Wagner, so Leach chose Louisville. (Louisville was in the National League then, and would soon move to Pittsburgh and become the Pirates.) On his first day with the new team, Leach sat, mouth agape, on the bench and watched his new team's third baseman make one great play after another. Leach turned to the guy next to him on the bench and asked who the third baseman was. "Why, that's Wagner," he was told. "He's the best third baseman in the league." Leach groaned, and wondered if his old manager had betrayed him. As it turned out, Washington did have a good third baseman named Wagner—Al Wagner. His brother, Honus, was right there at Louisville, starting his Hall of Fame career.

It eventually worked out well for Leach. He was good enough to start, so they moved Wagner to shortstop, where he played throughout his career. The Pirates won four pennants during the years when Leach and Wagner were on the left side of the infield. The point of this story is that Wagner was such a good fielder that he could have played anywhere. Leach said that Honus was the best third baseman, the best first baseman, the best shortstop and second baseman, and also the best out-fielder in the league. "And since he led the league in batting eight times between 1900 and 1911," Leach said, "you know that he was the best hitter, too, as well as the best base runner." (Wagner's numbers will be used to compare him with the short-stops on My Team.)

Although the third baseman doesn't get as many plays as the rest of the infielders, he may be involved in more highlight film plays. I still recall the incredible performance of Brooks Robinson in the 1970 World Series. And I recall two third base plays by others vividly: Doug Rader diving to his left for a sharply hit ground ball and throwing it to second base before he touched down, starting a double play, and Ken Caminiti diving for a ball across the foul line, deep behind the bag in San Diego, then throwing the runner out from his knees!

Graig Nettles made spectacular plays all the time, as did Buddy Bell. Ron Santo was a steady and sometimes spectacular fielder; Wade Boggs and Eddie Mathews and George Brett were all more than adequate with the glove. Chipper Jones is even better with the glove and he can also play the outfield well.

Here in Houston, I have seen two of the best fielders play every day. My teammate Doug Rader won five Gold Gloves in a row. And, when I was broadcasting, I watched Ken Caminiti making all the plays Rader made, but getting only three Gold Gloves for his effort. He had some tough competition during his years at the hot corner because Terry Pendleton and Matt Williams were also capable of making all the plays.

Mike Schmidt was simply the best I have ever seen at third base. He was often criticized for not diving for balls, but most of the ground balls the others would have to dive for, he caught without leaving his feet. He was cat-quick, and had soft hands and a strong, accurate arm.

Most positions at the major league level come with a hitting profile. Up-the-middle players can be good run producers and I will have speed and power up the middle on My Team. Even on lesser teams, the corner players, including the third basemen, are expected to hit for power and drive in a lot of runs. There are exceptions, however. Terry Pendleton was a good hitter, but he didn't hit as many home runs as most third basemen. Rader was a dangerous hitter, and Caminiti and Pendleton were even better. Both of them hit well enough to win National League MVP honors. Still, their offensive numbers, year by year, did not measure up to those of several of their peers. Matt Williams was a terrific fielder and a great RBI man for a few years. His slugging average is better than that of several of my candidates, but his OBA is very low, and he struck out at an alarming rate. Ken Boyer also played third base like he was born there, and his hitting was better than Brooks Robinson's, but his career was relatively short and I saw only the last part of it. Buddy Bell had several big seasons with the bat, but he didn't have ten good years. Nettles hit a lot of home runs. He was, perhaps, a little better than Brooks Robinson as a hitter, but he didn't drive in as many runs, or post as good an OBS as the rest of the candidates. Ron Cey was tough on me, but not quite good enough to qualify for My Team.

And so, my candidates are Mathews, Robinson, Santo, Brett, Schmidt, Wade Boggs, and Chipper Jones. (See table on next page.)

Strictly from a fielding standpoint, Robinson and Schmidt were the best, followed closely by Jones. The numbers don't show Brooks to be as good a hitter as most of the others, but he came up big when it counted most. His teammate Rick Dempsey called him "the ultimate team player." He also maintains that he was the guy the Orioles wanted in the batter's box with a man on second and two outs. "There is no doubt in my mind," Dempsey said, "he was one of the best clutch hitters in the league." Just as he helped the Orioles win ball games, he helped the young guys with their transitions into the major leagues. "I lockered right next to him and he taught me a lot and not just about baseball," Baylor said. "He was the player rep when I was there and I picked his brain. The first strike was

THE CANDIDATES

PLAYERS	OBA	SLG	OBS	R/PA	RBI/AB	SB	CS
MATHEWS	.384	.539	.923	1/6.3	1/5.5	44	21
ROBINSON	.341	.438	.780	1/8.6	1/7.1	16	13
SANTO	.378	.497	.875	1/7.7	1/5.8	24	31
SCHMIDT	.389	.554	.943	1/6.4	1/5.0	89	58
BOGGS	.428	.463	.891	1/6.8	1/9.1	15	27
JONES	.399	.535	.934	1/6.4	1/5.4	118	40
BRETT	.387	.526	.913	1/6.7	1/6.2	141	63
TRAYNOR	.374	.455	.829	1/6.8	1/5.6	130	?

tough because I wasn't making much money. Once he explained it to me, I felt it was my duty to stand strong. I later became a player rep myself and I think that helped me in becoming a coach and a manager."

It is difficult to ignore the positive attributes Brooks brought to the table. And intangible qualities are a part of my evaluation process. Still, there are others who did more with the bat.

Ron Santo, in my opinion, deserves to be in the Hall of Fame, but he still can't match Mathews, Jones, and Brett. Boggs recently made the Hall of Fame. He had a stratospheric OBA, but was not a power hitter. Neither was he ideally suited to the top of the lineup because he was a relatively slow runner, so it was difficult to get him around the bases, a fact that appears in the R/PA column. His fielding was suspect at the beginning of his career, but he was pretty good once he settled in. Still, he does not measure up to the power hitters at his position.

Based on what I know about Honus Wagner, the only player I have seen who matches his versatility is Michael Jack Schmidt. Schmidt probably could have played short or second. I know he could have played first base and left and right field. His hitting numbers are not like Wagner's. Mike hit a lot more home runs, and he walked and struck out more often. Wagner hit for a much higher batting average, but Wagner played in the dead ball era when most players hit very few home runs and didn't strike out much. If Schmidt had played in Wagner's time or vice versa, I think their offensive numbers would be similar.

Phillies fans often criticized Schmidt for walking too much. I guess they thought he could hit home runs off pitches that weren't even in the strike zone. I don't think he was ever fully appreciated for what he did while he was doing it, mainly because he made it look so easy. Almost all the great players make playing baseball look easy, when it is actually one of the most difficult and demanding of all sports. "Nothing was hard for him," said Larry Bowa, who played next to him at shortstop for many years. "He was a great golfer, a great bowler. He made everything seem so easy that, at least at first, some people didn't think he was giving it a full effort."

Among Schmidt's accomplishments are leading the league in home runs eight times, winning ten Gold Gloves, and winning league MVP honors three times. He played shortstop at Ohio University, where he was an All-American. When his magnificent career was finally over, Phillies fans, said to be "so tough that they would boo Santa Claus," voted Schmidt the best Phillies player of all time. He was elected to the Hall of Fame on the first ballot, collecting 444 of 460 possible votes. It is generally true that no single player can make a bad team into a contending team, but if you look at the Phillies record before he joined them and after he retired, it is possible to say that, in his prime years, he did just that.

No one saw him as much as his partner on the left side of

the Phillies infield, Larry Bowa. "He was so quick on the first step that he could get to everything without diving," Bowa said. "And he covered so much ground to his left that I could cheat and play further up the middle. I didn't see Brooks Robinson that much, but Mike was the best I've ever seen."

Despite his obvious athleticism and powerful swing, Schmidt really didn't hit that well at first, and was self-conscious about it. "He wanted to be perfect and we all know that nobody is perfect in this game," said Bowa. "At first, he seemed uptight before the game. As he got more experience and confidence, he loosened up a little. But he was still pretty intense. He may have looked like he was playing it cool because it was so easy for him, but he was still nervous when he faced a pitcher he hadn't seen before, even toward the end of his career. He didn't want to be embarrassed. He wasn't a leader so to speak. He did become one of the guys though. He'd play cards or do whatever everyone else was doing. Everybody liked him.

"Another time, he was in a slump. This was late in his career when he had a lot of confidence and didn't care as much about what other people would think or say. He had been ripped in the paper that day and so he came to the ballpark in disguise—with a wig. Everybody got a laugh out of that. It was so out of character for him, but then again, there was a fun-loving guy in there. He just didn't show it that often."

Though he may not have led the league in intangibles, Schmidt makes My Team on ability. One of the most difficult decisions I will have to make in choosing a 25-man team is who will back up Schmidt at third base. Baylor would vote for Robinson, even though he concedes that Brooks wasn't the fastest runner. "I usually hit fifth and he usually hit right behind me," Baylor said. "One time we were both in a slump and Earl put him in the seven hole and hit me eighth at Yankee Stadium. I hit two doubles in that game with Brooks on first. He didn't score on either of them. If he had hit the doubles, I would have scored. Fortunately, we got back to our normal places in the lineup the next day."

Looking at offense, Eddie Mathews has slightly better numbers than Chipper Jones and George Brett. Jones is probably the best fielder, but Mathews and Brett were pretty good with the glove. Looking at the stolen bases, it seems like Jones is faster than Brett and that George had a little more speed than Captain Eddie; they all had strong, accurate arms. In my view, the advantage Brooks Robinson had in fielding is not great enough to offset the others' hitting numbers.

Mathews was best known as a home-run hitter. I was actually surprised to find that he was not so one-dimensional. He walked enough to have an excellent OBA and, though he didn't attempt many steals, he had a pretty good success ratio. I was a little surprised that Chipper Jones was right there with him offensively. George Brett was perceived as a good all-around hitter and not a real home-run hitter, but he still had a great slugging average. He hit a lot of home runs, but it was the singles, doubles, and triples that pushed him over the .900 mark in OBS.

I'm sure most fans remember seeing the replay of Brett's game-winning pine-tar home run against the Yankees in 1983. That incident alone speaks volumes about his competitive spirit. Unlike Schmidt, he dove for ground balls all the time. He was one of those guys who seldom played a game without getting his uniform dirty. He was not real fast but fast enough to run aggressively. I would also guess that he helped more runners advance on long fly balls and grounders than Mathews, simply because he didn't strike out nearly as often.

Brett played with great energy, but was not the fighter that Mathews was. Eddie would throw a punch at the slightest provocation. He was a bona fide red ass. I'm sure his anger kept the Braves on the edge of hostilities all the time. During the dog days of August, it is hard to maintain intensity. But, with Mathews on the team, you don't have to worry about anybody slacking off. Brett was all business once the game started, but before the game, he was an affable guy who didn't mind shooting the breeze with teammates or opponents.

It is convenient that both of them were left-handed hitters because Schmidt hit from the right side. If I select Chipper Jones, he will hit from the left side most of the time, too. In terms of intangibles, George and Eddie were better than average. Eddie was intense and kept the pressure on all the time. Still, I would give the nod to Brett. George's anger on the pine-tar homer is somewhat misleading. He was willing to fight but was not looking for the chance. I think Brett's personality would be better for My Team. So does his longtime teammate Jamie Quirk.

"First of all," Jamie said, "everybody knew he was the best guy in the league. He played hard all the time and he loved the game. He was always the first guy to get to the ballpark and the last to leave. . . . George never got the big head, even after he became a star. He was really friendly, outgoing. He always wanted to be around a lot of people.

"When he first came up he had a strong arm but he wasn't accurate. If you were sitting in the box seats behind first base, you'd better be ready. He air-mailed the first baseman a lot. As the years went by he kept working at it and became a Gold Glove third baseman.

"During his rookie year, he was hitting about .200 at the All-Star break. He wasn't very consistent with the bat his first year either," Quirk said. "Our hitting coach, Charlie Lau, had seen enough. He challenged George to work extra every day. He moved him off the plate and had him close up and stride into the ball and hit from right center to left. He'd jump him when he pulled the ball. By the end of the year he hit .285. After he grooved his swing, Charlie didn't mind if he pulled the ball. Then, he started hitting more home runs. Charlie made George a great hitter and George made Charlie a great hitting coach. Early in his career, George was a good runner. Whitey Herzog even had him lead off a couple of years. One year he had something like 21 triples." (He hit 20 in 1979.)

In addition to being a winner on the field, he was also a great friend to his teammates. He took the rookies under his wing and helped them adjust to the big leagues. "When I came up he invited me to stay in his house," Quirk remembered with a smile on his face. "I stayed four years! During that time, Mark Gubicza and Brett Saberhagen moved in with us."

Although he was a friendly guy, he didn't hesitate to challenge a teammate—even Quirk. "One time, I grounded out to second base. I ran through the bag, but George still confronted me. 'Did you run as fast as you could?' he asked. I thought I ran pretty good. I was slow, but not that slow. I had to admit, though, on that play, I could have run faster."

Astros Coach Doug Mansolino remembered an opening day game in Chicago. "It was in the thirties and the chill factor was below freezing," Mansolino said, showing me his forearm. "Look at me, I've got goose bumps." (He did.) "That day Wally Joyner was hurt and George was playing first. He had a zipper on the inside of his pants leg so he could wear a big brace on his bad knee. The White Sox had a 9–0 lead in the ninth and they sent Roberto Hernandez out to finish up. Nobody wanted to hit against him. He threw 100 mph and didn't always know where it was going. George didn't have to hit. He could have just gone to the clubhouse to get warm and let somebody pinch-hit for him. But, no, George wanted to hit. He came up with two outs and nobody on base. Remember, we're down 9–0. So he hits this towering pop-up and takes off running. He got to second base by the time the ball was caught. I'm not talking about pulling into the base. He was standing on the bag. I'll never forget that."

"You know what he told me one time?" Quirk said. "He told me that he wanted his last at-bat to be a ground out to second base so he could run his ass off and end his career that way. I believed him."

Brett added more to the clubhouse chemistry than Mike Schmidt. But he is still known mostly for his hitting. "I think he had nine straight games with three hits or more in 1980 when he finished at .390," Quirk said. "In two of the games, he had five hits. He was greedy. If he got one hit, he wanted two, if he got four, he wanted five. He was relentless. He never said it but I think the whole time he was trying to do better than Schmidt. He knew he wouldn't hit as many home runs, but he always knew what Schmidt was doing.

"One day, we were playing in K.C. and it was about 100 degrees out there. George struck out his first two times and looked bad doing it. When we went out to the field, there was no third baseman. They found George in a trashcan in the runway with his head peering out over the rim. 'I stink,' he yelled. 'I really fucking stink.' But he sure wasn't going to quit. He got back out there at the last minute."

I think the little things about Brett, like base running and contact hitting, make up for the advantage Mathews had in the power department. Mathews was good for the team in terms of intensity. But Brett was intense and loose, too! If you wanted to create a fictional character for the ultimate ballplayer, you could start by describing George Brett.

Chipper Jones could be a better pick than Mathews or Brett. I don't think he is quite as good a hitter as either of them but he is a really good fielder. He gives a manager a lot of options because he can play virtually every position. I'm pretty sure he wouldn't hurt the chemistry of a good team. He has been playing on one team his whole career and is one of the reasons the Braves have such a long run of division championships. Chipper is not a rah-rah type, but you can count on him to do his job, whatever that job may be. Sometimes I think the players who try to lead by speaking are less effective than those who lead by example.

I really can't go wrong, no matter whom I choose. The only thing that works against My Team is that the other team will have a third baseman who is just about as good. Mathews would be like a caged tiger on the bench. Brett and Jones would be antsy, too, but they would probably be easier to tolerate. I won't gain much advantage at this position. Brett is my backup third baseman and he wouldn't play as much as Schmidt, mostly because of the defense. But if we came up against a pitcher who gave Schmidt trouble, I would be confident that Brett could hit the guy.

At some of the positions, I am willing to concede that the old-timers could be better. Lou Gehrig and Jimmy Foxx certainly posted better numbers than Jeff Bagwell. But at third base, I don't think there is any question that Schmidt, Brett, Mathews, and Jones were all better than anyone who preceded them.

THIRD BASE: SCHMIDT, BRETT.

5

Shortstop

These are the saddest of possible words:
"Tinker to Evers to Chance."
Trio of bear cubs, and fleeter than birds,
Tinker and Evers and Chance.
Ruthlessly pricking our gonfalon bubble,
Making a Giant hit into a double—
Words that are heavy with nothing but trouble:
"Tinker to Evers to Chance."

"*Baseball's Sad Lexicon*"——FRANKLIN PIERCE ADAMS

JOE TINKER was the shortstop, Johnny Evers the second baseman, and Frank Chance the first baseman when the Cubs were
at their best, nearly one hundred years ago. The poem proves
their eminence, or at least that's what some baseball historians
think. Others say only Chance could have made it to Cooperstown without the poem. But since this trio was so deadly in
combination, and since they won so many games together, they
were voted into the Hall of Fame together in 1946.

My Team

Tinker and Evers didn't like one another, but they formed one of the best double-play combinations in the National League. They averaged about 50 double plays per year, with a high of 73—not many by today's standards. Of course, they had tiny gloves and the infields weren't as well-groomed as they are now. The Cubs weren't the only team with a good double-play combination back then, but the other teams didn't win as often. Tinker stopped more rallies than most players because he seemed always to be in the middle of things, especially when the Cubs played their archrivals, the Giants. Like almost all shortstops, Tinker handled more ground balls than anyone else on the team. He played the one position that allows almost no margin for error.

Shortstop is a difficult position to play for obvious reasons. Most hitters are right-handed and most hitters pull the ball on the ground a lot more often than they hit a ground ball the other way. Other than the catcher and the first baseman, the shortstop gets the most action. He is also stationed a lot farther from first base than the second and third basemen. He has a lot of ground to cover and cannot afford even a hiccup of a bobble most of the time. He also needs a strong, accurate arm. A good shortstop is extremely important to an overall defense. If a guy is fleeter than a bird and steady with the glove, he can crack the lineup without being a good hitter. If he can do some damage with his bat, great, but that is not the primary consideration.

The best shortstop I had behind me in my thirteen years on the Houston mound was Roger Metzger. He was what I call a two-out shortstop. When the ball was hit to him with two outs, I didn't have to watch him make the play. It was automatic. I simply walked back to the dugout because I knew he would get the out every time. That is a comforting feeling, especially when the same fielder is capable of making the highlight film play. Roger could do that, too, but he was not a good hitter.

Shortstop

Since most shortstops are weak hitters, they have to hit at the end of the lineup. When you have an excellent fielding shortstop who is also a good run producer, you have a great advantage. The first five spots in the order are so important that they are usually occupied by outfielders and corner infielders. Oftentimes, the catcher is a weak hitter, too, because of the importance of defense at that position. If you can use your catcher in an RBI role and your shortstop is good at getting on base, it is easier to construct a good lineup. I will have no trouble coming up with a lineup in which the defensive positions are played by good hitters.

When I took over the Astros in the fall of 1996, one of the first things GM Gerry Hunsicker asked me was what we should try to accomplish in the off-season. We had finished in second place in 1996 without good pitching and I knew the prospects for getting three or four new and better pitchers were remote. So, I suggested that the way to improve our pitching was to improve our fielding. I knew the pitchers we already had would be better if we could give them better fielding support. "Even if we lose a little offense," I said, "we may be able to get over the hump with a better shortstop and a better catcher." We ended up getting Brad Ausmus to solve half the problem but we were unable to get the shortstop. Brad made us better and we won a weak division, but we still needed a shortstop. During my five years at the helm, we never got one. Ricky Gutierrez and Tim Bogar were pretty good, but neither of them covered as much ground as the premier fielders in our league. We weren't looking for a hard-hitting shortstop, merely an excellent fielder with good range and a good arm. Good shortstops are hard to find, and if you have one who can hit, you have a leg up on almost every team you play.

I don't know how to explain the relative surplus or lack of good players at various positions over the years. Sometimes it seems like these things go in cycles. When I was playing in the sixties and seventies, there were a lot of good starting pitchers and third basemen, but no hard-hitting shortstops. Dave Concepcion was about the best in the National League and he wasn't nearly as good a hitter as many of the guys who are playing the position these days. Now that situation is reversed. There aren't nearly as many terrific pitchers and third basemen but plenty of good shortstops. Several of them, like Edgar Renteria, Rafael Furcal, Miguel Tejada, Nomar Garciaparra, and Jimmy Rollins, could end up with 10 standout seasons; but I doubt that any but Tejada and Garciaparra will be Hall of Fame candidates.

Although there are a lot of slugging shortstops these days, there still aren't enough to go around. It is almost impossible to trade for one. You either have to develop one, trade for a minor league prospect and develop him, or wait for a current star to become a free agent.

There are a few playing now who have already had ten good years and are potential Hall of Famers. Alex Rodriguez (though he is playing third base now) and Derek Jeter come immediately to mind. Barry Larkin has recently retired and he had about as much talent as any of them. His career totals aren't quite as good as they would have been had he not been injured so much, but he still has a chance to make the Hall of Fame. If not for Ozzie Smith, Larkin would have won the Gold Glove just about every year. And, of course, he was a much better hitter than Ozzie, who has already been inducted into baseball's shrine. Tony Fernandez, Bert Campaneris, and Garry Templeton were good fielders and pretty good hitters, but not good enough to make My Team.

The Candidates

The players who did make the cut are Ozzie Smith, Ernie Banks, Derek Jeter, Alex Rodriguez, Cal Ripken Jr., Alan Trammell, Barry Larkin, and Robin Yount. For historical perspective I have included stats for Honus Wagner, but have omitted Joe

Tinker (in spite of the poem) because he wasn't good enough with the bat. I have omitted Hall of Famer Luis Aparicio for the same reason. Many would say that Aparicio belongs in the same class as Ozzie, but I was surprised to see that Luis wasn't better than Ozzie with the bat. I don't think anyone belongs in a class with Ozzie when it comes to the glove work, though I have heard scouts say that Aparicio was his equal. I'm sure there were many old-time shortstops who were terrific with the glove, but none of them provided much offense. Of the guys I have seen, most of the standouts are of recent vintage. Let's take a look at their hitting numbers.

THE CANDIDATES

PLAYER	OBA	SLG	OBS	R/PA	RBI/AB	SB	CS
BANKS	.344	.538	.882	1/7.1	1/5.4	40	37
LARKIN	.366	.451	.817	1/6.8	1/8.0	286	58
SMITH	.354	.348	.702	1/8.4	1/10.6	356	79
TRAMMELL	.361	.441	.802	1/7.2	1/7.6	176	90
RIPKEN JR.	.350	.468	.818	1/7.3	1/6.7	28	24
JETER	.386	.462	.848	1/6.0	1/8.1	215	57
A. RODRIGUEZ	.388	.585	.973	1/5.6	1/5.0	219	54
YOUNT	.364	.482	.845	1/6.7	1/6.9	160	47
HONUS WAGNER	.414	.505	.918	1/6.1	1/5.4	442	?

Ernie Banks had finished his career at shortstop by the time I came up with the Astros. I pitched against Ernie a lot during the second half of his career. A bum knee slowed him down halfway through his career and that's when the Cubs moved him across the infield to first. He won one Gold Glove playing shortstop but, if he had continued fielding that well, the Cubs would have left him at short. "He didn't have the best range once he hurt his knee," Cubs third baseman Ron Santo remembered. "When we got Don Kessinger, I was able to play a little closer to the line." Ernie's best years with the bat were during the late fifties: He was voted the MVP of the National League in 1958 and '59. He was still a dangerous hitter in the second half of his career and ended up hitting 512 home runs. He was not a great first baseman, but was good enough to play every day. "I never had to worry about a bad throw," Santo said. "He could dig them out of the dirt and he was tall enough to catch the high ones. He had great hands. Very soft hands." Ernie was fast in the early years, but he was not the best base runner late in his career. He could, however, keep things in perspective. He competed hard in the batter's box and at first base, but never appeared to be grinding. Instead he wore a perpetual boyish smile and said, "It's a great day for a ball game. Let's play two." He was known as Mr. Cub, and the fans voted him the greatest Cub player ever.

The thing that stands out in my mind when I think about Ernie is his graceful swing. He cradled the bat in the fingers of his large hands, massaging the handle as he waited for the pitch. He had good power even though his swing seemed effortless. I suppose five hundred home runs seem like more than good power, but I hesitate to say "great" because I never saw him hit a tape-measure homer. I did see him hit a few into the left-field pavilion in the Astrodome. Any homer hit into that part of the seats in that stadium had to be crushed. It was 390 feet to the fence and the ball didn't carry well in the Dome. Still, what amazed me wasn't his raw power, but his ability to make solid contact and hit the ball in the air. I saw him hit more than a few home runs at Wrigley Field and it looked like he just reached out and flipped them over the fence. Most of the homers he hit there went into the bleachers, not over them, while most of the home runs Sammy Sosa hit flew out into the neighborhood. The homers Ernie hit in Houston usually went into the first few rows of seats. It almost seemed like he swung just hard enough to get the ball over the fence—whether he was in a big ballpark or a small one.

In a way, Alex Rodriguez is an improvement on the Banks prototype: long, lanky, graceful, and able to hit a baseball out of the park with what looks like an easy swing. But A-Rod is faster than Ernie was. He steals a lot of bases and covers much more ground on the infield. Even though Joe Torre elected to move A-Rod to third base and keep Derek Jeter at short, Rodriguez would still be one of the best fielding shortstops in the league if he went back to his original position. And, if he stays healthy, he will surpass Ernie's 512 home runs. The sum total of Banks's career was good enough to get him into the Hall of Fame on the second ballot. But, because of A-Rod, Ernie isn't quite good enough to make My Team.

A-Rod will go in on the first ballot if he plays five to ten more years and continues his assault at the plate. If he plays long enough, he could get some votes for the best player in baseball history. As I have mentioned in discussing other positions, I consider range to be more important than great hands. With Rodriguez, you get both.

When I was managing and we played the Rangers in interleague games, I was surprised at his range. When you watch A-Rod run, you don't really appreciate his speed because he takes long fluid strides. What you notice is that he gets to balls you thought would be clean singles. You also notice that when he steals and your catcher makes a good throw, he is safe anyway. The great players make the game look easy and nobody makes it look easier than A-Rod. The only thing he lacks that Mays and Ruth had is showmanship, which doesn't help you win a single game but does add a dash of seasoning to the recipe. Henry Aaron didn't have much flair either and he was a pretty good player.

When I asked Jerry Narron who was the better fielder, Rodriguez or Jeter, he said, "What about Ripken?" This is the same thing I was hearing from several other players and managers who were in the American League during Cal's prime. Narron freely admits that A-Rod and Jeter, and the other candidates as well, could run faster than Cal, "but he was so sound fundamentally that he almost never made a mistake. He came from a baseball family and he was taught to play the game the way it's supposed to be played. He was just a very intelligent player." Still Rodriguez is a much better hitter and some of the other shortstops were a little better than Cal, too. "I'm not saying anything negative about A-Rod," Narron was quick to say. "I had him in Texas and what impressed me the most about him was his attitude. I knew he had great talent. But that doesn't say it all. I watched him prepare every day. He would take his ground balls, make the throws, take BP [batting practice], and sometimes extra BP. He didn't have to do all that but he did. He was the best player in the game and he prepared for each game like a utility infielder who was just trying to stay on the team by hustling all the time."

As a pitcher, I am sorely tempted to put Ozzie Smith on the team even though he was the weakest hitter of the candidates. I sure would have liked seeing him over my right shoulder when I was on the mound. Ozzie once said that one of the things that helped him develop the supersoft hands that took him all the way to Cooperstown was a game he played with himself as a child, lying on his back. "I would shut my eyes and throw the ball up in the air and then try to catch it without opening my eyes." If you think that would be easy, give it a try. I have also seen Ozzie taking ground balls while standing on his knees on the front edge of the infield during batting practice. He had a coach hitting hard, skimming fungos to him as balls from the batting cage whizzed by. To do this, you have to have complete confidence in your hands; you cannot jump out of the way. That drill was impressive, even to his peers. Sure, he had rare talent, but his practice routine refined his fielding day by day. The only thing he lacked was a powerful arm but, like Brooks Robinson, he was so quick on the release and so accurate that he didn't need to gun the ball across the infield. One of the things I remember most about his fielding was the way he could dive for a ball and come up throwing. It was like he was bouncing off a trampoline, not terra firma. One time I asked him why he dove when he could make the plays standing up. He said that it didn't take as much time to dive, hit the ground, and pop up throwing, all in the same motion. "If I stay on my feet," he said, "I have to take a couple more steps to get my feet under me so I can throw." He did it all so quickly and so consistently that he was more than a two-out shortstop. He was a vacuum cleaner. Anything hit in his direction was an out every time.

In contrast, A-Rod is more like Mike Schmidt. He plays a lot of games without getting his uniform dirty. That doesn't mean he isn't hustling. As with Schmidt, his clean uniform only makes him look better, because he still makes all the plays. I think Ozzie got outs on some plays that no one else could make. A-Rod could probably dive and keep ground balls in the infield, preventing further advances, but I don't think he could do the trampoline act that Ozzie did.

During the second half of his career, Ozzie became a much better hitter. He learned to work a walk, which was not easy for him as a singles hitter because pitchers were not afraid to throw the ball down the middle if they got behind in the count. Most of the time he had to foul off a couple of pitches and run the count to 3-2 before finally drawing the free pass. He was always a good base stealer and bunter, but until he improved his on-base average, he had to hit at the end of the lineup where his bunting and base stealing were less valuable to the team. During his best ten seasons, he had a .358 OBA, which is marginally adequate for a number-two hitter who can bunt for a hit and steal a base. If I played him and put him in the two-hole with a great hitter in front of him and another great hitter behind him, he could be a reasonably productive hitter. But no matter where I put him, he wouldn't produce runs like A-Rod. I can infer from Banks's base-stealing numbers that he wasn't much more than an average runner, even when he played shortstop. I would pick Ozzie over Ernie on My Team on defense alone, and let all the other sluggers drive him in. But I can't put Ozzie ahead of A-Rod, who is clearly the best all-around shortstop since Honus Wagner. And I cannot put him ahead of Derek Jeter or Robin Yount either. Ozzie is the best shortstop I have ever seen, but the others are capable fielders and much better with the bat.

In terms of athleticism, Barry Larkin may be the best of them all. But it would be difficult to place Barry Larkin ahead of Ozzie, because Larkin spent so much of his career on the disabled list, while Ozzie was durable. When Larkin was healthy, he was a better fielder than all of them but "The Wizard of Oz." He was fast, perhaps faster than Ozzie, and I think he could cover more ground than Jeter or A-Rod. He had a stronger arm than any of them, and he was a good teammate, on and off the field. If he hadn't been injured so much, I might pick him over Jeter but, when you pick a team, you have to consider durability.

Cal Ripken Jr. was another story—a long one. His consecutive game-playing streak will never be broken. I know *never* is a strong word, but I don't think I will have to eat it. In the first part of his career, Cal was similar to Banks. He didn't hit quite as many home runs, but was an excellent RBI man. Like Banks, he won his league's MVP award twice. Banks won one Gold Glove; Ripken won two. I am skeptical when someone says that Cal or any other player has good range because he knows how to position himself for the various hitters. I have heard this about Ripken and I'm certain that some players are better than others in this regard, but I'll still take the guy who can cover more ground. If you have a fielder like Cal, who knows where to play, it is great, but if you don't, you can always move him by signaling from the dugout.

Shortstop

. . .

I didn't see Cal play as much as his contemporary at shortstop, Robin Yount. Robin made a good point: "He played on a lot of teams with good pitchers. It's a lot easier to position yourself when you know how the pitcher is going to pitch to the hitter. The Orioles almost always had pitchers who could coax hitters into hitting the ball into the area where the fielders were stationed. If your pitcher can't make the pitch, you can't possibly shade the hitter to pull or to go the other way." As a hitter, Ripken was way above average for a shortstop, but his numbers aren't quite as good as Larkin's. Since Cal played every day and Larkin missed a lot of time with injuries, I have to favor Ripken. His teammate Rick Dempsey thinks Ripken changed baseball by proving a big hard-hitting player could do a good job playing short. "He wasn't as fast as most of the great shortstops," Dempsey said. "But he was a very smart player and he knew where to play. The Mariners might have played A-Rod at third if Cal hadn't proved that a tall guy can play the position." (Actually, the Orioles already knew a tall guy could play short because Gold Glover Mark Belanger played short before Ripken arrived.) Larkin wasn't quite as powerful and not nearly as durable as Ripken, but I would rate him as one of the top ten baseball athletes I have seen in my forty years. Cal isn't in my top fifty. Of course, Babe Ruth and Ted Williams weren't the best all-around athletes either.

The thing I found the most interesting in rating the offense of the shortstops using statistics is that Ozzie had the same ten-year OBS as Dave Concepcion. In my opinion, this can only be because Davey played in an era when there were more good pitchers. Davey was the best defensive shortstop before Ozzie came along. He invented the one-hop Astroturf throw, he had good speed, he was limber and relatively tall and could stretch out his glove to get to some balls that seemed destined to be singles. Even though Ozzie played a little later than Davey and

didn't face as many good pitchers, I would take Ozzie on fielding alone. Still, the hitting numbers don't lie. Ozzie's OBS was
achieved mostly by getting on base. Davey didn't get on as often
but had more power. Statistically, they were equal. But, at his
best, Ozzie was a top of the lineup hitter; Davey was a second-
tier RBI man who hit toward the end of the lineup. I will have
plenty of RBI men at the end of My Team's lineup. After considering all the candidates, I took Davey off the list.

Alan Trammell and his double-play partner Lou Whitaker
were among the best infielders in the American League for
many years. Trammell was faster than Ripken and covered
more ground. He was also a two-out shortstop—very steady.
His hitting was well above average at his position, about the
same as Ripken's. He was also one of those guys who is not
only talented but sets an example for the rest of the players on
the team. When your stars play hard, the lesser lights have to
play hard, too. That was one of the Astros' strengths during the
Bagwell and Biggio era. The marquee players set the tone.
Everyone else has to harmonize with them. And Alan Trammell
was definitely a marquee player. "He had the most accurate arm
I've ever seen at short," Yount said. "He made a good throw
ninety-nine point nine percent of the time. And he was a good
hitter, too." In fact, I can't think of a reason to leave Alan off My
Team except that a few of the other candidates are even better.
Yount himself was a player who could be described in almost
the same words. Toward the end of his career with the Brewers, he said that he didn't care about the Hall of Fame, but
would be thrilled if his number were retired. He got both. Rob
was a great all-around athlete and was durable, too. He came
up young and ended up playing for 20 years. He amassed 3,142
hits, playing shortstop at first, then in center field, and, finally,
near the end of his career, he was a DH from time to time.
When a great player gets traded a lot, you begin to wonder if
he is a bad apple. Conversely, when a great player plays 20
years for the same team, you wonder how that team could be

so lucky. Rob didn't play a full ten years at shortstop but, like Banks, he played his prime years at that position and is worthy of consideration. His OBS is very good, but not in a class with A-Rod's. If I were to choose him as the backup shortstop, I could also use him in the outfield. With the outfielders I will have on My Team I probably wouldn't need him there, but it would be comforting to have that option in an emergency.

One thing that helped the Astros finish first or second for over a decade was the presence of Craig Biggio at the top of the lineup. The same thing can be said of the Yankees leadoff man, Derek Jeter. It is a great advantage to have a good RBI man hitting first because it forces the opposing pitcher to throw strikes to the hitters at the end of the lineup when there are men on base. As a pitcher, I was aware of Bobby Bonds, Pete Rose, and Lou Brock when they were batting leadoff. I much preferred to let the eighth batter have a pitch to hit than to face these strong leadoff men with runners in scoring position. I would have looked at Jeter the same way. Conversely, when the leadoff hitter was weak, like Maury Wills or Felix Millan, I could pitch more carefully to the hitters at the end of the order. The outfielders can play shallow for the weak leadoff hitters. As a result, the runner on second base can't always score on a single. Wills and Millan didn't have any extra-base power at all. They afforded the pitcher another way to get out of a jam. Sometimes, the number-two hitter is weak as well. This won't happen on My Team, but it is a factor for many major league ball clubs.

Having good hitters in important defensive positions made the Big Red Machine dominant, and did the same for the Tigers in the Sparky Anderson years. Sparky was blessed with great up-the-middle hitters in both Cincinnati and Detroit. They made him look very smart. The Yankees have the same situation with Derek Jeter. He can get on base, steal a base, and drive in runs, too. He has home-run power but is also a good bunter and a contact hitter who can execute the hit-and-run play. I can't remember any hitter I've seen deliver as many clutch hits in the postseason as Jeter. When my former bench coach Mike Cubbage was coaching at third base for the Red Sox, he saw Jeter win Game 3 of the 2003 league championship game with a home run off Pedro Martinez. Cubby thinks Jeter is one of the best clutch hitters he has ever seen. Yount concurs: "Jeter is one of the most talented athletes in the game, and his talent goes way beyond what he does on the field. He's just a winner. What more can you say?" You can't say much more but you can say it again. "He's one of the best hitters I've seen in a pressure situation," said Roger Clemens. "If I had to pick five guys out of all the hitters I've seen in the clutch, he would be on the list. He's a winner. That's all you need to say."

Jeter is such a good fielder that he would be a starter even if he weren't a good hitter. He has soft hands, good range, and an accurate arm. Like Trammell, there is nothing not to like about him. The intangibles only make him better. It would be easy to get a big head if you were a star on the best team in baseball in the city of New York. But Jeter has a wonderful personality and is not inclined to draw attention to himself. I think one of the Yankees hidden assets has been the way he and center fielder Bernie Williams carry themselves. It's a class act, all the way. Like Ripken and Yount, Derek may play his whole career with the same team. He is a two-out shortstop, and a two-out-with-a-man-on-second-base hitter. He has been a lot like Larkin, and a lot more durable. "He's the total package," said Mets manager and former Yankees infielder and coach, Willie Randolph. "His arm isn't as strong as it used to be, but it is still more than adequate. And he's off the chart in terms of intangibles."

Still, I keep coming back to Alex Rodriguez. The only other shortstop who could hit in the middle of my lineup is Banks. And even Ernie can't compete with Rodriguez as a power hitter, fielder, or base runner. Of all the positions on My Team, shortstop, left field, and right field are the easiest for me to declare a winner. Both Randolph and Torre felt that A-Rod would adapt to third base better than Jeter, mostly because he has a stronger arm. Jeter has certainly benefited by having good hitters around him, but even if I rate him down a little for that, I still have to pick him as A-Rod's backup. Yount rates slightly below Jeter, as do Ripken and Trammell. I have to place Larkin one notch lower because of his injuries. Ozzie wasn't nearly as good a hitter as the rest, but no manager would complain about having him at short.

When I was pitching, there were no shortstops that could even make this list. Now there are so many great ones that I can hardly separate them, except for A-Rod, who is in the rarefied air of the sport, along with Barry Bonds. I could select Jeter, Yount, Trammell, Ripken, or Larkin (since he wouldn't have to be durable). It really doesn't matter because I will have a distinct advantage with A-Rod as my starter, but I am going to go with Jeter. Only George Steinbrenner could have two of the best shortstops in the history of the game on the same team at the same time.

It was difficult to separate Jeter from the field of candidates. It was not hard to pick A-Rod as the starting shortstop. It will, however, be extremely difficult to pick a starter for the Dog squad. More on that later.

SHORTSTOP: A. RODRIGUEZ, JETER.

6

Left Field

THERE MUST BE a reason for the expression, "He was way out in left field." Why not right field or center field? My guess is that the stereotypical left fielder is a slugger but a poor fielder. He is a Greg Luzinski type, a Jeff Burroughs type. He's a guy who spends most of his time in left field thinking about his next at-bat, or perhaps wondering what he is going to have for dinner. He's daydreaming out there. He doesn't worry too much about defense and doesn't think he should be required to be a great fielder. He is getting paid for what he does with his bat. As long as he hits, he'll be okay.

I know the type well: At various times in my career, I pitched with sluggers in left field who were indifferent about defense. Like most pitchers, I would prefer a decent-hitting left fielder who can run a little bit and chase down fly balls, a guy who charges hard on base hits and throws out a runner once in a while. Lou Brock, Vince Coleman, Rickey Henderson, and

Tim Raines weren't gifted outfielders; they often took the great circle route on their way to a fly ball. They were so fast that they usually got to it anyway. Sometimes they got a good jump and took a direct route and made a play that most left fielders are incapable of making. None of them threw well, but they got a lot of assists because a lot of runners tested them. Sometimes a weak throwing left fielder can throw out more runners than a strong-armed right fielder.

One year I moved Richard Hidalgo from right to left field when our regular left fielder got hurt. Richard had a good arm. I think he had about twenty assists in half a season. If a left fielder has sprinter's speed or a strong arm, he can be a real asset to the overall defense. I will not take a left fielder who is a poor fielder. I'm in a position where I don't have to make concessions on defense. Manny Ramirez is perhaps the best active hitter after Barry Bonds, but I am not even considering him for a spot on the team because of his desultory play in left field and on the bases.

It is no secret that the best fielders are usually in center field and right field, but left is important, too. The only difference in left field is that you don't need a strong arm. Otherwise left field requires the same talents as the other outfield positions.

One reason to play good defense is to win and the other is to avoid being embarrassed. In baseball there is no place to hide. An interior lineman in football can make a mistake and nobody will notice. When there is a jumble in the lane at a basketball game, it is sometimes difficult to see exactly what happened. In baseball, you are naked as Adam with a half-eaten apple. The gods of baseball are almost always unforgiving. You can really look foolish if you misjudge a fly ball in the outfield. Perhaps the most embarrassing play I have seen occurred when Joe Gaines was playing left field for the Astros at Crosley Field in Cincinnati. The batter hit a line shot over the left-field fence and, for some reason, Joe charged it. He came racing in while the ball was racing out. At least he didn't cost us a run on the play. It would have ended up the same way if he had broken back on it.

Lance Berkman wasn't so lucky in left field when he encountered the restless winds of West Texas in a game between Rice and Texas Tech. The wind on this day was blowing everything from right to left. There were two outs in the bottom of the ninth inning and the tying run was on first base. The batter hit a high fly ball that looked like it was headed for left center. Lance will never forget. "I broke to the left, but then had to turn around and race toward the line because the wind was carrying the ball in that direction. I got to the ball just as it landed near the line and near the fence. I dove for it, but came up empty. At this point I knew the tying run was going to score and I was just trying to prevent the hitter from scoring to win the game. I tried to scramble to my feet, but my left foot got caught under the fence. When I reached to pick up the ball, I came up with a hot-dog wrapper, too. I knew I didn't have time to get rid of the hot-dog wrapper or get my foot out from under the fence, so I just threw the ball and the wrapper flat-footed. The ball only carried about sixty or seventy feet. By the time the infielder was able to get it, the batter was turning third with the winning run. The relay throw was wild and late and I could hear coach [Wayne] Graham yelling at me all the way from the dugout."

When I was managing the Astros, I made it a point to talk with the outfielders every spring before we did our cutoff and relay drill. They all hated the drill because they had to run a lot. Knowing this, I gave them a pep talk. I told them that they should know what to do with the ball before each pitch is made. They need to know what they will do if it is hit to them, to their right or to their left. They also need to preconceive balls that are hit hard and loopers that land like dying quail. This is especially important with men on base. The outfielders need to be aware of the base runners' speed to make good decisions. And they need to do this on every pitch even though the vast majority of pitches will not be hit in their direction. Since there aren't as many plays, there aren't as many chances to mess up. But occasionally you will see an outfielder catch a fly ball and lob it back in toward the mound because he thinks it is the third out, not the second. I told our outfielders, "An error in the infield will likely allow the opponent one extra base. An error in the outfield usually allows him two or three bases. If you make an error out there, you put a runner in scoring position almost every time." It is also possible to allow an extra base without making an error. If you don't charge the balls hit in front of you, the good base runners will advance another 90 feet. I'm not sure I had a captive audience for this spiel. I should have had Lance tell his story first.

It isn't easy to play the outfield with sharp focus on every pitch. It is easy to let your thoughts wander. In fact, if you watch enough games, you will see outfielders who are practicing their swings between pitches. You know what they are thinking about.

To give you an idea what casual outfield play can mean in the context of a game, consider this situation: The left fielder runs over toward the line on a looping single but doesn't run fast. The base runner hustles down the line in case the outfielder bobbles the ball. When he sees the outfielder loafing, he sets sail for second and makes it safely. The next hitter hits a ground ball to second base. The runner on second goes to third, then he scores on a sacrifice fly. If the left fielder had hurried over to get the ball in the first place, the runner would have stayed at first and would have been erased in a double play on the ground ball to second. The sacrifice fly would have been the third out. What if you lose that game by one run?

Two slugging left fielders, Jeff Burroughs and Barry Bonds, provide a clear contrast between playing left field and just standing out there. When I was broadcasting, Burroughs was with the Braves. When you looked down from the booth in Atlanta, you could see a patch of dead grass in left field. That patch marked the spot where Burroughs played no matter which batter was at the plate. It was funny to us, but I'm sure it wasn't so funny to the Braves pitchers. Bonds, however, makes an effort to play each hitter based on where he thinks that hitter will hit the ball. One night, he was playing left field at Houston's Minute Maid Park. Lance Berkman was hitting left-handed with a right-handed pitcher on the mound. Bonds stationed himself deep and about 100 feet from the left-field foul line. Lance hit the ball about 390 feet, up against the wall in left center. Barry was able to catch it without too much trouble. If Burroughs had been out there on his little spot of grass, it would have been a double or a triple. Later in the year, we had another switch hitter, Jose Vizcaino, at the plate, also hitting left-handed. Since Jose was more of a contact hitter and didn't have much power, Bonds took a chance and moved in about ten steps, playing only about 40 feet off the line. There was a gaping hole in left center, but Jose hit a blooper to left, near the line, and Bonds caught it. I don't think any other left fielder in the league would have made that play. The rest of them wouldn't have the nerve to leave so much open space in left center in the event that Jose hit one out there, even though he seldom did.

All of my candidates for left field are or were good enough in the field to avoid embarrassment and make some great plays. Bonds won the Gold Glove all but two years in the 1990s and had 129 assists in his first 14 years. When he was young and playing with the Pirates, he had a center fielder's speed. So did the Bucs' center fielder Andy Van Slyke. The two of them covered everything between the left-field line and right-center field. You really had to hit a line drive to get it between them in left center. Frank Robinson was not as fast, but he was not slow. He was also a hard-hitting outfielder (he played left and right) who cared about defense. His range was above average and his arm was good enough to discourage flagrant advances. Rickey Henderson wasn't a great outfielder but he covered more ground than most of his peers. Carl Yastrzemski wasn't nearly as fast as Henderson, but he learned to play the Green Monster in Fenway Park like he was born there and won seven Gold Gloves for his effort. Billy Williams was good enough that you seldom noticed him in left field. The Indians played Manny Ramirez in right and left field and were unable to hide him in either position. The Red Sox have him in left. I would get a real outfielder and let Manny DH. Finally, there is a candidate that almost slipped by me. He flew under the radar for most of his career, probably because he had his best years with the Expos and didn't get much action in the postseason. When you look at the records, Tim Raines was a better hitter than Lou Brock. He was also a better base stealer. Lou played longer and had a hundred more stolen bases, but he got caught twice as often as Tim.

No matter how much emphasis is placed on fielding, every left fielder knows he is in the game to hit. At this position I have some truly great hitters. Henderson was the premier leadoff hitter of his generation and possibly of all time. The rest were great RBI men. I have calculated Bonds's record before his alleged use of steroids to prove his merit. I have also included his ten best years overall, including those of recent vintage, and listed them below Ted Williams's statistics. (See table on next page).

Obviously, Bonds is the best hitter in my universe of modern players. Ted Williams appears best overall, if you don't count Bonds's recent home-run spree. I can only shake my head at Bonds's alleged use of steroids. If anyone needs steroids, it's the guy who doesn't have quite enough ability and may be able to play in the major leagues with a little boost. Barry didn't need a boost, as you can see from the numbers he posted earlier in his career. It is unfortunate that his final career record is going to be clouded. He claimed that he just took the

THE CANDIDATES

PLAYERS	OBA	SLG	OBS	R/PA	RBI/AB	SB	CS
ROBINSON	.393	.567	.960	1/5.9	1/5.4	139	49
B. WILLIAMS	.367	.514	.881	1/7.0	1/6.2	60	27
YASTRZEMSKI	.397	.503	.900	1/7.1	1/5.9	113	70
HENDERSON	.406	.454	.860	1/5.5	1/8.8	724	138
BONDS (BEFORE '01)	.431	.595	1.026	1/5.7	1/4.8	327	97
RAINES	.391	.435	.826	1/6.6	1/9.5	581	96
T. WILLIAMS	.489	.634	1.123	1/5.1	1/4.1	17	14
BONDS (BEST TEN)	.493	.702	1.196	1/5.3	1/4.2	219	58

medicine his personal trainer dispensed. That admission will prevent him from being considered with Ted Williams and Babe Ruth. When I include 2001–05, the years when Bonds started hitting a lot more home runs, he appears to be as good a hitter as the Splendid Splinter. But even if I exclude all of his hitting numbers since 2001, when he allegedly started taking steroids, he is still the best hitting left fielder in the last forty years. We know Williams didn't take steroids—I doubt he ever heard of them—but he did miss several years during what should have been the prime of his career due to military service. Still, Barry Bonds won three MVP awards in the early 1990s, before he got bigger and started hitting more home runs. I considered him to be the best hitter in the National League every year since 1990 when he moved to the middle of the lineup from the leadoff spot.

Frank Robinson wasn't quite as devastating as Bonds, but he hit in an era when it was tougher to score. He would likely have come closer to Barry if he had played in the next generation.

Billy Williams and Carl Yastrzemski are legitimate Hall of Famers, but they played in the same era as Robinson and were not quite up to his standard. Rickey Henderson will probably make the Hall of Fame on the strength of his stolen bases alone. He would have a better RBI ratio if he hadn't batted leadoff throughout his career, but he may not have scored quite as many runs. Many experts think he is the best leadoff hitter of all time, but the limited value of the stolen base is clearly revealed in the numbers. Even with all the steals, he is only slightly better than Bonds and Robinson in runs scored per plate appearance. Stolen bases seem to be very important when you are watching a game but, statistically, they aren't worth that much. Psychologically, the running game can be disruptive and even one steal can win a close game. Over time, when you judge the value of a player, it is a mistake to fall in love with larceny. Outfield assists are worth even less. I have seen outfielders lay back to encourage a runner to advance so they could try to throw him out. That's like passing a police car at 75 mph for the thrill of seeing if you will get a ticket. When I judge an outfielder's defense, I'm looking for a guy with good range who charges hard to prevent runners from trying to take the extra base. I am also looking for total offense.

In terms of intangibles, two candidates really stand out. Billy Williams didn't say much. He let his bat do the talking. If you were on his team, you could expect him to play, and play well, day in and day out and year in and year out. At one point in his career, he played in 1117 straight games, one of the longest streaks in the history of the sport. He was a good outfielder and a pretty good base runner. He didn't steal a lot of bases but he was fast enough to score from first on most doubles. And he was the type of guy who wouldn't say anything about a teammate or opponent unless he had something nice to say. One time I threw him a get-ahead curveball and he hit it over the right-field bleachers at Wrigley Field. I thought it was a pretty good pitch—for the first 59 feet. After that I stuck with fastballs inside of the inside corner, tight on his hands, and sinking fastballs low and away in the strike zone. I had pretty good luck containing him that way. He got plenty of singles to left field, but he didn't kill me. About five years later, I got the brilliant idea of throwing him another get-ahead curveball and he hit it over the right-field bleachers again.

Yastrzemski was a lot like Williams. He played hard in the field and ran the bases well. If he made a mistake, he would admit it instead of blaming someone else. Many of the great players are so contentious that they rub opposing players the wrong way. Not Carl or Billy. They were respected and admired by teammates and opponents alike. Yaz hit a long home run off me in spring training at Chain O' Lakes park in Winter Haven. I didn't mind. It was an honor just to compete with him, but I'm glad he was in the American League. I didn't have to face him during the regular season.

"Yaz was special," his former manager Eddie Kasko recalled. "He was intense about the game. I mean really intense. If he got into a slump, he would hit extra before and after the game until he got straightened out—even before day games. He'd be out there at nine in the morning."

He would also be out there when he was hurt. "He hardly ever missed a game," said Kasko. "He was an iron man. As a base runner, he reminded me of Frank Robinson. He'd go for the extra base every time he could and he almost always made it, even though he wasn't that fast."

He was also good in the field. "You know people talk about how well he could play that wall (the Green Monster), but they don't know he had to learn it twice. It was sheet metal when he started and later they changed it to wood. He spent a lot of hours out there after they changed it. But what I remember most about his fielding was the way he charged the ball. He came in full speed and I don't remember a single ball getting under his glove. He threw some guys out and prevented a lot of advances."

When Yaz was not on the field, he was totally different. He was the life of the party. "He was the best practical joker I've ever seen," Kasko said. "He and Gary Peters and Luis Aparicio always had something going. They played jokes on their teammates and on themselves. He was just a great guy to have on the club."

Billy Williams didn't seem as intense, but he was tough. Like all everyday players, he got hurt occasionally. But he wouldn't come out of the lineup. I don't think words can say as much as deeds. When a player sees a teammate going out there in pain, it sends a strong message. And when that teammate hits .300 or better every year, he becomes a hero on his own team. "That's the way it was with Billy," Ron Santo said. "He was a great player and he was a lot tougher than most people realize. He didn't talk about himself very much. He just kept going out there. He was a very good fielder and base runner. And he worked at it. On a windy day at Wrigley Field, he would take extra fly balls before the game. He was always well prepared and it showed."

Tim Raines came up as a second baseman but, when he struggled at that position the Expos sent him to the outfield. He was like Brock and Henderson out there—a lot of speed but not much of an arm. What he brings to the plate is similar to the other two players. He hit for a good average, stole a lot of bases, and scored a lot of runs. He wasn't quite as good a lead-off hitter as Henderson but he was a little better than Brock. He is not, however, in the Hall of Fame. As with Ron Santo, I could make a case that he should be.

Henderson is a different story. He played with passion and helped several teams win championships. But he was often accused of being selfish, caring more about his own records than the team's success. When he broke Lou Brock's career stolen-base record, Rickey took the bag out of its mooring and held it over his head. He spoke about being the greatest base stealer of all time, but he did not acknowledge Brock, who was at the game to congratulate him. His manager, Tony La Russa, saw a different side of him. "Rickey is a very smart guy, but it was more street smarts than wisdom," he said. "He knows exactly what he is doing and how he can do it best. He did push-ups and sit-ups when other guys were doing weight machines. He had his own running routine. He was a great teammate and for a couple of years I thought he was the most dangerous hitter in the league. He could beat you in so many ways. I think he got a bad reputation because he didn't always express himself well. He came off as being more selfish than he really was. Believe it or not, he was a lot of fun—a great guy to have on the team."

I would be glad to have him, if I were managing, but he would have raised my hackles if I were pitching against him. It even made me mad to watch him on television. It wasn't just the defiant glare. A lot of hitters affect that pose. But Rickey squatted low and stuck his head out. It was nearly in the strike zone. I never threw at a hitter's head, but from my point of view, throwing fastballs about letter high and six inches inside is a common and acceptable strategy. That's where Rickey's head was! My attitude would be that he was asking for it, and I might just oblige. Pete Rose was the same way, but at least he kept his head back. He was accused of being selfish, too, but it is no coincidence that the teams he played on often won championships. I think it helps to have players like Henderson and Rose who are intense at all times. Their passion may make the manager's job a little tougher because he is likely to have to intervene in some sort of squabble from time to time. Talented players who play with passion help teams win, however, and in the end, they help the manager keep his job.

Bonds has been a lightning rod, too. He has a high opinion of himself and doesn't hide it. He is not media friendly and doesn't give the fans the time of day. When he came up with the Pirates, Bill Virdon was his outfield coach. Bill once told me that he didn't think Barry was a problem in the clubhouse. "He's not a bad guy," Virdon said. "He keeps himself in shape and does his job. He didn't have many friends on the team, but he didn't bother anybody." Barry doesn't play with the intensity of Henderson but, like Billy Williams, he has been durable. During the last few years, he has suffered some injuries and his defense has slipped a little bit, but he has still won eight Gold Gloves. And even in recent years, he has made some great plays coming down the stretch and in the playoffs. No, he doesn't play the outfield with the energy he had when he was younger, but he can still play it well when he is inspired by the situation.

Toward the end of his career, he started hitting more home runs. His manager, Dusty Baker, had nothing bad to say about him and plenty of admiration. "He's a loner. Everyone knows that," Dusty said, "but he is always ready. Sometimes he doesn't take batting practice. He takes a nap. Then he gets up and hits a home run the first time up." The home runs are obvious, but the way he prepares explains a lot. "He is better at pitch recognition than anyone I've ever seen," Baker said. "If a guy was doing something to tip his pitches, Barry would know it in two or three pitches. Then he'd go up there, knowing what was coming.

"Another thing he told me is something I will never forget because it makes too much sense. He said he saw an imaginary tunnel between the pitcher's hand and the strike zone. If he saw the ball coming down the tunnel, he knew it was going to be a strike. If it was down the middle, he would take the home-run swing. If there were two strikes in the count, and a pitch was coming down the edge of the tunnel, he would slap it up the middle or to left field. I wish I had known about the tunnel when I was hitting, but I'm not sure it would have helped me much." Another thing Barry told Dusty was that he didn't try to hit the ball, he tried to catch the ball on the meat of the bat and sling it.

In terms of team chemistry, Barry seems to be neutral. He doesn't do anything to help anyone else, but he does his own job as well, or better, than anyone else. It would be nice if all players acted like Billy Williams and Carl Yastrzemski. But I wouldn't play them over Barry Bonds. Every manager would like to have Barry Bonds and all the baggage he brings with him.

Even though I concede that there is no way to compare players across generations, I do feel that Barry is the best hitter since Ted Williams. In fact, I can still remember talking about him on a broadcast from Candlestick Park around 1991 or '92. Xavier Hernandez came in from the bullpen for the Astros and had to face Barry right away. X had a good sinker and a good forkball. His job wasn't necessarily to get Bonds out, just to get him to hit a ground ball. I can't recall the count, but I can recall the pitch vividly because I watched it in disbelief and had to look at the replay to make sure I wasn't hallucinating. It was a sinking fastball, right at the knees on the outside corner. Ordinarily, a left-handed hitter would either take the pitch, swing and miss it, or hit it on the ground. But Barry hit it over the left-field fence. It was a perfect pitch and he hit a home run. I still remember saying, "This guy is the greatest hitter I've ever seen. I've seen him turn on a Nolan Ryan fastball, I've seen him hit slow stuff, fast stuff, curving stuff, and sailing stuff in every part of the strike zone. And he almost never swings at a pitch that isn't in the strike zone."

After watching him for all these years, I still don't know what I would do if I had to face him. I faced every great hitter who was in the National League between 1965 and 1977. I've also faced a few of the American League greats in exhibition games and watched them on television. And I've watched every National League hitter from 1965 through 2005. I faced Willie Mays and Hank Aaron. I faced Willie McCovey and Willie Stargell. When I was at my best, I could get a riding fastball by any of them. I struck them out many times. But I don't think I could strike Bonds out unless it was on a called strike, probably a pitch that started out wide (out of the tunnel) and moved to the corner. I have also seen Manny Ramirez a lot during inter-league play and in the postseason. He is almost as good a hitter as Barry, certainly in a class with Frank Robinson, and he has played on a lot of winning teams. When I was managing the Astros, we never found his weakness. Like Bonds, he may not have a glaring weakness at the plate but, in the field and on the bases, he is way below average—too far below to make My Team. In my opinion, Barry Bonds is in a class of his own. No one else is even close.

That said, if I wanted someone on the team who could confront Bonds when he was acting selfish, I would pick Frank Robinson. If you're looking for a stand-up comic, Frank is not your man. If you're looking for a guy to help you win a ball game, Frank is just about as good as anybody, ever. I was lucky. I only had to face him a few times with the Reds before he was traded to the Orioles. Then I faced him a few more times at the end of his career with the Dodgers. I don't remem-ber having too much trouble with him but I know he would have gotten to me if I had faced him more in his prime.

In baseball, we have a term for players who lose concen-tration when the game is out of hand. Sometimes, it seems like they don't really care what they do because it doesn't make any difference. We say that this guy "gave away an at-bat." I doubt anyone ever said that about Frank Robinson. His effort was full on, all the time. *Los Angeles Times* columnist Jim Murray once wrote of Frank, "He plays the game the way the great ones play it—out of pure hate." Toward the end of Joe Morgan's career he played for Robinson in San Francisco. Joe and Frank both came out of high school in Oakland and Joe had a great deal of re-spect for the way Frank carried himself. He summed it up in one sentence when he said, "He can step on your shoes with-out messing up the shine."

Don Baylor remembers Frank as a leader and also as an

unselfish teammate. "He used to have the best wood from Louisville. Good hard wood. He would always let you use one of his bats. Some players won't do that." He also remembers one game at Fenway Park. "Frank ran into the wall on a play in left field and jammed his wrist. He couldn't swing, but he didn't tell anybody. When he came up, the lead run was on third base. So what does he do? He bunts. The only time I saw him bunt, and it was a good one. He got the runner home and was safe at first. I'll never forget that."

When Frank was with the Orioles, he was the judge at kangaroo court. He presided with a mop of hair and a robe. He doled out fines for such things as not advancing a runner or looking at a pretty girl in the stands. It was an unusually comic role for such an intense competitor, but he was a master at it, and it was one of the things that helped those great Orioles teams click.

If Frank was on your team, you knew you might get in a fight at any time—and he would be right in the middle of it. I don't recall anyone saying Frank was selfish or driven by his stats. But his stats don't lie. He wasn't quite as tough an out as Barry. He wasn't quite as good as Willie Mays or Hank Aaron either, but it would be difficult, if not impossible, to find another outfielder who played better between 1965 and 2005.

In many of the positions, including the starting pitchers and relief pitchers, I have found it difficult to gain a significant advantage. In left field, that is not the case. Over the course of a 162 game season, Bonds and Robinson would outperform any other combination of left fielders.

LEFT FIELD: BONDS, F. ROBINSON.

7

Center Field

Snider, Mantle and Mays—you could get a fat lip in any saloon by starting an argument as to which was best. One point was beyond argument, though. Willie was by all odds the most exciting.

——RED SMITH, SPORTSWRITER

ON MOST TEAMS, the center fielders and shortstops are the best all-around athletes. To play center field well, you have to be a fast runner, get good jumps on fly balls, take direct routes to get to the ball, charge hard, and throw quickly on base hits in front of you. All three of these storied center fielders were doing these things in New York in the 1950s. Down the road in Philadelphia, there was another Hall of Fame center fielder, Richie Ashburn. Ashburn didn't play on as many championship teams as the others and he was a leadoff man, not a home-run hitter. He was, however, exceptionally fast, and led the league in putouts almost every year. I don't know how to explain how four center fielders playing so close to one another at the same time could make it to Cooperstown. To questions like that, we just say: "That's baseball."

The center fielder is the captain of the outfield. Though he doesn't have to make inspirational speeches, he is the leader and the flanking outfielders have to follow him. The other outfielders do have to yield to him on fly balls in the gap, and also have to station themselves based on where he sets up in order to get the best coverage. Occasionally, corner outfielders do not position themselves in relationship to the center fielder. In the case of Barry Bonds, this can be a positive variation, whereas, with Jeff Burroughs, it is exactly the opposite. For defending most hitters, it is best for the center fielder to play straight away or to shade a hitter a little to one side or the other. Then the other outfielders station themselves accordingly.

Most people think that center is the most difficult outfield position. That is certainly true if you are not a fast runner, because there is more ground to cover. If you *are* fast, center might be the easiest outfield position. I have heard many outfielders testify to this. They say it's about perspective. Looking in from center, you can see the pitch fly toward the plate and see the hitter swing. From this angle, you get a better view of where the ball is heading when it leaves the bat. Most of the plays in center are on fly balls that are not hooking or slicing, which makes it easier to predict where the ball is going to come down. A speedy center fielder can allow the corner outfielders to play a little closer to the foul lines. Mantle and Mays both qualify as speedy center fielders, even in a universe of speedsters.

I saw Duke Snider play only when he was with the Los Angeles Dodgers. His career was just about over at that time; his best years had been in Brooklyn. He had a glorious Hall of Fame career, but his numbers don't quite match those of Mays and Mantle. The Duke was probably exciting if you were a

Dodgers fan, but I doubt he could light up a stadium like Mantle and Mays. All three were good with the glove. If they hadn't been, they would have played left or right.

Mantle had a flair for the dramatic. He was the first batter in the first game at the Astrodome and he hit a Turk Farrell fastball over the center-field fence to christen the stadium. I watched it sail over the fence but it wasn't as impressive at that time as it is now. (It took a couple of years for everyone to learn how hard it was to hit a homer to dead center in the Dome.)

Both Mays and Mantle possessed great raw power, but they were also apt to bunt for a hit. You won't find many home-run hitters doing that these days. "Mickey was a great drag bunter," teammate Tony Kubek recalled. "I don't think I ever saw him thrown out on a bunt. He could get down the line on a bunt faster than anyone I've ever seen. And he almost always did it leading off an inning when we needed to get something started. But that's the way he was. He wanted to be a good teammate. In fact, that is what he wanted to be printed on his tombstone and it was. I can't remember the exact wording but it was something like, 'Here lies the perfect teammate.'"

Mantle had even more power than Mays and could run faster, too. As a base runner, though, he was more conservative. He didn't steal very many bases because he didn't need to. With the hitters that came behind him with the Yankees, there was no reason to take a chance on a steal. Mickey had a great success ratio when he did steal. I imagine Casey Stengel and Ralph Houk wanted him to stay put and let the other hitters drive him around the bases most of the time.

I suppose the best way to describe the Mick is to tell a few stories. One rainy spring training day in Kissimmee, Florida, Bill Virdon and I were in a batting cage and he started telling me about Mantle. Bill was not prone to exaggerate. He was my manager when I pitched a no-hitter and, after all the hoopla, he came by my locker, shook my hand and said, "Nice game." Virdon was one of the best defensive center fielders of his time, but he was shocked the first time he saw Mickey play, in the spring of 1955. Mantle had already had several good years; his power and speed were legendary right from the start. But this was the first time Virdon actually saw him in person. It was at Bill's first big-league camp and he thought he would have to measure up to Mickey if he wanted to play every day for the Cardinals. He was standing in center field the first time Mantle came up. "He hit one so far over my head," Virdon recalled, "I barely got turned around before it went sailing over the fence. There was no sense running after it. It was the longest home run I had ever seen." Later in the game Mantle hit one in the gap. "He was so fast that we didn't have a chance to hold him to a double. That was back when they still had those canvas bags and Mickey tore them up. No kidding. He kicked up big clumps of infield dirt when he ran—like a horse. And then he ripped holes in the canvas bags as he went around. Now I'm just a kid, trying to make the team and the whole time I'm thinking, 'If I have to play like that to make the major leagues, I've had it. I have no chance.'"

My own experience was a little different. I faced Mickey in an exhibition game in the Astrodome right at the end of his career, probably 1968. I was throwing at my absolute best that night. All of my pitches were working. I could have pitched a low-hit shutout if it had been a regular-season game. As it was, I pitched seven scoreless innings and struck out ten or eleven batters, including Mantle three times. The next day he was quoted saying it was the best stuff he had seen in a couple of years. Considering the source, that was the biggest compliment of my entire career. Of course, it was just an exhibition game. If he really felt that way, he probably would have bunted the third time up. I've heard several people say that he could go down the line in 3.5 seconds from the left side on a bunt. With a running start out of the batter's box, it's no wonder he seldom got thrown out. During my five years as the Astros manager,

Kenny Lofton was the fastest player we timed. He got down the line in 3.8 seconds.

To better understand the dynamics of Mantle's career—early and late—you have to understand the New York fans. "I think they resented him at first," Kubek said. "He was playing right field because Joe DiMaggio was playing center. Mickey was a lot faster than Joe, but Joe was the conquering hero. When it seemed like Mickey was upstaging Joe, the fans resented it, and they didn't take to him right at first. In 1961, Mickey was in that dramatic home-run chase with Roger Maris. Mickey got an infection and had to take a penicillin shot. It got abscessed and became swollen and angry. Mickey was willing to shut it down and rest up for the World Series because we already had the pennant won. He finished with 54 homers, but Roger Maris kept playing and eventually hit 61, to break Babe Ruth's record. At that point, the fans turned on Roger. They didn't like him upstaging Mickey and didn't want him to break Ruth's record. When we got into the World Series against the Reds, Mickey wanted to play. When the doctor pulled off the bandages, he pulled some of Mickey's skin with them. It was ugly. But Mickey played. In the first game, he slid into second base and tore the bandages loose. It seemed like his pants were full of blood. Ralph Houk took him out of the game and he didn't play after that. We couldn't believe he would play in the first place, but that was Mickey.

"I think a lot of people are skeptical when they hear that he was always playing with pain. How could he hit like a superstar and run like a deer with a bad right knee? But I'll tell you, his right knee buckled every time he swung the bat left-handed. When he got out of a car, sometimes he had to reach down and grab his thigh to lift the leg, just to get out. He had to tape both knees every day. In fact, he was classified 4F ineligible when he took his army induction physical. Anyone who thinks he wasn't hurt that bad is crazy."

"Mickey may not have been as good in center field as

Mays," Kubek said. "He was just as fast if not faster, but he mis-judged a ball from time to time. Early in his career, he got into a throwing contest with Jimmy Piersall, trying to throw the ball over the center-field fence from home plate, and he hurt his shoulder. That took away some of his arm strength, but he still threw pretty well. Later in his career, when we were playing the Braves in the World Series, he stole second and the throw sailed over second baseman Red Schoendienst's head. Red fell on top of Mickey and tried to hold him down. Mickey pushed up with his right arm as he tried to go to third. That's when he really hurt his shoulder. He was only an average thrower after that."

It has been written that Mantle was sometimes surly with the fans, but he did a lot of unselfish things for his teammates and the club in general. "In terms of being a good teammate," Kubek said, "he was almost perfect. He always stopped where the families waited after the game and spoke to the wives and children. He wasn't a cheerleader type, but he had a good sense of humor and was a great storyteller, kind of like Will Rogers. When we needed a run late in the game, he would come up to the front of the dugout and you could hear his high-pitched Okie twang over the crowd noise. 'C'mon, you can do it,' he'd say. We all knew he was pulling for us. For him the team and the game were more important than his personal stats. And at spring training, he would go out of his way to be-friend the rookies. He took them under his wing. DiMaggio didn't do that.

"After he retired he did a lot of card shows. And, when he made his deal, he made sure the promoter would let him bring a teammate or two so that they could make a few bucks," Kubek said. He still remembers Johnny Blanchard telling him, "I don't know how he knew, but a few times when we got into a little money squeeze, Mickey would call and take me to a card show."

Kubek acknowledges that Mickey had a drinking problem, but resents people saying that he was a sad case. "I've seen him mad, but not sad," he said. "He didn't like to strike out with men on base. It made him furious. If he was sad, it was only late in his life when he realized he hadn't been the best family man."

Kubek couldn't help but notice the irony of the final chapter of the Mantle and Maris story. "Several of Mickey's male relatives died young with Hodgkin's disease," Tony said. "I think Mickey just assumed he would die young. Then Roger Maris died first—with Hodgkin's disease."

It would be impossible to imagine a more exciting player than Mickey Mantle if it weren't for Willie Mays. Willie was more exciting because he played with a big smile and a mischievous twinkle in his eyes, and you never knew what he would try next. Sometimes, it seemed like he invented new strategies on the fly. Once, I saw him bunt for a double. Astros third baseman, Bob Aspromonte, had no play so he was letting the ball roll, facing the third base dugout, hoping it would go foul. He forgot to watch Willie, who turned first and raced to second. "I still remember that play," said teammate Jack Hiatt. "I was down by the third base end of the dugout in the Dome. I remember it like it was yesterday."

Mays's signature play was the basket catch. One of his managers said that he was reluctant to suggest the conventional catch because he never saw Willie drop the ball. He probably dropped a few (even the best outfielders drop easy fly balls), but I never saw him do it either.

I saw Willie play, and pitched against him a lot during the second half of his career, which was almost as good as the first half. In fact, I faced him in the first inning of the first game I pitched and struck him out. He got me back a few times. One time, he hit two home runs in one game against me. It was an early day game at Candlestick Park. In the first inning, at about high noon, he pulled a slow curve down the left-field line. There was very little wind at the time and the ball barely crept over the fence. Later in the game, a stiff wind blew hot-dog wrappers from the left-field foul pole across to the right-field pole. That's when Willie took a slashing swing at an inside fast-ball and sliced it over the fence in right center. If he had hit that one in the first inning and the other one later, they both would have been caught. I felt, and still feel, that he played the wind on me that day.

That's the way Willie was. Most of the time, he instinctively did whatever it took to win the game. More than a few times I saw him jog into second like he was going to pull up, then turn on the burners and take third. I also saw him win the first All-Star Game in the Astrodome. He led off with a hit, and kept juking off the bag until Luis Tiant threw over to first. When the ball got by Harmon Killebrew, Willie raced to second base. He advanced to third on a wild pitch, Curt Flood walked, Willie McCovey grounded into a double play, and Mays scored. It turned out to be the only run of the game.

On August 22, 1965, when Giants right-hander Juan Marichal hit Dodgers catcher Johnny Roseboro over the head with a bat, Mays ushered Roseboro to the dugout and comforted him. A few innings later, Willie hit a game-winning home run off Sandy Koufax. In another game, Marichal and Warren Spahn went 16 shutout innings against one another at Candlestick in a night game. Mays homered off Spahn in the bottom of the 16th to win that one 1–0. I agree with Robert Creamer's observation. Willie Mays was, by all odds, the most exciting player I have ever seen. Mantle was scary, but at least you didn't feel like he was going to trick you.

Mickey and Willie were both friendly with the rookies. They were secure in their own stardom and tried to make the younger players feel at home on the team. "When I came up," Hiatt recalled, "we had to wear a sports coat on road trips. I only had one coat and Willie must have noticed, because he was always well dressed. He handed me a card when we were in New York. 'Go see this guy and tell him I sent you,' he said. Well, I go to see him and the next thing I know I have two nice suits. Willie paid for them." His generosity extended to his opponents as well. "He had this big ring with diamonds all over it and the number twenty-four in the middle," said Hiatt. "I remember Jimmy Wynn coming into our clubhouse to see it. Jimmy looked like a little Willie Mays anyway. Willie was his idol, and he copied everything he did. So Willie showed him the ring and Jimmy was dazzled by it. Willie took it off and gave it to Jimmy, who also wore number twenty-four. He was just that way. He was the nicest, most generous man I have ever known."

Willie was always good-natured and, unlike Mickey, he didn't need a drink to loosen his tongue. "One time we were on the road on his birthday and the people with the airlines found out about it," Hiatt said. "So, they decorated the plane and put a case of champagne on ice. We all sang 'Happy Birthday' to him and raised a glass. Willie put it to his lips but didn't drink it. He just wasn't a drinker. With all the beer in the clubhouses and on the airplanes, he never touched it."

In the years that followed the retirement of Mantle, Mays, and Snider, there were no center fielders who had great home-run power until Ken Griffey Jr. arrived in 1989. Junior had overarching power and speed. It didn't take a great scout to evaluate him. I would guess that most scouts knew he would be a Hall of Fame candidate even before he got called up to the major leagues by the Mariners. He made it to the big leagues at the age of nineteen and had his first 100 RBI season at age twenty-one. He has won ten Gold Gloves and hit over 500 home runs. During the first half of Griffey's career, it looked like he, not Barry Bonds, would be the one who could challenge Henry Aaron's career home-run mark of seven hundred fifty-five. But Junior has been slowed by injuries the last few years. He already has the credentials for the Hall of Fame and is still playing. Junior was like Mays in the beginning, always smiling and having fun, but even the young Griffey had to take a backseat to Willie in the area of showmanship. In recent years, Junior has been more like Mantle, who was not so exuberant. It's a lot harder to smile when you're in pain.

To be honest, I have only three candidates for center field because there are no others who even come close to Mays, Mantle, and Griffey (Snider retired before 1965). Bernie Williams and Jim Edmonds have great numbers, too, but they are not in the "immortal" range. Griffey and Mantle have a slight edge on Willie in RBI per at-bat, but they played their home games in ballparks that favored home-run hitters. The Mick has the best OBS of the three, and Mays is second. All of them were good fielders, but most experts would pick Griffey or Mays over Mantle in the outfield. Mays was clearly the best base runner. In my estimation, Mays has the overall edge because of what Branch Rickey called the "frivolity in his bloodstream." That may not be much of an edge, but it's a tie-breaker for me.

I have included Joe DiMaggio's statistics, as he is my pick for the best center fielder before 1965. The Yankee Clipper also patrolled center field at Yankee Stadium. Another player I considered has been one of the best in the business over the last fifteen years. Bernie Williams doesn't measure up to Mantle or DiMaggio, but he is certainly in contention for the Underdog team. He is so smooth you may not have noticed him but, believe me, the pitchers he faces notice him and so do his teammates. Bernie Williams has quietly assembled a glittering resume, helping the Yankees get to the playoffs year after year. He is a gifted fielder and his numbers indicate that he is a very dangerous hitter. Jim Edmonds has played in both leagues during the same era as Williams and his numbers and fielding ability are remarkably similar.

There are also two players from the Negro Leagues who deserve to be mentioned. The first, speedster Cool Papa Bell, was more like Richie Ashburn, and actually took himself out of consideration by extolling the virtues of the other, Oscar

Charleston. "I could outrun Oscar a bit and maybe others might do this or that better than him," he said. "But putting it all to-gether—the ability to hit, run, field, throw, and hit with power—he was the best I ever saw. He didn't have a strong arm, but he covered more ground than Willie Mays." Another Hall of Fame player from the Negro Leagues, Judy Johnson, who later became a major league scout, described Charleston as a combination of Tris Speaker and Ty Cobb, but with more power.

Some baseball historians would favor Tris Speaker or Ty Cobb over DiMaggio. Speaker was a great hitter and generally thought to be the best defensive center fielder of his era. Ty Cobb was the best hitter among the center fielders of his day, but both of them played so long ago that the comparison with the modern players is more difficult to make.

THE CANDIDATES

PLAYERS	OBA	SLG	OBS	R/PA	RBI/AB	SB	CS
MAYS	.396	.612	1.008	1/5.5	1/5.2	217	68
MANTLE	.440	.605	1.046	1/5.3	1/4.9	119	20
GRIFFEY JR.	.385	.585	.970	1/6.2	1/4.8	153	55
DIMAGGIO	.402	.597	.999	1/5.3	1/4.3	29	8

It is possible that Griffey Jr. will surpass them all if he gets healthy and mounts a major comeback. He played in a hitter's park in Seattle and is still playing in one at Great American Ball-park. For now, I am picking Mantle to go with Mays. One thing that gives the Mays/Mantle quinella a bit more credence is that the pitching in baseball was better during the time they played than it is now. Since Mantle and Mays nearly overlapped with

DiMaggio, and the Yankee Clipper had similar hitting numbers, it is clear that he deserves to be put in the same class. Like Mantle, he was burdened by injuries and didn't steal much. Unlike the Mick, he did not have the Yankee Stadium advantage because he was a right-handed hitter.

As with most of the other positions, I've got two great players (Mantle and Mays) to play center field, but have omitted another player (Griffey Jr.) who is so good that it is hard to leave him off the team. If he were on the Underdogs, I would feel like My Team would have only a slight advantage.

Since I am only getting a slight advantage in center field, I may have to resort to legerdemain in right field. I am not considering players who have primarily been designated hitters and I will not play any games on Astroturf. I am, however, not so much a purist as it may seem. The great sportswriter Heywood Broun once said, "The tradition of professional baseball always has been agreeably free of chivalry. The rule is: Do everything you can get away with." I wasn't clever enough to cheat when I was pitching; I didn't throw spitballs or scuffed balls or step forward and pitch from 60 feet instead of 60 feet 6 inches, but I did consider it. This time, I'm going to do it. Watch what happens in right field.

CENTER FIELD: MAYS, MANTLE.

8

Right Field

IN CENTER FIELD, it doesn't matter whether you are a left- or right-handed thrower. In left and right field, it does matter, but there is some disagreement about which alignment is best. Some people think it is easier to get a ball down the right-field line and throw it back in if you are a left-handed thrower. However, some believe that a right-handed thrower, with his glove on the foul-line side, can get to a ball faster, then spin counterclockwise and get more momentum behind the throw.

I am of the latter persuasion—even if the outfielder turns clockwise. I think an outfielder has more range if he has the glove hand on the foul-line side. Most of the balls that hook and slice move toward the foul lines. Hits to the gaps don't waver as much. I think it is easier to play the hooks and slices on the forehand side. I don't think the backhand play is as tough in the alleys. The only corner outfielder that I have seen play hundreds of games in both left and right field is Jose Cruz. I think Jose did a better job in left field, and he was a left-handed thrower. In the end, the only way you can be sure is to try a player in both positions, then decide where he is the best.

The conventional wisdom is that your right fielder should have a strong throwing arm to discourage runners from going from first to third on a single. It is quite an advantage if you can prevent such an advance. Most of the time, however, even a strong-armed right fielder can't keep a decent runner from taking third base on a single, unless the ball is hit sharply right to him. In many cases it is best for an outfielder to think like an infielder and put more emphasis on getting to the ball and getting rid of it quickly, rather than on winding up to launch a hero throw. The fans really admire a low arching powerful throw because it looks so majestic, like a home run, but those throws are usually in vain. Many times they sail over the cut-off man's head and allow the trailing runner to advance 90 feet. Vladimir Guerrero is a case in point. Guerrero can get to the ball in a hurry, and he also has a rifle arm. Still, our scouting report said to run on him for two reasons. First, he took a lot of time on the transfer, which gave runners an extra step or two. Second, his rifle was more like a shotgun, spraying pellets in the general direction of the base. If he made a good throw, he would throw our runner out, but he didn't make many accurate throws. So we ran, and most of the time we were safe.

Two of my right-field candidates, Roberto Clemente and Al Kaline, had strong arms and made accurate throws, and also got rid of the ball quickly. Runners didn't take any liberties with them. They didn't run on Andre Dawson or Dave Winfield either, even though Winfield did take a little extra time on the transfer. The key to stopping a runner is getting the ball in the air. If an outfielder with an average arm gets to the ball and gets rid of it quickly, most third base coaches will hold the runner, assuming he is coming from first base and there are no outs or two outs. Once the coach sees the outfielder throwing, he stops the runner. He has to make that decision before he has a chance to see if the throw is on line. The best weak-armed outfielder I have ever seen is Tony Scott. Tony got to the ball in a flash and immediately threw it to the cut-off or relay man. It was really hard to take liberties with him, even though he had very little arm strength.

With one out, the third base coach might gamble. His decision is based on the adage, "Never make the first or third out at third base." This is the logic behind it: With no outs, you already have a runner in scoring position at second base; why risk an advance? With two outs, a runner at second base will score on most singles. Why would you take a chance trying to get him to third base? That's why you play it safe. With one out, you might take a chance on getting to third, since a sacrifice fly, ground ball, or squeeze bunt could allow you to score on an out.

Sometimes, the risk factor applies to the outfielder as much as to the base runner or to the third base coach. Let's say you're the right fielder. There are two outs and a runner on first with the pitcher or another weak hitter due next. First of all, all the outfielders should play a little deeper to prevent a run-scoring double. On a looping ball over the infield you should play it safe to make sure the ball doesn't get by you. You have to believe that your pitcher can get the next guy out. When Lance Berkman started playing in the outfield, he was often out of position. He spent his college career at first base, but the Astros already had Jeff Bagwell at that position. One night, Lance was playing right field and there was a man on first with the eighth hitter at bat with two outs. The hitter looped a soft fly ball to right and Lance came charging in and dove for the ball, but missed it. It rolled all the way to the wall and the runner scored. Then our pitcher retired their pitcher. If Lance had played it safe, the other team would not have scored. His attempt to make a diving catch was unwise with the pitcher coming up.

Outfielders need to know when to take a chance and when to play it safe. If the runner is on second base instead of first with two outs, gambling on a diving catch is warranted. The runner will be running on contact, and if you don't try the diving catch, the runner will score. It is hard to decide what to do as you are approaching the ball unless you have thought about it first. There aren't many outfielders who are thinking about the on-deck hitter, but the best of them seem to know when and where not to take a chance.

The same is true for the third base coach. Next to the umpire, the third base coach is the biggest villain on the field. If he sends ten straight runners and they score and holds ten straight runners that would have been thrown out, he is merely doing his job. But if he sends a runner home and it turns into an easy out, or if he holds a runner and the outfielder bobbles the ball, he is vilified. Still, most coaches like that pressure. When you are coaching third base, you actually participate in the game.

Some ballparks are deeper in one field or the other. When this is the case at your home ballpark, you will probably want the fastest corner outfielder to play where there is more ground to cover. All of the outfielders I am considering for right field on My Team can cover a lot of ground. Roberto Clemente and Al Kaline may not have been the fastest runners but they were the best fielders in their respective leagues during their prime years. In the next generation of great right fielders, Andre Dawson won eight Gold Gloves and Dave Winfield (who also played left field) won seven. Tony Gwynn won five Gold Gloves and eight batting titles. He led the league in OBA once, but his slugging average was relatively low. If I were looking for a number one or two hole hitter, I would consider him, but I will likely have my right fielder hitting in the middle of the batting order. Dawson's speed would give him one significant advantage. He could cover more ground than the rest of the candidates. If he caught a ball that would otherwise be an extra-base hit, it would be a huge defensive play. It would take the air out of a rally like a George Foreman body blow would knock the air out of an opposing boxer. But this wouldn't happen all that often. With Dawson, it might happen about once every ten games.

Henry Aaron had a good arm, but was not in the same class as the other candidates. I am including offensive numbers on Babe Ruth for purposes of comparison. I don't know if he was tough to advance on or not, but I know he was a great pitcher, so I assume he had a strong arm. He may have been quick on the transfer and accurate, too, but I have no way of knowing about that. Still, his hitting was awesome.

Gary Sheffield is another guy who must be considered. His hitting numbers are better than those of most of the candidates but his defense, though not bad, is below par for My Team. I would say that he had slightly less range than Aaron and a little better arm. He couldn't throw as well as Dawson, Winfield, Clemente, Kaline, or Larry Walker. His arm strength and accuracy are about the same as Sammy Sosa's, but his hitting is a lot better. In fact, I was surprised to see that he was a better offensive player than both Clemente and Kaline.

Still, there is one thing that sticks in my craw. Kaline and Clemente both played their entire careers with one team. Sheffield has bounced around like a pinball. My guess is that he has been less than an inspiring teammate. I still recall reading about his first trade from the Brewers to the Padres. At the time of the deal, he said that he really hadn't played his best in Milwaukee because he was unhappy there and wanted to be traded. I don't know if he was unhappy in San Diego, Florida, Los Angeles, and Atlanta, but they all let him go, too. As with Robbie Alomar, I have to ask: Why would a team trade a guy who is prolific with the bat and a reasonably good fielder and base runner? Now he is in New York and he has continued to produce in Yankees pinstripes. But he is getting close to the end of his career and his production will probably decline. Still, it's hard to ignore his OBS which, for ten years, is almost 1000. If he were a left-handed hitter, he would make it tough on me, but like all the other candidates, he swings from the right side. I'm not going to take him on My Team because I just can't abide a player who admits to playing less than his best. Sure, he was just a kid then, and he's an old pro now. I guess I could forgive what might have been a lack of maturity. But with so many good right fielders to choose from, I am willing to let him go to the Dogs. Gary had also played a lot in left field, and I could use him there if I didn't already have Barry Bonds and Frank Robinson. Except for Manny Ramirez, Sheffield is probably the best hitter who didn't make My Team.

All around, Sammy Sosa has the most standout seasons with the bat. Like Sheffield, he is a pretty good fielder, but not a great one. He has never won a Gold Glove. In addition, I was surprised when I looked at his hitting record. Sosa doesn't even have the ten good seasons necessary to qualify for My Team. His monster years seemed to start when he arrived at the Cubs Hohokam Stadium in Mesa, Arizona, in 1998, looking more like Hercules than like Sosa. He hit 66 homers that season, breaking Roger Maris's all time record by five, but falling four short of Mark McGwire for the home-run title and new single-season record. McGwire gained a lot of upper-body strength that same year and, when the two sluggers played against one another in September with the record in the balance, it was like magic. It couldn't have been scripted any better. Their home runs were in the spotlight; hidden in the shadows was the specter of steroids. McGwire admitted to using a supplement, but it was something one might buy at a health-food store. I'm not sure if Sammy ever admitted to taking anything. Yet he followed his 66 homer season with totals of 63, 50, 64, and 49, his upper body bulging like that of the Michelin man. The next season, after the steroid scandal came into focus, he looked like the old Sammy and had a decent year. In 2005, he did about the same thing for the Orioles. With or without the big seasons, I don't think Sammy is worthy of consideration for My Team. Without those big seasons, he isn't much better than an ordinary outfielder.

Another right fielder I'm not even considering, despite his great fielding and hitting, is Larry Walker. Even without the Superman build, he has slightly better numbers than some of the others named in this chapter. However, he amassed a great portion of his statistics in a mile-high hitter's heaven, Coors Field. Considering what he has done at sea level, Walker doesn't quite make it. Aaron was a great hitter, but even Hank didn't measure up to the Babe. Let's see how the rest of them did.

THE CANDIDATES

PLAYERS	OBA	SLG	OBS	R/PA	RBI/AB	SB	CS
Clemente	.376	.502	.879	1/6.7	1/6.4	60	23
Kaline	.385	.513	.898	1/6.6	1/5.9	75	40
Winfield	.360	.503	.863	1/7.0	1/5.5	89	49
Dawson	.338	.512	.851	1/7.3	1/6.0	220	70
Aaron	.388	.602	.990	1/5.9	1/5.0	136	43
Gwynn	.397	.473	.871	1/7.1	1/8.1	226	77
Sheffield	.418	.557	.975	1/6.3	1/5.0	114	56
Ruth	.504	.751	1.255	1/4.4	1/3.5	96	97

Ruth is obviously off the chart, but Aaron is clearly the best hitter among my candidates. Kaline and Clemente are almost equal. When I consider that Tiger Stadium was a better hitter's park (even for right-handed hitters) than Forbes Field and about the same as Three Rivers Stadium, I have to give Clemente a little boost. And when I consider that the National League seemed to have more good pitchers than the American League during their respective careers, I have to split hairs to say that Kaline was still a tiny bit better hitter than Clemente.

I didn't have much trouble with Roberto. I threw him a few fastballs inside to keep him from leaning in. One of those fastballs broke his wrist in my rookie season. I saw him that night at a banquet in our hotel, the Pittsburgh Hilton, and tried to apologize, but he waved my words away. "Don't worry about it," he said, "It's part of the game." It was also part of the game that I continued to throw fastballs inside of the inside corner to him as a reminder and got him out mostly with outside sliders. I still remember facing Kaline in an exhibition game at the Astrodome. I threw him a good slider, right on the outside corner at the knees, and he slapped it sharply up the middle. He was at the end of his career at the time and I was really impressed. I still remember it after all these years.

I know they were both great outfielders. Clemente won twelve Gold Gloves and Kaline won eleven. Both of them hit better than Andre Dawson and Dave Winfield, who were also Gold Glove outfielders. The problem I have is that if I select Aaron, who do I pick to back him up, Clemente or Kaline? Actually, if Andre Dawson had been a little more patient at the plate, he could have made my decision easier. With a better on-base average, he would have leapfrogged Clemente and Kaline. Of course, if he had drawn more walks he would have scored more runs and would be in the Hall of Fame with the rest of them.

I saw Clemente and Aaron play a lot of games, Dawson and Winfield quite a few, but I didn't see much of Kaline. Perhaps Kaline was as good as Roberto in right field, but it is hard for me to believe he was better. In Pittsburgh, it was risky to go first to third on a single to right field—even on singles that almost any runner could advance on. I can still see our third base coach putting up the stop sign as soon as the runner coming from first rounded second, even before Clemente had gloved the ball. Roberto had such a strong, accurate arm, and he unleashed his meteoric throws so quickly, few runners dared to challenge him. Most of the time, they didn't even round the bag. Just the threat of being thrown out was enough.

It was probably the same with Kaline. I know Dave Winfield and Andre Dawson were tough to advance on. They both had powerful and accurate arms. Aaron had a good arm, but he couldn't throw like the rest of the candidates. I guess I can forgive him that, especially when I consider that even the best throwing right fielders don't throw out many runners at third base.

Aaron didn't throw out many runners at third, but that's about the only thing he didn't do. If you look at the hitting statistics, however, and consider that Hank was good but not great in the outfield, you already know that he makes My Team. It is interesting that the two most prolific home-run hitters of all time, Babe Ruth and Henry Aaron, played right field. That's where their similarity ends. Ruth was loud and brash; Aaron was soft spoken and easygoing. He didn't like to draw attention to himself, which is not what you would expect from the all-time home-run king. If you wanted to typecast the personality of a home-run hitter, you would most likely pick a guy who didn't make My Team, but did hit a lot of home runs and played right field—the flamboyant Reggie Jackson.

Home runs for a hitter and strikeouts for a pitcher are the gaudiest of all baseball records. I find it ironic that the all-time strikeout and home-run records are held by Nolan Ryan and Hank Aaron. When the Dodgers won the World Series in 1981, Dodgers broadcaster Vince Scully said that Burt Hooton would probably go out and paint the town beige. Aaron and Ryan are beige guys, too. Ruth and Mays were more entertaining. They were worth the price of admission, even when they didn't get a hit. I think Ruth's personality would have been better suited to center field, but he couldn't run fast enough. Center field is a showboat position. The fastest outfielders play center and make the most spectacular catches. They also steal bases and, in Mays's and Mantle's cases, hit home runs.

Aaron was no showboat, but he was aware of his accomplishments and had plenty of pride. Five years after he retired, he said, "If I had to pay to go see somebody play for one game, I wouldn't pay to see Hank Aaron. I wasn't flashy. I didn't start fights. I didn't rush out to the mound every time a pitcher came near me. I didn't hustle after fly balls that were 20 rows back in the seats. But if I had to pay to see someone play a three-game series, I'd rather see myself."

I'd like to see him out there, too—on My Team. When I came into the National League in 1965, Henry was about halfway through his career, and the Braves were still in Milwaukee. He hit a home run off me the first time I faced him at County Stadium. I lasted 13 years, and he hit six more homers off me during that time. I had a chance to go into the record book with him in 1973. I had been injured and not pitched in a game in more than a month when Leo Durocher called me in from the bullpen to face Aaron. It was the last series of the year and Henry had 713 home runs—one fewer than Babe Ruth's record. I didn't want any part of that record and managed to jam him; he got a broken-bat single. It was the happiest I had ever been after giving up a hit.

Hank taught me one thing about hitters: When they are successful against you, you have to figure out why and change your plan of attack. He hit most of his homers off me on inside fastballs during my first few years in the league. If I threw toward the outside corner, he would just let it go by, waiting for me to make a mistake. I think he rightly assumed that I wasn't good enough to hit the outside corner three times. Over the years, my control improved and once he realized that I could stay on the outside corner all day, he started swinging at outside strikes and I had a little more luck. At that point, I found that I could also pitch him inside occasionally, but I sure didn't want to come inside very often. He was as good a fastball hitter as I have ever seen. His teammate Lew Burdette once said, "Trying to sneak a fastball by Henry Aaron is like trying to sneak the sunrise past a rooster." Joe Torre hit behind Henry for the Braves in 1966, '67, and '68. "The thing that I remember most is watching him when I was on deck. Most pitchers like to go up and in on a hitter with an 0-2 count. I don't know how many times I saw him turn that pitch around and hit it out of the park. It's a good pitching strategy, unless you're facing Hank Aaron." The other thing that Hank could do was pull the ball down the left-field line without hooking it. I remember him hitting one off me in the Astrodome. The pitch was up and in and he pulled it right down the third base line. I was sure it would hook foul but it did not. It just shot straight into the left-field mezzanine seats like a rocket. No hook at all. This is something that only a few modern hitters, like Albert Pujols and Barry Bonds, can also do.

"The only guy that really gave Henry trouble was Curt Simmons" (a left-handed pitcher who threw mostly slow stuff), Torre said. "He'd throw that changeup so slow and Henry would try so hard to hit it but he'd end up hitting a little pop fly off the end of the bat. It was funny. Even Henry laughed. Finally, he tried to run up on it and he hit it out of the park in right field. The home plate umpire that day was Chris Pelekoudas. He called him out for stepping out of the batter's box. Simmons got Henry out—even when he hit a home run!"

Aaron made the N.L. All-Star team 21 times. I'll never forget the first time I made it, in 1969. The game was in Washington, D.C., and I was perusing the gifts laid out on a table in the locker room before the game. Each player could pick from an array of maybe ten items, including a silver punch service, watches and other jewelry, crystal goblets, and the like. I was trying to decide what to take when Henry strolled by and said, "I wonder when they're going to come up with some new gifts. I already have all of this stuff."

In 1966, the Braves moved to Atlanta and played their

games at the launching pad, Fulton County Stadium. I was told that Henry was a tougher out earlier in his career because he hit a lot of line drives to right field. Once he got the lay of the land in Atlanta, he became a pull hitter. His batting average suffered a little, but his assault on Babe Ruth's career home-run record began. While it was hard to pick Willie Mays over Mickey Mantle, it is easy to pick Aaron over everyone else.

You may recall that Aaron didn't look like a big, strong guy. He was listed at six feet and 180 pounds, which seems about right. If you shook his hand, you would immediately know that he was much stronger than he looked. Aaron was a great all-around player. He could hit for average and power. He could steal a base. And he was a very good outfielder, even though he only won three Gold Gloves. "He was a great outfielder," said former teammate Dusty Baker. "But he made everything look so easy. He got to the ball quickly and threw to the cut-off or relay man immediately. He had good arm strength, but he almost always hit the cut-off man." All outfielders are taught to do this but some of the strong throwing guys go for the hero throw—and let the trailing runner advance. Henry didn't give them that option. Another misconception about him is that he was a quiet, unassuming guy. "He was quiet on the field," Dusty said, "but in the clubhouse and away from the ballpark, he had a lot of personality. He loved to laugh. If you watched him play, you might think he was serious, but that's the attitude that was most respected in the game."

Another thing that was seldom talked about in the players of the past is conditioning. "We had a little basketball game in Atlanta," Dusty said. "I know he would have been good if he played, but he just ran around and around the gym the whole time we were playing. Sometimes he played handball and racquetball. He took great care of himself and that's why he lasted so long."

I expect there will be some disagreement over my picks at

some positions. I can't imagine anyone making a case that any right fielder in the last forty years is better than Hank Aaron. That said, I still have to select another right fielder. Should I pick Clemente or Kaline? Because I can't decide and because it is the manager's prerogative to move a player to another position to improve the team, I am going to take a player that would be on the Dogs team and put him on My Team. No disrespect is intended toward Roberto or Al, but I need another left-handed hitter and I am going to take Ken Griffey Jr. I won't play him every day, but at least My Team won't have to face him. Check it out.

PLAYERS	OBA	SLG	OBS	R/PA	RBI/AB	SB	CS
CLEMENTE	.376	.502	.879	1/6.7	1/6.4	60	23
KALINE	.385	.513	.898	1/6.6	1/5.9	75	40
GRIFFEY JR.	.385	.585	.970	1/6.2	1/4.8	153	55

So, I cheated. So what? In baseball there has always been cheating. I consider this a misdemeanor. I don't think Junior would be quite as good as Kaline and Clemente in right field, at least not at first. But I do think he would be very good out there and I think he would have a better chance to succeed against even the nastiest right-handed pitchers, when I would want to give Aaron a break.

Once you see a player at a position for maybe thirty or forty games, you begin to get a feel for what he can and can't do. If Griffey had trouble adjusting to right field, I could try Mays or Mantle or Frank Robinson out there. The kicker is that I can play Bonds, Mantle, and Griffey Jr.—an all left-handed hitting outfield. Against a tough lefty, I could go with Robinson, Mays, and Aaron. With Griffey Jr., I have another base stealer— a small edge, but still an edge. Because I do not have a left-handed hitter at shortstop or catcher, I need one everywhere else. Now, I have one in right field.

When Griffey was traded to the National League, I was eager to see him play. He was clearly the best all-around player in the junior circuit and Bonds was the best hitter in the National League by far. Now, I could compare them. Reds manager Jerry Narron saw Griffey in his prime years in the American League and has seen Bonds now in the National League. "Considering everything, Griffey was the best all-around player in the American League by far. But I think Barry is a better hitter. Junior doesn't always get around on the good fastball and Barry does. Junior swings at some bad pitches and Barry does not. I didn't see Barry in the outfield, but I don't think he could play it as well as Griffey."

In Seattle, there were some mumblings about Junior being a selfish player. "I don't know about Seattle," Narron said. "But with us, he is great. He does all his work and the players really like him." I really like him, too. And, let's face it, on My Team it would be hard for anyone to play the prima donna.

After Clemente emerged, Aaron didn't win any more Gold Gloves, but he was still an asset in the field. "He was anything we needed," Dusty said. "He hit big home runs, got big hits with the game on the line, and he could have stolen a lot of bases, but he only stole when we needed a steal."

"What about bunting?" I asked. "I've never seen him bunt for a hit like Mays."

"Well, you got me there," Dusty said. "He didn't bunt. That's the only thing he didn't do."

There is one thing that I know to be true. With Bonds and Robinson in left, Mays and Mantle in center, and Aaron and Griffey in right, I will have all the outfield positions well covered—and I won't have to bunt very often.

RIGHT FIELD: AARON, GRIFFEY JR.

9

Starting Pitcher

Good pitching beats good hitting and vice versa.

——YOGI BERRA

COMPARING PITCHERS across the last three generations is more difficult than comparing hitters and fielders. Having participated in the first of the three generations included in this study, I have to admit to being biased toward my own contemporaries. Still, it would be hard for anyone, no matter how objective, to analyze pitching across generations, especially given the great surge in power hitting in the last fifteen years. I sometimes wonder how I would have fared in this current period of power hitting. And I wonder why the best modern pitchers have better winning percentages than those who came before them.

All but one of my candidates for the starting rotation have ten years with an ERA below 3.00, but the recent crop, though thin, is just as stingy in a harder-hitting environment. Greg Maddux, Randy Johnson, Roger Clemens, and Pedro Martinez are like skyscrapers in the village of modern pitching. Or, maybe these four guys are just better than the pitchers that came before them. It's got to be one or the other. I tend to think that with 30 teams, there aren't enough pitchers to go around. Today's hitters are hitting against a lot of guys that would have been in the minor leagues 30 years ago. I do have to admit, however, that there are enough good hitters to go around. Most teams have guys who can hit home runs batting seventh and eighth in the order. That was not the case when I was pitching. Still, those four pitchers have been able to dominate hitters in an era that is second only to the 1930s in run production.

There are only a few active starters who have a chance to make it to the Hall of Fame, but there are 10 Hall of Famers from the sixties and seventies on my list from the first and second generations of starting pitchers. There are other old-timers, like Catfish Hunter, who are not on my list but have already made it to Cooperstown. After twenty years of drifting in the doldrums, talented pitchers are finally washing ashore. Perhaps the pitchers are making a comeback. Time will tell. Still, I haven't included some great pitchers from the sixties and seventies like Tommy John, who won 288 games; Bert Blyleven, who won 287; or Jim Kaat, who won 283. If hitting is better now than it was in the sixties and seventies, and even to an extent than in the eighties, Pedro Martinez, Roger Clemens, Greg Maddux, and Randy Johnson are perhaps the best pitchers ever to take the hill. They have exceeded the league ERA by wider margins than any of their predecessors, which suggests, at least to me, that high-quality pitching is ankle deep these days. Why don't these pitchers give up more runs than say, Tom Seaver, Jim Palmer, and Bob Gibson? Shouldn't Maddux et al. have ERAs that float up toward their peers like a boat on a rising tide? No one can answer this question unequivocally. The only way for me to make an educated guess is to imagine how the old pitchers would have fared against this generation of hitters and how the great modern pitchers would have done against the old-time hitters. And that is just a guess. Sometimes there is little comfort in the numbers.

My opinion is that Juan Marichal, Steve Carlton, and Don Sutton would have a little higher ERA pitching to today's hitters, but not much. A diluted current crop of pitchers may also explain why the best of them have such high winning percentages. Again, this could be because contemporary pitchers are better, or it could be because the old-time pitchers faced tougher opposing pitchers and thereby didn't get as much run support. When Bob Gibson posted a 1.12 ERA in 1968, he won 22 games, but he also lost nine. I beat him 3–2 that year and I also beat every National League pitcher on the list of my peers at one time or another. Did this make me a great pitcher? Of course not. But I *was* a good pitcher who could pitch a shutout (25) and a complete game (106). There were a lot of guys like me around back then. There aren't many good second-tier pitchers now.

There are twelve pitchers from my era who won more than 250 games, but only five 250 game winners among those who played mostly between 1980 and 2005. A big part of the reason for this is the emergence of the closer and, in recent years, the set-up man. Roger Clemens has won seven Cy Young Awards and leads all active pitchers with 118 complete games. If all these games were wins, he would still have had 213 wins in games he did not finish through 2005. And I know they aren't all wins because the one complete game he pitched in 2005 was a loss.

The easiest way for me to select a five-man rotation would be to count Cy Young Awards. Using this method, Roger Clemens would pitch on opening day. Steve Carlton, Randy Johnson, and Greg Maddux would be in the rotation, and either Pedro Martinez or Tom Seaver would be the fifth starter. I wish it were that easy, but it is not. As you can see from the chart on the next page, none of these pitchers really stands out from the others. How do you compare Maddux, who won four Cy Young Awards, while averaging seven innings per start, with Gaylord Perry, who won only two Cy Young Awards but averaged 304 innings per year in his prime with an ERA of 2.70? There is no question that Maddux stood out from his peers more than Perry did from his. Maddux's ERA from his best ten years was 1.58 runs per game better than that of the entire league; Perry's was only .82. Maddux lost only 82 games in his 10 years; Perry lost 133, probably because he pitched more innings and pitched mostly for ordinary teams. Spend half an hour with this chart and you will end up more confused than you were to begin with.

Trying to come up with the best five-man rotation by using these statistics is maddening. I know Maddux had better teams behind him than Perry did, but I don't know how to account for this statistically. Perry was the ultimate workhorse, while Maddux was a silent assassin. Perhaps it will be of some avail to break down the numbers to get the top five pitchers in various categories. Let's see if that clears the water or just makes it murkier.

Wins

Marichal, Carlton, Palmer, Jenkins, and Clemens. As you can see, this category favors my first-generation pitchers, who pitched many more innings per start and per season. The guys who pitched more innings got more wins.

Winning Percentage

Clemens, Martinez, Johnson, Maddux, and Seaver. Four out of five are contemporary. This category is influenced greatly by the quality of the teams they pitched for, although Jim Palmer pitched for a lot of great Orioles teams and didn't make

THE CANDIDATES

PITCHERS	W	L	W%	IP	ERA	LG ERA	DIFF	BR/IP	HR/IP	GS	IP/ GS
MARTINEZ	162	62	.723	1954	2.62	4.47	1.85	1.07	1/12.9	269	7.3
CLEMENS	198	72	.733	2478	2.65	4.25	1.60	1.12	1/17.2	335	7.4
MADDUX	185	82	.693	2399	2.46	4.03	1.58	1.07	1/20.0	329	7.3
JOHNSON	186	72	.721	2374	2.69	4.48	1.79	1.11	1/11.5	324	7.3
GIBSON	193	111	.635	2792	2.64	3.55	.90	1.15	1/15.8	338	8.3
MARICHAL	202	97	.676	2804	2.65	3.54	.89	1.07	1/11.3	352	8.0
PERRY	195	133	.595	3044	2.70	3.52	.82	1.13	1/15.2	382	8.0
PALMER	200	94	.680	2818	2.53	3.69	1.16	1.13	1/14.6	359	7.9
CARLTON	201	95	.679	2680	2.76	3.59	.83	1.16	1/13.7	348	7.7
SUTTON	169	95	.640	2521	2.85	3.70	.86	1.10	1/13.3	344	7.3
SEAVER	192	88	.686	2585	2.51	3.65	1.15	1.08	1/13.5	337	7.7
JENKINS	200	133	.601	2889	3.09	3.61	.52	1.12	1/10.3	376	7.7
RYAN	163	117	.582	2459	2.87	3.68	.80	1.22	1/17.3	337	7.3
P. NIEKRO	169	132	.561	2794	2.86	3.50	.64	1.18	1/13.3	353	7.9

W: wins; L: losses; W%: winning percentage; IP: innings pitched; ERA: earned-run average; LG ERA: league earned-run average; DIFF: differential; BR/IP: base runners per inning pitched; HR/IP: home runs per innings pitched; GS: games started; IP/GS: innings pitched per game start

the top five. Nolan Ryan did not pitch for many good teams, and it shows in his win percentage.

ERA

Maddux, Seaver, Palmer, Martinez, and Gibson. How can you win seven Cy Young Awards without making the top five in ERA? Easy. Pitch in the American League, where you have to face a designated hitter. If it weren't for the DH, Randy Johnson and Roger Clemens would likely be in a class with Maddux.

ERA Differential

Martinez, Johnson, Clemens, Maddux, and Palmer. Hats off to Palmer for making this list. As you can see, the modern pitchers do better in this category. Do they stand out so much because of their ability or because of their opponents' lack of ability?

Base Runners per Inning Pitched

Maddux, Marichal, Martinez, Seaver, and Sutton. Once again, it appears that either the old-timers faced a higher percentage of weak hitters or that Maddux and Martinez were simply more efficient. Maddux's efficiency rating is enhanced by his ability to keep the ball in the ballpark and to field many of the would-be hits up the middle.

Home Runs per Innings Pitched

Maddux, Ryan, Clemens, Gibson, and Perry. Big home ballparks helped Ryan and Gibson. Clemens and Maddux made this list on their own in a more prolific home-run era. It would take a sabermetrician to figure out how home ballparks influenced Perry because he played for so many teams. Suffice it to say that when he had the wet one going, it was pretty hard to hit the ball in the air.

Innings Pitched per Game Start

Gibson, Marichal, Perry, Palmer, and Niekro. I consider this an important category for My Team because I am only carrying nine pitchers. Palmer pitched both before and after the DH. He probably stayed in some games longer because Earl Weaver didn't have to pinch-hit for him and also because the Orioles didn't have any relievers that could outpitch him. Gibson and Marichal were both good hitters and probably got to stay in some games for that reason. Why would you pinch-hit for a guy who is a good hitter to begin with and gives you the best chance to prevent your opponent from scoring? Niekro falls into that same class. He didn't hit for power, but he did hit for average and seldom came out of a game because he was tired. Perry's manager may have been afraid to take him out of a game. Among the pitchers who did not make the top five, Seaver and Carlton were good hitters, too; Jenkins was the type of pitcher who got better late in the game. Martinez is clearly at the bottom of this list. He only averaged 27 starts per year and only 7.3 innings per start. The rest of the field averaged about 34 starts per year.

Cy Young Awards

Clemens, Carlton, Johnson, Maddux, Seaver, and Martinez. (Seaver and Martinez are tied.) The Cy Young Award is the best measure of a pitcher's effectiveness during a single year. It, too, can be misleading because the quality of the pitchers, hitters, and fielders has a major impact on his wins and ERA.

Obviously, these categories shouldn't carry the same weight in the analysis, but here are the men with the most top-five mentions: Maddux, Seaver, and Clemens. Johnson, Gibson, Palmer, and Perry are just a step behind them.

I would like to be able to end this discussion right here, but I cannot. If I did, I'd have a fifteen-man rotation. To get it down to the last five, I have to do some interpolating and exercise some judgment.

It's hard for me to think of Gaylord Perry as a better pitcher than Juan Marichal because I saw them on the same Giants staff for seven years and, at that point, Juan was better. But Gaylord just kept trudging out to the mound until he finally eclipsed a lot of pitchers who seemed better than him at the start, like Jerry Koosman, Catfish Hunter, Mickey Lolich, Bert Blyleven, Dennis Martinez, Jim Bunning, and Luis Tiant. He finished up at age 45 with his ninth major league team, the Kansas City Royals.

Gaylord had the wide-hipped, hunched-shouldered body of a guy who has spent some time behind a plow. As the summer wore on and the casualties of the long season started dropping away, Perry just got stronger. He featured the spitball and everyone knew it. The hitters he faced were half psyched out before they even stepped into the batter's box. He threw hard, but that wasn't the whole story; there were many who threw harder. He had that dour, inscrutable half-smile that made you wonder what he was thinking. He was ornery and irascible, and he could be just plain mean. His repertoire was simple: fastball, slider, changeup. He actually changed speeds on all his pitches and, of course, he threw the spitter when he really needed an out.

The spitter and the split-fingered fastball are pitches that have *late life*—they don't have tight spin, which informs the hitter about which way the pitch is moving. Pitches that spin loosely seem to move just as they approach the hitting zone. The pitch that has the most late life is the knuckleball. Sometimes it doesn't spin at all. The spitball is held on the smooth part of the ball with the index and middle fingers moistened with one substance or another. The split-fingered fastball has loose spin, too, because the index and middle fingers are off to the side of the seams. A good split lurches downward at the last moment. With the spitball you get the same effect; it squirts out of your hand like a bar of soap.

Back in the sixties, when I was pitching, there was no

such thing as a split-fingered fastball. I wish I had known about it because I threw my changeup with a split-fingered grip. If I had thrown it hard instead of loosening my grip and trying to make it go slow, I would have had a much better weapon. My changeup was decent, but the splitter can be devastating.

Gaylord Perry used to pick at his uniform and his hat a lot between pitches. Everyone watched him, trying to figure out where he was getting the grease. The spitter also helped him indirectly: I think he got more outs with his legal pitches because the hitters were looking for the spitter. He also got a lot of outs because he consistently pitched at or just below the knees. He had great control. Actually, I think the reason Gaylord lasted so long is that he didn't throw many pitches per inning. He would be perfectly pleased if a hitter hit his first pitch sharply and made an out. He wasn't out for glory, just wins.

A couple of stories say a lot about his personality: Giants catcher Jack Hiatt was traded to the Astros in 1971. Jack told me that one time, when Giants manager Herman Franks sent pitching coach Larry Jansen out to the mound to take Perry out of a game, Perry wouldn't give him the ball. Jansen reached for it and Perry shoved him back toward the dugout and said, "If he wants to take me out of the game, tell him to come out here himself." Jansen was a pretty good pitcher in his day, a winner of 122 games. I can't help imagining that he was both upset and amused when he retreated to the dugout. No amount of coaching could make a pitcher that competitive.

"He was a tough SOB," Hiatt said. "I couldn't believe some of the things he said when the manager came to the mound to take him out. There were a few times when he talked him out of it."

Several times, according to Hiatt, the Giants were tied late in the game and Gaylord went into the clubhouse and put his spikes on, then went to the bullpen and started warming up.

He knew that if he could get in the game, he would have a chance to be the winning pitcher. "He never thought about losing, only winning," Hiatt said. "He had five daughters to feed and he wasn't afraid to lose. He wasn't afraid of anything." I imagine the Giants relievers were somewhat aggrieved by this, but Gaylord didn't care what anyone thought.

"I remember a lot of guys worrying about their arms, getting treatment from the trainer, talking to the team doctor," Hiatt said. "Gaylord never got treatments or talked to the doctor, he just kept pitching. He must have had a sore arm at times, but you would never know it. He just got in the whirlpool, heated himself up, and went out and pitched." Another thing that helped him get warm was a reddish ointment called Capsulin. I used it, too, and it was a lot hotter than Red Hot. It came in tubes, like toothpaste, and when I first started using it, I only needed about an inch to feel like my arm was on fire. "Gaylord used so much of that stuff," Hiatt said, "his undershirts started getting sticky and turned red. The next thing you know, the rest of us started getting hot. We had to tell the clubhouse guy to wash his stuff separately." Capsulin wasn't the only ointment Gaylord used. When he first started using slippery-elm lozenges to moisten his fingers, his fastball started dive-bombing into the catcher's mitt. No one could hit it hard, just strikeouts and ground balls. The league had to add a rule about pitchers touching their mouths with their pitching hands. After that, Gaylord started putting slippery salves and ointments all over his hat and uniform. Facing Gaylord was no picnic, but his ten years stat totals leave him on the outside, standing in front of a window to the home clubhouse, looking in. My Team may have to face him, but I am comfortable with that because the Underdogs will have no picnic with My Team's pitchers, either.

Greg Maddux throws pitches that have a lot of late life, too, and he doesn't throw a spitter. He does have small hands, though, and I think he gets loose spin on his sinker and changeup without even trying. Hitters have trouble with pitches that seem to dart one way or another just as they reach the hitting zone because they can't predict how the ball will move. They have to start swinging or decide not to swing before the ball moves. Maddux gets them to do this all the time.

Most good pitchers have a knack for getting the hitter to swing at pitches that are not in the strike zone and to take pitches that are strikes. Maddux is the best I have ever seen at doing this. He throws a sinker inside to a left-handed hitter and, just as the hitter checks his swing, the ball moves in to catch the inside corner for a called strike. Then he throws a slider (or cutter) on the next pitch that looks like a fastball and appears to be a strike. By the time the hitter's bat is in the zone, the ball has moved in on him and is just below his hands, not in the strike zone. He either hits it foul or hits it weakly on the ground. Maddux is not about power. He is about late life and control. As he gained experience, he threw fewer curveballs for a very good reason. When you throw a curve, it is most effective down around the knees, but the curve is a hard pitch to control. Sometimes it hangs and is easy to hit. Sometimes it snaps into the dirt and gets by the catcher. In the second half of his career, Maddux started throwing more sliders and changeups—pitches he could control much more easily.

Next time you watch Maddux, pay close attention to how many batters swing at balls and take strikes. If most pitchers could do this, the league ERA would drop back to 3.50 or less.

It is tempting to say that Greg Maddux is at the other side of the attitude spectrum from Perry because of his studious demeanor. Maddux typically pitches fewer innings than Perry and seems to be less selfish. I have seen him come out of many games in the seventh inning with a lead. I've even seen him come out with a shutout in progress. Though Maddux looks more like a technician than a workhorse on the mound, he is win-hungry, too. All first-rate pitchers are. If he is ahead, he doesn't mind coming out of the game. If he is a run behind or tied going into the seventh, he wants to continue unless he is out of gas.

When you look at Maddux on the mound, he looks like a professor, with his studious, benign gaze. When things are caving in around him, especially due to errors and weak hits, he still seems placid. But if you watch him go back to the dugout when the inning is over, he will usually slam his glove into the bench and expel more than a little hot air.

One game I will never forget took place in the Astrodome. Greg was pitching against rookie Donne Wall and the game was scoreless after nine innings. Maddux seemed to get angry in the tenth. He started throwing 91 and 92 mph, much harder than he had been throwing. Naturally, his control suffered and we scored and won the game. They don't call him Mad Dog just because of his last name.

In his own way, Greg Maddux is as tough as Perry; he just doesn't show it on the mound. According to the numbers, Maddux makes My Team. However, the numbers reveal one thing that makes me hesitate. In one way, he is a workhorse because he seldom misses a start and usually pitches 240 or 250 innings in a season. In another way, he doesn't measure up. In his average start during his 10 best seasons, he pitched only 7.3 innings, tied for the fewest of any of the candidates. Since I have only four relief pitchers, I have to consider this. I also have to consider the situations. Playing for the Braves, he often had a comfortable lead after seven innings. He was willing to come out and save on the wear and tear to be stronger the next time out. I have a feeling he could have finished a lot of those games, and would have if necessary. In the summer of 2005, the Cubs had lost eight straight games in August, when he took his start against the powerful Cardinals. Talk about a stopper. He pitched his first complete game of the year throwing 115 pitches, about 15 more than he had thrown in any game to that point of the season. His team needed a win so he pushed himself, went the distance, and won 11–4. It was his 106th complete game, the same number that I had during my career. The difference is that he has won more than twice as many games as I did. He often didn't finish games because he didn't have to.

His pitching coach in Atlanta, Leo Mazzone, told me a story that speaks volumes about Greg Maddux. "It was about the seventh inning and he was in trouble. Bobby (Cox) went out to either take him out of the game or have him intentionally walk the batter. So Greg says, 'Give me two pitches. I think I can get him to hit a pop fly to third. If it's 2-0, I'll walk him.' So Bobby comes back to the dugout and the hitter hits a pop-up to third on the second pitch." Leo also remembers the 1995 season, one of Maddux's best. "Near the end of the season, I'm looking at his record and I notice that he has more wins than walks. He didn't quite make the whole year like that. I doubt anyone has ever done it." Maddux won 19 games that season and walked 23 batters, three of them intentionally. I'm not going to leave him off the team because of his innings per start. I think he could have pitched more innings in a lot of those games if the bullpen needed a rest, or if he needed to snap a losing streak.

The guy who is really at the other end of the spectrum from Perry and Maddux is Nolan Ryan. Unlike most of the pitchers in this book he didn't have good control as a young pitcher. Nolan did, however, pitch seven no-hitters and he struck out 2,000 more batters than Walter Johnson, the pitcher who had the career record before Nolan broke it. But Nolan never won the Cy Young Award. Some of the seasons he had with the Angels have Cy Young written all over them. But when I looked at the guy who won it three of those four years, I found that there was, indeed, a better pitcher in the league. In the other year, 1977, Sparky Lyle won the Cy Young Award while pitching for the Yankees. I suppose Sparky's team's success influenced the vote. In my opinion, Ryan had a better year. But it is hard to compare a starting pitcher to a relief pitcher. See what you think.

PITCHER	W	L	W%	IP	ERA	LG/ERA	DIFF	BR/IP	HR/IP	GS	IP/GS
RYAN '77	19	16	.543	299	2.77	4.06	1.29	1.37	1/25	35	8.5
LYLE '77	13	5	.722	137	2.17	4.06	1.89	1.21	1/19.7		

It's hard to believe that Ryan did not win the Cy Young Award and it is also hard to believe that Roger Clemens has pitched in over 600 games and has won seven Cy Young Awards without pitching a single no-hitter. Steve Carlton won it four times and he didn't pitch a no-hitter either.

Ryan learned the hard way. He was wild when he first joined the Mets in 1968. They had a weak offense. No matter how many guys he struck out, it seemed like it was still hard to win a game. After he was traded to the Angels, his control improved and he started winning more games. But it was still tough. The Angels hit as weakly as the Mets. Many years later when Nolan was with the Astros, I asked him, "Did you ever go out to warm up and find that you had great stuff and great control and then look across the field where a rookie pitcher was warming up and say to yourself, 'Man this is going to be fun today?'" His answer was, "Not once."

I have to imagine that his it's-not-going-to-be-easy mentality came from circumstances. The Mets and the Angels just weren't that good. I think Nolan threw harder than any pitcher I have ever seen, and I've seen a lot of hard throwers. He is also the only pitcher I have seen who could impress a blind man because sometimes you could actually hear him pitch; he grunted when he threw the ball, much like a shot-putter. You can only imagine how much fun this was for opposing hitters in the days before his control improved.

By the time Ryan was forty, his control was much better and he had developed a nasty changeup; he was a complete pitcher. Many pitchers don't last long enough to reach their potential. I didn't. By the time I learned what to do, and how to do it, I no longer had the arm strength to do it. Ryan lasted long enough to learn while he was still a hard thrower. His Rangers years were good, but I wonder what he would have been like in his prime with that changeup.

To give you an idea of what it was like to face Nolan in his early to midcareer years, it is necessary only to listen to the hitters who faced him. One of those hitters, Oscar Gamble, said, "A good day against Ryan is go 0-4 and don't get hit in the head." Reggie Jackson explained it this way: "Sure I like to hit the fastball, but with Nolan it's different. I like ice cream, too. Everybody likes ice cream. But that doesn't mean I want someone stuffing it down my throat by the gallon." When Nolan was in the late stages of a 17-strikeout no-hitter in Detroit, Norm Cash didn't say anything. He just stepped to the plate with a piano leg for a bat.

The only pitchers I have seen who are as intimidating as Ryan are Randy Johnson and John Candelaria against left-handed hitters, and J. R. Richard against right-handers. Candy was about six-foot-seven and he had a wide, sweeping slider that seemed to start out heading toward a left-handed hitter's thigh and end up on the outside corner. J. R. Richard gave right-handed hitters the same treatment. I wouldn't describe Nolan as a mean pitcher, but I saw him give hitters what he calls "a bow tie" many times. I saw him hit Pedro Guerrero on the helmet with a fastball at Dodger Stadium. After that, Nolan threw him mostly curveballs, starting them toward Guerrero's left shoulder and breaking back over the plate; Guerrero bailed out every time. He wasn't going to take a chance on another beaning, so he didn't get any hits, which was probably an acceptable tradeoff, from both his and Ryan's point of view. As with the Cy Young Award, Nolan comes up just short of making My Team. But the thing that is most disconcerting is that if he's not on My Team, he's on the other team. I can predict what Nolan's adversaries would have said if they were ever asked if it was fun to face him: "Not once!"

Another guy I liked to watch was Don Sutton. Sutton had his best years with the Dodgers, but he won a lot of games with the teams he played for in the second half of his career. In 1981, he signed with the Astros as a free agent. J. R. Richard had suffered a stroke in 1980, so the Astros signed Sutton to replace him in the rotation. Don doesn't get as much attention as some of the others because he had only one twenty-win season. But look at his efficiency. He had two years where his opponents averaged fewer than one base runner per inning. In 1972, the league had a .189 on-base average against him!

One of the things I liked about Sutton was that he was clever. I bet he would say that there were games when he thought it was going to be fun before it started. Don had a great curveball, and he showed me something about the curve that I didn't know. When he came over to the Astros, I was broadcasting his games, and I probably watched him pitch 25 or 30 times that year. I was amazed at how many called strikes he got on high curveballs. To do this you need tight spin and Don had it. When most guys hang a curve, it doesn't break very much. Don's did. He also had an upright delivery. Tom Seaver had what he called a "drop and drive" delivery. His release point was rather low. Sutton wasn't any taller than Seaver but Don's release point was relatively high. When he heard that Seaver was a drop and drive pitcher, he said, "I prefer the tilt and topple." If you get a mental picture of him on the mound, leaning back and then vaulting forward, that's exactly how it looked.

One thing that alerts a hitter that a curveball is on the way is when it pops out of the pitcher's hand heading up instead of straight. Guys with low release points have trouble throwing big-breaking curveballs for strikes. (Seaver's didn't break as much as Sutton's.) They actually have to throw the ball up so it will be a strike when it comes back down. Good hitters notice how the ball comes out of a pitcher's hand. When Sutton threw his curve for a high called strike, it was with the knowledge that it would come out of his hand looking like a high fastball. The hitters would assume it was too high, until they wised up—too late. Sutton didn't really have a sinking fastball, but, as I said, he was clever. He did have some fastballs that moved sideways. Hitters accused him of doctoring the ball, and he just gave them that sly smile. I doubt Don threw many fastballs harder than 90 mph. Like Maddux, he was fast enough. And like Clemens, he got a lot of strikeouts with his fastball. He is one of seven pitchers on my list that passed Walter Johnson's old career strikeout record of 3508. Like Maddux, Don could make a lot of hitters swing at balls and take strikes. He may not have been quite as masterful as Maddux, but he did win 324 games. Among all modern pitchers, only Warren Spahn, Steve Carlton, and Roger Clemens won more. Still, I can't put Don in my top five. He was fun to watch and hard to beat, but not quite as hard as some of the others.

Speaking of masterful pitchers, Juan Marichal was number one in my book. "In an era of power pitchers, Juan was all fi-nesse," said his catcher, Jack Hiatt. "He had so many pitches, it was hard to call a game for him. He knew exactly what he wanted to do, but sometimes I didn't. We had a few shake-off wars." Juan struck out a lot of hitters with his fastball and I'm not sure he ever threw a pitch faster than 90 mph. A lot of hit-ters who faced him would rather hit against Sandy Koufax. He had about 18 pitches and even on a windy day at Candlestick, he could hit corners with all of them," Hiatt said. "Pete Rose could hit anybody, but he couldn't hit Juan with a frying pan." I guess it's easier to admit you have been overpowered than to accept being tricked and looking foolish.

Over the years, I have seen many pitchers try to put more variety into their repertoires by changing arm angles. None of them could hold Marichal's jock (nor would they want to). Juan threw five pitches, and he made them into 11 by throwing straight overhand (90 degrees), three quarters (45 degrees), and sidearm (0 degrees). He couldn't throw his screwball sidearm and he didn't throw his changeup from that angle. But he could throw his fastball, slider, and curve from all angles. If most pitchers tried to achieve this type of variety, they wouldn't throw many strikes. But Juan would throw any pitch, from any angle, in any count. He didn't walk many batters, and he changed patterns enough to make a hitter dizzy.

Juan had a relatively short career compared to the others, but he was mighty stingy. During his ten best years, he averaged only 1.07 base runners per inning. And he averaged 8 innings per start. For me, it was more fun to watch Sutton and Marichal than Ryan and Koufax. I have had Juan on my top-five list and taken him off several times. I finally decided to take him off because he hit Dodgers catcher Johnny Roseboro on the head with a bat. That has nothing to do with pitching, but I found it so difficult to trim the rotation that I used this incident to help decide.

Another guy who often gets compared to Koufax is Bob Gibson. As a matter of fact, Koufax set the standard of excellence in the 1960s and is still rated by many the best of all modern pitchers. He doesn't make my list because he didn't have ten good years; he was like a left-handed Nolan Ryan but with better control. Gibson gets mentioned with another Dodgers pitcher, too, Don Drysdale. I suppose he is linked to Sandy by strikeouts and Don by batters struck. Actually, he didn't hit near as many hitters as Big D., but he was every bit as scary. The apocryphal story has a hitter digging his back foot into the batter's box and Gibby yelling at him from the mound, "Dig it deep, because I'm going to bury you in it."

One thing about these pitchers is that almost all of them were dead serious. Gibson wouldn't speak to an opposing player, let alone chat with one. A lot of pitchers don't talk to opposing hitters, but Gibson wouldn't even talk to opposing pitchers. One day, in my rookie year, I passed by him when I was running in the outfield. "Hi, Bob," I said. He just went on by as if I hadn't spoken. At least you knew where you stood with him. He wasn't interested in tricking a hitter or outguessing him. He simply threw one tough pitch after another—mostly darting fastballs and sliders—until the game was over. The word on him was to get him early because you couldn't get him late.

There was some truth in that. I think it was part of the mentality of that generation of pitchers, especially when teams were using four-man rotations. I know I felt better in the ninth inning than in the first in many of my complete games. The idea was to start out by making good pitches, on or near the corners, and to offer a variety of different speeds with a little movement this way and that, in some sort of random order. Mix it up and move it around, as they say. A lot of times Gibby wouldn't be throwing all that hard in the first and would just blow you away in the ninth. I wasn't as extreme as he was but I was always thinking about pitching the whole game, which meant that if I could save some energy early, I would have more later. The good thing about this approach is that it tends to stress accuracy over strength in the beginning. It's a lot like golf. If you get into a good rhythm early, you can add a little power later without losing your accuracy. It also gives you another place to go if you are in trouble early. Gibson didn't always look overpowering when the game started, but if you got him backed into a corner—voom!—he'd let you have it, full bore. The one thing that separated him from all of his peers was his pace. He had an up-tempo delivery and didn't waste much time between pitches. Dodger's announcer Vin Scully once said, "Gibson pitches as if he's double-parked."

Gibson radiated defiance on the mound. He was an impressive athlete, not real big, but strong and well coordinated. And there was that hard piercing stare. A lot of hitters didn't even like to look at him except when they had to because he was throwing a pitch. As a hitter, he had the power to hit the ball out of the ballpark. And he had the sheer strength of will to have things his way on the mound. I doubt many hitters were tempted to charge the mound.

Mike Shannon played third base and outfield behind him and saw Gibson's act firsthand. "He was smart," Shannon said. "Most people don't realize how intelligent he was. He used to tell me to be ready with a man on first base and less than two outs. I can't count the times he ran that sinker in on a right-handed hitter and the ball came right to me on one hop for a double play. Everyone says he was a winner but what I remember is the other side of the coin. He hated to lose. I don't think I've ever seen a guy who hated to lose that much. I know I'm biased, but I'd take him as my number one, even over Koufax."

It isn't often that a pitcher is a team leader; that honor is usually assumed by an everyday player. Tim McCarver caught Gibson a lot and has remained a friend. He has seen a different Bob Gibson than all but the inner circle of Cardinals players. "He seemed like the easiest guy to typecast as a tough-minded fierce competitor," McCarver said. "And he was. But there is another side to him. He could tell a story better than anyone. He could imitate anyone and when he got started, he'd have guys rolling on the ground laughing." There was no question about his fierce competitive desire. When he was on the mound, he was a leader by example. When he was in the clubhouse, on a bus or an airplane, he was one of the guys. McCarver thinks that Gibson was the leader of the sixties-era Cardinals even on a team with a lot of great stars. They were a hard-driving team, and they were belly up to the bar for a Budweiser team, with all the jokes and stories. When Bob Gibson was on the mound, though, there was no nonsense. McCarver reminded me of how Pete Rose used to circle around after grounding out and run across the mound to intimidate the pitcher. I never minded that; in fact, I thought it was funny. He was the one who made an out. But "when he did that against Bob," McCarver said, "he would say, 'get off of my mound.' Then he'd hit him the next time he came up. We are still good friends," McCarver said, "But sometimes, back then, Gibby was a difficult friend to have." Mc-Carver wouldn't have to be friends with Gibson on My Team. Tim didn't make it, so he will have to give up that pitcher/catcher relationship to Johnny Bench.

If he was a difficult friend as a teammate, he could be impossible for an opponent. When Merv Rettenmund was asked if he would rather face Nolan Ryan or Bob Gibson he said, "That's like asking me if I would prefer the gas chamber to the electric chair." Gibson had a reputation for hitting a lot of batters on purpose. Looking at his record, he really didn't hit many more than I did or than anyone of his era did. Nonetheless, most of the guys who stepped into the batter's box against him thought they were as likely to get hit as to get a hit. It's the thought that counts. Gibson and Tom Seaver had some memorable confrontations and neither could establish superiority. In one game, Gibson threw a pitch over John Milner's head. Seaver waited for Gibson to come up and after getting ahead in the count, he buzzed Gibson twice. Gibson stepped in front of home plate and said to Seaver, "You're not that wild." Seaver told Gibby that he wasn't that wild when he pitched to Milner either. Cardinals catcher Tim McCarver said that Seaver was the only pitcher who had the guts to challenge Gibson. I disagree. Gibby and Tom Terrific may have had some classic confrontations, but I think most of the pitchers in this study would be capable of challenging Gibson—perhaps not in a fight, but on the mound. That's one of the reasons they all won so many games.

Former Mets catcher Jerry Grote recalled a similar incident when Gibson was facing Seaver. "One day, Gibson drilled a couple of our guys," Grote said. "Tom said, 'Don't worry about it, I'll take care of it.' So, when Gibby came up Tom flipped him. That took some courage because Tom was the leadoff hitter for us when we came back up. Well, Gibson throws the first pitch behind him. Then the second pitch is in the same place. Tom walked about two steps in front of the plate and said, 'If you do that again, you're dead.' That was the end of the war that day." Gibson was mean, but he was not stupid. Seaver could throw every bit as hard as Gibby and had great control. He was not mean by nature, but was fiercely competitive. I know. We had a few throwing contests when we played the Mets in the late sixties. Seaver was right in the middle of them.

Gibson is the most contentious pitcher on the list. He would give any team he pitched for a sharp edge. His performance in the World Series is legendary. In 1967, he beat the Red Sox three times, all complete games, and his ERA was 1.00. The next year the Cardinals returned to the Fall Classic. This time he faced the Tigers and they didn't have much more luck with him than the Red Sox. In the first game of the Series, he struck out 17 batters, and won 4–0. He came back in game four and beat Denny McLain 10–1. His winning streak came to an end when Mickey Lolich outpitched him 4–1 in game seven. But you get the idea. In a big game, Bob Gibson was almost unbeatable.

Cardinals Manager Red Schoendienst left Gibby in to finish the last game against the Tigers. When asked why he didn't pinch-hit for him, Schoendienst said, "I had a commitment to his heart." It's hard to understand all the nuances of the sport, but one thing that you could do without exception is to make a commitment to Bob Gibson's heart. If his pitching wasn't enough, he added a little extra to the winning formula. His lifetime batting average was .206. And he hit 24 home runs and stole 13 bases. He also won the Gold Glove nine years in a row.

Pedro Martinez is defiant, like Gibson, but a few hitters have charged Pedro. He doesn't present an intimidating visage like Gibby, but he throws about as hard. He hasn't instructed batters to "dig it deep for a burial" or told anyone to "get off of my mound," but he doesn't give in to threats. He has pitched in a hostile environment of his own making many times, and he has continued to strafe right-handed hitters nonetheless. He just keeps pounding the ball in on their hands. Pedro hasn't started as many games or pitched as many innings as the others, but he has hit more batters per inning than any of the other candidates. He is short and slim but not afraid of anything. It's odd how that works. You might think the big, strong pitchers would be the most aggressive, but that isn't always the case. Bruce Kison, one of the skinniest pitchers I have ever seen, was also among the most aggressive.

My guess is that most of the guys who pitch aggressively and hit a lot of batters throw sinking (two-seam) fastballs. Coming from a right-handed pitcher, this pitch will run down and in on a right-handed batter and will usually be chopped on the ground. If you get it up too high, it doesn't sink as much, but it runs in more. A lot of hitters have trouble with fastballs on the hands. Some of them can handle a riding (four-seam) fastball in there but cannot deal with a pitch that tails in on their hands. For that reason, guys like Gibson, Martinez, and, for that matter, Kison, try to run the ball in under the hands and, when they miss their spot, they often hit the batter. If they were concerned about hitting a guy, they could start the pitch farther out over the plate, hoping it would curl in to the inside corner. However, if they did that and the ball didn't move much, it would often be hit very hard. So, for the intrepid, the preferred margin of error is inside, off the plate, rather than out over the plate on that pitch.

In addition to being defiant, Pedro does one thing that is exceptional: He deliberately lets the ball pop out of his hand with an upward trajectory. If this only happened on a breaking ball, it would help the hitter. However, Pedro's release point is so low that his fastball and changeup come out of his hand heading up, too. The fastball just keeps riding up (and sometimes in), and hitters usually swing under it. His other pitches start up and then drop, the breaking ball angling toward the first base side of the plate and the changeup just the opposite. Hitters can't guess anything from the way the ball leaves his hand because all three pitches leave the same way. The low release gives him an added advantage because most pitchers who throw from that low are sidearmers—sinker-ball pitchers. Pedro can make the fastball ride or sink. He is a master of late life.

Toward the end of my pitching career, my release point was low, too, not by design, but by necessity. It was the only way I could throw without pain. I still recall reading something in the Philadelphia paper after one of those late career games. It was a quote from Mike Schmidt saying about me what I said about Pedro. Mike said that when he saw a pitcher slinging the ball from the side, he expected the fastball to sink. He said he was surprised my ball was sailing instead of sinking. Learning to make it do that was about all I had left. My arm position had pretty well taken the curveball and changeup away from me, and also flattened my slider. Enough of that talk. It hurts just to write about it.

In the last few years, Pedro has had some arm problems too. It became an issue when he signed with the Mets in 2005, but he passed their physical exam and had another good year, despite losing a little velocity. It will be interesting to see how much he has left in the tank. One thing that anyone who has faced him will tell you is that he is a warrior and that his arm is a deadly weapon. From 1997 through 2003 his ERA was microscopic, like Sandy Koufax's in the 1960s. In 2004, Pedro's ERA leaped to 3.90, not bad by today's standards, but twice what it had been in the preceding years. In 2005, he got it back down to 2.82 pitching for the Mets. The advantage of not having a DH and pitching at Shea Stadium helped him a lot.

Thinking about sidearm pitches that sail and sink, I can't avoid another painful memory—a game the Padres' Kevin Brown pitched against the Astros in the 1998 playoffs, beating Randy Johnson 2–1. Brown was flat nasty that day. His splitter was coming in at 90 mph and his fastball at 96 and 97. His pitches were sailing and sinking so much that our hitters were coming back to the dugout shaking their heads. Brown pitched two-hit shutout ball for eight innings and struck out sixteen. We got our run off Trevor Hoffman in the ninth. From what I have seen of Pedro, he threw that type of stuff most of the time during his best seasons. Pedro is probably the toughest pitcher on the list when it comes to preventing solid contact, but his starts per year bother me enough to let him go to the Dogs. I wouldn't want to face him, but they wouldn't want to face my guy either and my guy would likely still be pitching after Pedro had given the ball to the bullpen.

The guy on my list who was probably the least impressive in terms of stuff is Ferguson Jenkins. Fergie didn't throw as hard as a lot of lesser pitchers. He didn't have a wide array of pitches either. I am still amazed that he was able to keep his ERA so low, while pitching half his games in Wrigley Field. The thing that he did better than any of the others, except perhaps Clemens, was to keep the ball out of the power zone without walking batters. He could hit either corner, up or down, at will, with a fastball or a slider. He probably threw in the low nineties, but that was enough. He could hit either corner with his fastball, and most hitters were looking for his slider. That didn't necessarily help them when he threw it because it was almost always low and away. Every once in a while, he came in hard to back a hitter off the plate. But, most of the time, he just nipped the outside corner. I have seen a lot of pitchers who could win just by throwing the ball low and away consistently. All but Fergie were lefties, like Randy Jones, Tom Glavine, Tommy John, Jamie Moyer, and Kirk Rueter. All of these lefties had sinking fastballs. Fergie was right-handed, and his fastball was pretty straight. But trying to hit Fergie was like eating broth with a fork. You never got a pitch you could sink your teeth into and he issued very few walks. He gave up a lot of singles, but most of the runners died on the basepaths.

When the Cubs got Fergie from the Phillies in 1966, he was a throw-in player with Adolfo Phillips. "He was in our bullpen," Ron Santo remembered. "And he was doing pretty good. But one day Leo (Durocher) came out of our clubhouse, down the left-field line and Fergie was throwing in the bullpen.

Leo stopped and watched and decided Fergie was going to be a starter. Fergie didn't really want to start, but Leo started him anyway. That changed his whole career."

One time I was watching him pitch against the Pirates on television. He struck out Matty Alou three times with sliders down and in. The pitches didn't appear to be that nasty, but they were perfectly placed and Alou couldn't hit them. I couldn't get Matty out with a slider or any other pitch. I thought I had a sharper slider than Fergie, but I made a lot more mistakes with it. He could throw it into a soup can from sixty feet, six inches.

Fergie was an easygoing guy, not the warrior type, not apt to become enamored of strikeouts. He did strike out more than 200 batters in a season six times, however, and more than 3000 during his career. As much as anything, he was an innings eater. He almost never got knocked out of a game. He pitched over 300 innings in a season five times. And he also had six 20-win seasons in succession. He is often overlooked because he never pitched for a championship team and wasn't as flashy as many of his contemporaries. But he did win a Cy Young Award and did throw almost everything low and away while walking fewer than two batters per nine innings throughout his career. I am not going to put Fergie on my staff, not because he didn't pitch on championship teams, but because I don't think he was quite as good as the rest of the pitchers.

Another guy who ate up innings was Phil Niekro. Knucksie worked about 280 innings per season during his ten best years. He seemed to last forever, probably because the knuckleball didn't take much out of his arm. He could even pitch in relief between starts, and he ended up saving 29 games. His ERA for the ten years was 2.86, which is higher than that of most of my candidates, but certainly low enough to win with My Team. (In fact, he'd have an easier time winning with My Team than he did with the Braves.) Even though it wasn't much fun to lose to him, I have to admit that it was funny to see the expressions on our hitters' faces after trying to hit his break-dancing pitch. Fast base runners can almost always steal bases on knuckleball pitchers for two reasons: the pitch takes longer to get to the plate and the catcher sometimes has trouble making a clean catch, which makes it harder for him to throw quickly. Knucksie didn't have a big problem with runners because he had an extremely fast move to first base. Runners had to stay close to the bag or risk being picked off. They still ran on him some, but not as much as you might expect. He was one of the best fielding pitchers I have ever seen, and was a good bunter and hitter.

Niekro's numbers aren't quite as good as most of the others' in this comparison, but when you consider the fact that he pitched in a small ballpark and with a weak team most years, his Hall of Fame credentials are legit. It would be a hoot to have him on your team so you could watch the opposing hitters embarrass themselves. And for my hypothetical team, including Knucksie would be a conservative move because, with only four relief pitchers, there might come a time when I would need a starter to pitch in relief between starts. Having him would be like having a player who could serve as a third catcher in emergencies—not a critical need, but certainly an asset. However, I have not selected Niekro. It would be nerve wracking watching him pitch. When his knuckleball didn't move much, it was a home-run pitch. And, with men on base, there was the constant fear that a ball will get past the catcher, allowing a runner or runners to advance a base. I could learn to live with those potential problems, but with the other guys I have to choose from, I won't have to worry about passed balls.

Among the older pitchers, Tom Seaver and Jim Palmer come closest to matching the modern pitchers statistically. Tom's ERA compared to the league ERA is clearly better than that of anyone else of his generation besides Palmer's. His base runners per inning numbers are impressive as well. Tom told me one time that he was more proud of his ERA than anything else. Certainly there are a lot of other things for him to be proud of, but keeping his career ERA below 3.00 for the entire span of a long career is probably his most impressive accomplishment. All of the pitchers I am considering, except Jenkins, have ERAs below 3.00 for ten years, but half of them are above 3.00 for their whole career because of their performance in the first and last few years.

"Tom was a veteran when he was a rookie," Jerry Grote said. "When I worked with a young guy, I always stepped out in front of the plate and made him aware of the situation. After a couple of starts with Tom, I knew I didn't have to do that. He was aware of everything. He was a perfect pitcher."

Seaver had a pretty good slider and curveball, but it took him a while to develop a good changeup. "One day I was in the outfield shagging," Grote said. "Tom said, 'Come over here, I want to show you something.' So, I got down in a crouch and he said 'fastball,' and threw it. Then he said 'changeup' and threw a good one. 'That's what you've been looking for,' I said. It was a circle change. The next game he pitched was against the Reds. Johnny Bench came up with the bases loaded and two outs. Tom got two strikes in the count and threw his new pitch. Bench about fell over trying to hit it. I ended up having to block it because it landed a couple of feet in front of the plate. From that point on, he had a good changeup."

I still recall the first time Seaver pitched against the Astros. It was at Shea Stadium in 1967, his rookie year. He beat us that day, but our hitters weren't that impressed. I have to admit, I couldn't have forecast his rise to prominence from that game. He wasn't throwing real hard that day. He did, however, have exceptionally good control for a rookie. Seaver ended up winning 16 games his rookie year. Obviously a lot of other teams got the same treatment we did. He won the Rookie of the Year Award, pitching 250 innings and striking out 170 batters. The next year he started throwing harder and began a streak of nine straight years with more than 200 strikeouts, leading the league in that department five times.

At six-foot-one he wasn't the tallest pitcher. And he made himself even shorter with his drop-and-drive delivery. His legs were so strong that he could drop his weight on the right one to get a powerful push off the pitching rubber. His right knee actually brushed the mound as he drove into the pitch. This helped him in two ways. First, it made it easier for him to throw low strikes. And second, it allowed him a better angle for throwing the four-seam, riding fastball. That was usually his strikeout pitch. Hitters swung under it all the time, and when they didn't strike out, they usually hit a pop-up or a lazy fly ball. Seaver was another of the serious, no bullshit performers. He would retaliate, as he did with Gibson, and he would pitch hard and tight inside to set up the fastball and breaking balls away. Because of his low-profile delivery, his curveball couldn't break very much and stay in the strike zone. To be honest, his breaking balls didn't look that impressive at first. After a few years, we all realized that they were effective. He didn't strike out as many batters with sliders and curveballs, but he threw them so consistently at or below the knees that he got a lot of easy ground-ball outs. Seaver is the only pitcher from my generation who stands out from his peers as much as Clemens, Johnson, Maddux, and Martinez stand out from theirs. He gets the nod on My Team, even though I know that if I could beat him, the rest of the pitchers in this study could do it, too.

Jim Palmer started two years before Tom Seaver, and they were alike in many ways. Each was able to maintain a sub-3.00 ERA throughout a long career. Each had the bright, wholesome, polished look of a high achiever. Palmer was long and lean, while Seaver had a more blocky build. I suppose that's why Palmer got to model underwear and Seaver did not.

Palmer had an erect delivery, like Sutton, but his delivery had a steeper angle because he was several inches taller and threw with his arm further extended, like a catapult. If you have watched many good starting pitchers over the last 40 years, it is easy to see that there is no model delivery. From the length of the stride to the angle of the arm, each of these guys had a unique way of throwing a pitch. Likewise, there is no standard demeanor. Some of the candidates are aggressive and defiant, while others prefer the even-keel approach. All of them, however, could concentrate for nine innings. Palmer, like Sutton and Jenkins, appeared nonchalant, while sending batters back to the dugout empty-handed. Jim had the four-seam fastball and threw it over the top with backspin and riding action. He was the best I have ever seen at getting hitters to swing at a pitch that was a little too high to hit well. He could pitch around the knees, too, down and away to the dangerous hitters. The high fastball and big overhand curve were his strike out pitches, but there was more to him than that. Rick Dempsey says, without hesitation, "He was the best pitcher I ever caught. In fact, he helped me learn how to call a game. I think I caught over 200 of his wins. He was so smart. He would move fielders around all the time and the hitters usually hit it where he thought they would."

Don Baylor remembers Palmer moving him around in the outfield. "He had his own way of doing things and he didn't always agree with Earl (Weaver). In fact, he used to needle him. He called him Mickey Rooney. He didn't always pitch to guys the way Earl wanted him to. And he would sit right next to him on the bench when he wasn't pitching. I remember one time when it was late in the game and we were tied. Jim said, bunt, Earl. B-U-N-T! But Earl didn't give the hitter the bunt sign. He didn't like to bunt. He liked to hit away. He was stubborn, like Jim, and we won."

Palmer had some arm problems early in his career. He even went back to the minor leagues, briefly. He went to winter ball in Puerto Rico to get more work in and the pain in his arm mysteriously went away. After that, he averaged about 280 innings pitched per year for eight years. He is one of only 18 pitchers who have won 20 or more games eight times. He also pitched a no-hitter and won the Cy Young Award three times.

"He was the whole package," Baylor said. "He was a good fielder; he was a good hitter; he could get a bunt down. And he was all business when he pitched. He wanted to control everything. I think he was good for our other pitchers, too. I don't think Jim Hardin could have won 18 games without Jim helping him. People say Jim was selfish but I disagree. He may have been self-centered, but he cared about the team, too. He wasn't just about Jim Palmer. He was about winning—just like Earl."

Even after he became one of the best pitchers in baseball, he continued to have flare-ups with his combative manager. Weaver liked to move players around, too. One time he said that he sometimes moved his outfielders over six steps to the right so that when Palmer moved them back three to the left, they would be in the proper position. (I'd hate to be one of those outfielders.) No matter where they were stationed, it usually worked out well for the Orioles. They were loaded with good pitchers year after year. They also had good hitters and fielders, and, though Jim might not be the first to admit it, they had one of the best managers, too. Theirs was a friendly disagreement most of the time and after too many arguments in Baltimore, they finally became neighbors in Cooperstown when Weaver was elected to the Hall of Fame in 1996.

About the only critical thing I can say about Jim Palmer is that he is not one of the top five candidates in winning percentage. He is sixth behind Clemens, Johnson, Martinez, Maddux, and Seaver. Still, 68 percent is pretty good in baseball. Palmer is also tied for fourth on top of the list in innings pitched per start at 7.9. He hardly ever had a bad game.

Jim Palmer was only 20 years old when he won his first World Series game, shutting out Sandy Koufax. He finished his postseason career with a record of 7-5 and a sparkling ERA of 2.61. I am torn between Marichal, Palmer, and Gibson. However, for the sake of team chemistry, Gibson gets the nod.

Palmer was aloof and Marichal did hit Johnny Roseboro over the head with a bat. When you come right down to it, attitude is all I have to go on. They were all great pitchers and their numbers are almost identical.

I consider the Marichal/Roseboro incident an anomaly, because Juan played his whole career with the Giants. If he had been a bad actor, the Giants probably would have traded him. But that's all I have to go on statistically. Palmer, Gibson, and Marichal are all so closely bunched that I eliminated Palmer because he played in the American League when the National League was stronger. He also played for the Orioles when they had great teams every year. He got a lot of help both at the plate and in the field. With Brooks Robinson, Mark Belanger, Bobby Grich, and Paul Blair behind him, many would-be hits were turned into outs. And with Brooks and Frank Robinson, Boog Powell, Don Baylor, Ken Singleton, Lee May, Reggie Jackson, Eddie Murray, Cal Ripken Jr., and Grich in the lineup, Palmer had a lot of power-hitting teammates, too. Most of these hitters overlapped and did not play with Jim throughout his career, but he did have good offensive support just about every year.

Roger Clemens has a variety of tough pitches that are just about as nasty as Pedro's. When it comes to painting the corners of the plate with wicked stuff, they are about even. Unlike Pedro, Roger has been a workhorse, seldom missing a start. All in all, Roger is the toughest pitcher I have ever seen, except for Sandy Koufax. Clemens makes my squad on the Cy Young Awards alone. By the numbers, he would have made it anyway. Unlike Ryan, Clemens pitched mostly with good teams. I doubt he ever thought it was going to be easy to get a win, but I'm almost sure he didn't think he'd have to work as hard as Nolan to get one. Nevertheless, he pitched like it was going to be tough. In 2004, when he won the Cy Young pitching for the Astros, I saw most of his games. I have never seen a pitcher as uncompromising as he was that year. Most of the time, he had better than average stuff, and all of the time he tried to hit corners with it, even against the lesser hitters when he was behind in the count. He simply would not give in. Call it "refuse to lose" or whatever you'd like, the result was 18-4 that year. His career winning percentage is in the top ten all-time—almost 70 percent. And he pitched most of his innings in a hard-hitting era. In 2005, the Rocket was even stingier than he was in 2004, but he didn't get much support from the Astros hitters. Still, an ERA of 1.87 isn't bad for a 43-year-old pitcher.

I think Roger is a little more competitive than Ryan was in terms of those things you do that aren't related to throwing a pitch. Both were dedicated to conditioning, but Roger seemed more determined to master the nuances of the job. Early in that first year in Houston, I watched him take batting practice. Most pitchers just try to hit home runs in BP. But Roger was choked up on the bat and trying to hit the ball where it was pitched. He approached hitting the same way a hitter would—dead serious. He also worked runners harder than Ryan worked them. Nolan was indifferent to runners. His fastball was a fly-ball pitch and his curve was usually chopped on the infield or missed completely. He didn't have a medium speed ground-ball pitch, so it was hard for him to induce a double play. He worked cattle harder than base runners. As a result, it was easy to steal on him, but it was still tough to score. Roger, on the other hand, had a sinker, a slider, and a splitter, three good double-play pitches. For this reason, he threw to first base often and sometimes tried to quick pitch to keep runners on first base. The man wanted to be in control of every little thing from the first pitch to the last. He didn't throw quite as hard as Nolan, but he still got most of his strikeouts with the fastball. He had to be in great physical condition to go all out on all of his pitches, running deep counts to a lot of hitters. As a result of the energy he expended and the number of pitches he threw, he didn't pitch as many complete games as you might expect. Part of it was the emergence of the closer during his era and part of it was that he, like Maddux, was willing to take an early exit if the game was in hand. Ryan seldom had that luxury. Roger stands out, even in this elite group of pitchers. He would start for My Team on opening day.

Because Sandy Koufax did all of his amazing pitching in only nine years, I have only two left-handed pitchers on my list: Steve Carlton and Randy Johnson. Both of them could be intimidating, Carlton mostly with his breaking pitches and Johnson with his fastball. And both of them could be scary without even throwing a pitch. All you had to do was look them in the eye to know that you were in trouble. Randy has the advantage of being six-foot-ten—all knees and elbows. And with that monomaniac glare, he could make a hitter wish for a "real job." Carlton was also tall and had an upright delivery that gave him a great angle on his curveball and slider. One opponent said of him, "When you mention 'Lefty' and every player in both leagues knows who you are talking about, that guy must be pretty good."

When he was with the Cardinals, Lefty was an excellent young pitcher who won a lot of games. He threw mostly fastballs and curves then. The nasty slider would come later. At that point, he was not considered to be in a class with Koufax, Marichal, Don Drysdale, or even his own teammate, Bob Gibson. Carlton was traded to the Phillies and started killing the Cardinals from that day forth. In Philadelphia, he launched an alternative strength program with Gus Hoefling, who was one of the first of the professional strength coaches. Once Gus got him, he was a different animal. The word got around. He started doing all kinds of different conditioning drills, like digging his hands into a barrel of dried beans. The idea was that the farther he could dig the stronger his forearms would get. McCarver claims that Lefty was the strongest man he has ever known from the hands to the elbow.

And his focus was pure. It was almost a trance. As Phillies announcer and Hall of Fame outfielder Richie Ashburn once said, "You could have run a herd of elephants across the field and he wouldn't have seen them."

The first time I encountered him in person was the night before the Houston baseball dinner in 1970. Steve was in town to collect an award, and we went to a party in Astros owner Judge Roy Hofheinz's penthouse. The judge had a pool table up there like none I had ever encountered in a pool hall or a honky-tonk. The felt was smooth and it really took hold of the spin on the ball. The bumpers were livelier than any I had ever seen. Watching Carlton play, I learned why he had such a sharp curve and slider. It was all in the wrist, as they say. One time he made a shot from about three quarters of the way down the rail and he had so much backspin on the ball that it backed up all the way to the rail it had come from. I'm talking about four feet of green and six feet of backspin. I'll never forget that.

After Carlton became a Philly, he became more than a good young pitcher; he became a monster. Before every pitch, he would clench his neck and, from the dugout, you could see the cords running from his collar to his jawbone. It looked like he was twitching and sucking air through his nose. This was in 1972, when he won 27 games for a last place Phillies team that won only 59 games overall. It was a *piece de resistance* nonpareil in the annals of the sport. That year he collected one of his four Cy Young Awards, pitching 347 innings, striking out 310 batters, hurling eight shutouts, and finishing with an ERA of 1.97. At one point in the season he won 15 straight games.

The first half of that season, Steve pitched to Tim Mc-Carver. They worked well together, as they had in St. Louis, and became good friends. McCarver was traded to the Expos that year, but Carlton was already in the winning zone. After Mc-Carver left, Steve started pitching to John Bateman and pitched even better. McCarver moved on to the Red Sox and was released in June of 1975. Carlton suggested that the Phils sign him as a backup to the Phillies young starting catcher, Bob Boone. The Phils complied. After that, McCarver became Carlton's personal catcher, and they worked together the rest of the decade. The Phillies won their division four of the next five years, and Carlton picked up two more Cy Young Awards. He ended up pitching more games to McCarver than any other catcher, prompting Tim to say that he and Steve would be buried sixty feet, six inches from one another. Carlton was in his heyday in the late seventies, but he had also pitched to McCarver in the sixties with the Cardinals. Pitching to his favorite catcher, he went 97-46 with an ERA of 2.75.

Carlton had great breaking stuff, and that's what most hitters were concerned with, but he also had a good fastball. He didn't throw as hard as Ryan, Gibson, or Koufax, but he homed in on the outside corner at the knees against right-handed hitters and he could hit that spot with regularity. He could run the ball in under a right-handed hitter's hands, too. Steve had one of those fast balls that come again. Palmer and Seaver had the same type of deception. Many of the great pitchers have this quality and it is hard to explain unless you have seen it from the batter's box. It usually comes from a fluid, seemingly effortless delivery. When a hitter sees this type of fastball it appears to have ordinary speed. Then, when it gets about three-quarters of the way to the plate it seems to surge. You think you have it timed and then, whoosh! It breezes right on by you like the second stage of a rocket. The first stage is steady until the booster kicks in. It is the opposite effect from that of a junk-ball pitcher: He comes charging off the mound like a maniac, looking like he's throwing the ball 100 mph, and then when the ball gets to the plate it just rolls over and dies. Either way is deceptive. What you see is not what you get.

Carlton limped to the finish line in his last two years, but still won 329 games. The only left-handed pitcher in the history of the sport who won more was Warren Spahn. What McCarver remembers most about going to Carlton's Hall of Fame induction was something that happened the night before. There was a dinner at the Otesaga Hotel and several people got up to talk about Lefty. When it was McCarver's turn, he said that Carlton had the best slider ever. Afterward, as guests were filing out, he saw Gibson, swimming upstream against the flow. When Gibson got to McCarver, he said, "Best left-handed slider."

Roger Clemens and Randy Johnson are the only pitchers who have won more Cy Young Awards than Carlton, and Clemens is the only modern pitcher with more wins. On top of everything else, Carlton was a good hitter. He batted .201 with 13 homers during his long career.

Despite all this, I'm not going with Carlton for two reasons. One, I don't subscribe to the notion that you need to have as many left-handed starters as possible and, two, his efficiency numbers don't quite measure up. I toyed with the idea of selecting McCarver and Carlton as a tandem. But Maddux likes to pitch to a back-up (or personal) catcher, too, and Mike Piazza is a much better hitter than McCarver. I'm not sure I'm getting a better pitcher when I select Maddux and Piazza over Carlton and McCarver, but I know I'm getting a harder-hitting catcher.

Randy Johnson isn't such a good hitter, but he is the most intimidating left-handed pitcher I have ever seen. His numbers do measure up and, boy, was I wrong about him. After we traded for him in 1998, he went 10-1 to help us get into the playoffs. But Randy had a chronic back problem. He couldn't run with the rest of the pitchers. Instead he had his own workout plan. It was mostly weight-room stuff; you knew when he was in there because the heavy-metal music was cranked up and it rocked the room. When he was pitching, he would lie on his back between innings in the runway between the locker room and the dugout. In his last two starts that year his velocity dropped from near the century mark to the low to mid-nineties. He threw a little harder than that in the first game of the play-offs but lost to Kevin Brown. His second start in the playoffs was in San Diego and he never even reached the mid-nineties as the Padres, behind Sterling Hitchcock, eliminated us.

That off-season, the Astros offered Randy a lucrative contract for three or four years. I was privately hoping he would not accept it. My fear was that his back wouldn't last as long as the contract and that we would have a lot of money tied up in a guy who couldn't pitch. Looking back, it reminds me of what the Astros said when they traded Rusty Staub to the Expos. They claimed that Rusty had a chronic ankle problem that would shorten his career. After that, Rusty played seventeen more years. Randy has done the same thing. He won the Cy Young Award in his first year with the Diamondbacks, then went on to win it the next three years, too! Outside of wins and losses, he had a better year than Clemens in 2004. But the D'backs were rebuilding that year and Randy didn't get much run support. Still, he went 16-14 with an ERA of 2.60, and allowed fewer than one base runner per inning. He also struck out 290 batters! If he had won the award, it would have been his sixth and, since Roger already had six, they would have been tied. So much for my ability to predict the future.

One of the many things that makes Randy so tough is his release point. His posture during his delivery is erect. His arm angle is low three-quarters to sidearm. Because he is so tall, he releases the ball from a higher level than most pitchers. Because he throws from the side and his arm is so long, he also throws from a wider angle than anyone else. There is no comfort zone for a hitter, as the ball comes from an angle he sees only when he is facing the Big Unit. Randy has an electric fastball and a wide, sweeping slider. If his delivery and the stuff that comes out of it aren't enough, his attitude makes him even scarier.

Randy is a quiet, private man most of the time. He does

his work between starts and doesn't bother anybody. But, on the day he pitches, he seems to get even bigger, and he also seems to be angry. His long, stringy hair throws off a rooster tail of sweat when he turns the ball loose. You almost feel like you have to ask permission to get in the batter's box, even though you don't really want to get in there. Standing up on the hill, he looks like a giant bird of prey, even a pterodactyl. Hitters scurry to and from the dugout like lab rats; they are defenseless.

Of all the pitchers in this study, only Pedro Martinez has an ERA differential that is better than Randy's. Only Pedro and Nolan Ryan have given up fewer hits per at-bat. The only area where Randy isn't one of the best is in average innings per start. In this regard, he has the same problem as Ryan. It's a good problem because it suggests that hitters have trouble hitting the ball, which leads to a lot of foul balls and a high pitch count, which makes it difficult for him to pitch a complete game. Nolan pitched most of his career in an era when pitchers were expected to go the distance if they could. Randy has pitched most of his career in an era when managers would call on a relief pitcher to finish up an easy win. I believe that Randy, like Maddux, could have finished a lot more games if he'd wanted to, and I believe he could do it on command if the bullpen needed a rest.

I doubt there has ever been a more fearsome left-handed pitcher than Randy Johnson. And I doubt anyone would disagree with that statement. No, I didn't do a very good job of estimating his longevity, but I think it is safe to say that his ultimate destination is Cooperstown.

No matter which five pitchers I select for My Team, there will be five others who are just as good. That's why I think My Team would be hard pressed to win more than 60 percent of its games against another all-star team. My Team will have a rotation of Roger Clemens, Randy Johnson, Greg Maddux, Tom Seaver, and Bob Gibson. Putting these pitchers into a rotation will be challenging. But no matter which way I line them up, the Underdog hitters will be whining.

STARTING PITCHER: CLEMENS, R. JOHNSON, MADDUX, SEAVER, GIBSON.

10

Relief Pitcher

 WHEN WHITEY HERZOG was asked what a major league manager needed the most, he said "A good sense of humor and a good bullpen." He said that in the 1980s and it is even more apropos now. Relief pitching may not be as important on a team with so many good starting pitchers, but having a bad bullpen is no laughing matter. I didn't use my bullpen as much as most managers, but we couldn't have won four division titles without a closer. Although I don't anticipate many early exits with my starting rotation, I know I need at least one pitcher who can go three or four innings in the unlikely event of one my starters getting knocked out or sustaining an injury early in the game.

As with the other positions, I have numerous worthy candidates and there will be some great closers that won't make the cut. The eight-year requirement to qualify works against a few great pitchers, like John Franco, who had far more than eight good seasons, but did not have eight stellar seasons. Among the candidates, there are two pitchers, Dennis Eckersley and John Smoltz, who served as starting pitchers for many years before moving to the bullpen. Even though Smoltz has now moved back into the rotation and did not pitch the required eight years to qualify for My Team as a reliever, I will still consider him for the bullpen because that is the way I would use him. Eckersley never went back to the rotation after becoming a closer, but I will give both of them bonus points in my evaluation because I know they could pitch three or four innings if needed. I will also consider Rollie Fingers and Rich Gossage for the same reason. Fingers's career started when there was no such thing as a closer. At that time, the best reliever almost always pitched last when his team had the lead. In other words, Fingers, Sparky Lyle, Tug McGraw, Hoyt Wilhelm, Elroy Face, and others were closers before the term came into common use. They all pitched two or three innings from time to time and they had the stuff to do just that. By the time Smoltz and Eckersley moved to the bullpen, the closer's role was defined as the guy who pitches the ninth inning to save the game. It is a windfall to have closers who are durable enough to pitch more than one inning.

These days, some closers still work more than an inning occasionally, but they don't enter the game nearly as often as Fingers and his predecessors did, so their chances of blowing a save are not as great. Since I have decided to go with a nine-man staff, including only four relievers, I have a difficult decision to make. Should I take two closers who can act as long relievers or serve as their own set-up men by pitching the last two or three innings of a game? Or should I take one such pitcher and three ninth-inning guys? I could take Wilhelm, or make Phil Niekro a long reliever and spot starter to cover the unlikely need for a pitcher who can either start or pitch in relief. I am inclined to take two guys who can pitch more innings, if necessary, which means that I will still have two true closers. Ideally, one of the closers will be right-handed and one left. I'm not concerned about being undermanned because I will get a lot of complete games from my starters. I am somewhat concerned about having too many pure closers because the save opportunities may not be plentiful. It might be difficult to keep two closers sharp without using them in nonsave situations. I would either have to designate one of them to be the ultimate closer (which may create a chemistry problem) or help them stay sharp by using them in some nonsave situations. How would you feel if you were Trevor Hoffman and you were told that Mariano Rivera was the primary closer, knowing that you have a better save percentage than he does?

I have the longest list of candidates for these positions and there are more worthy closers than there are places for them on My Team. You can see the difference between the old and more modern closers by looking at the number of innings per appearance. I will consider innings per appearance for the long relievers and save percentage for the closers. After I examine my options, it seems like the left hand versus right hand issue didn't make much difference. As with the starting pitchers, my four relievers may not be much better than the next four. In fact, I think I could easily fill three teams with great relievers. My job is to pick them. Your job is to evaluate my picks. (See chart on next page.)

Dennis Eckersley is the most obvious first choice. He is fourth on the all-time saves list and could pitch long relief if necessary. His save success ratio is slightly lower than that of John Smoltz, Trevor Hoffman, and Mariano Rivera, but it is still excellent. And his presence on the team would be a chemist's dream. Eck was a great teammate and a great guy. When Don Zimmer was his manager in Boston, he summed him up nicely when he said, "Of all the people I've managed in the game he's the one kid I'll always remember, because he always approached the game the way it's supposed to be approached. He had fun, he was competitive, and he loved it." Eck was popular with fans and the media, too.

THE CANDIDATES

PITCHERS	G	IP	ER	ERA	W	SV	SVO	SV%
AGUILERA, RICK	473	516	182	3.17	28	268	325	.825
BECK, ROD	502	526	165	2.82	26	269	311	.865
ECKERSLEY, DENNIS	484	588	160	2.45	31	302	344	.878
FINGERS, ROLLIE*	510	865	238	2.48	64	176	223	.789
FRANCO, JOHN	476	556	151	2.44	40	257	309	.832
GOSSAGE, RICH	435	785	168	1.93	53	206	256	.805
HENKE, TOM	473	560	147	2.36	23	253	290	.872
HERNANDEZ, ROBERTO	539	582	199	3.08	33	262	318	.824
HOFFMAN, TREVOR	502	537	152	2.55	36	325	356	.913
MYERS, RANDY	481	550	170	2.78	27	276	316	.873
NEN, ROBB	575	601	176	2.64	38	299	353	.847
REARDON, JEFF	492	600	208	3.12	34	266	341	.780
RIVERA, MARIANO	506	554	131	2.13	34	331	375	.883
SMITH, LEE	532	671	209	2.80	37	267	314	.850
SMOLTZ, JOHN**	246	285	84	2.65	6	154	168	.917
SUTTER, BRUCE	497	806	226	2.52	52	250	325	.769
WAGNER, BILLY	480	525	136	2.33	28	240	273	.879
WETTELAND, JOHN	497	550	155	2.53	34	295	348	.848

*Fingers save percentage and save opportunities for only six years, no stats available on blown saves for 1972 and '73 when he had a total of 43 saves
**Represents four best years of relief pitching, all others are eight best years
G: games; IP: innings pitched; ER: earned runs; ERA: earned-run average; W: wins; SV: saves; SVO: save opportunities; SV%: save percentage

Relief Pitcher

What amazed me about him was his ability to come into a game and burn the corners of the plate from the first pitch. It didn't take him any time at all to get into a groove. His fastball had riding life even though his arm slot was three-quarters, somewhere between overhand and sidearm. His breaking ball was always around the knees or lower and he didn't walk many batters. Conversely, he struck out a lot of them (more than a strikeout per inning between 1987 and 1994). During his prime years in Tony La Russa's bullpen, he helped the Oakland A's win the Western Division four times. In 1992, he made a clean sweep, winning the American League Reliever of the Year, the Cy Young Award, and the League MVP Award.

He has no better fan than his manager, La Russa. "He really made my job a lot easier when we had a one-run lead," La Russa said. "A lot of times he got three outs on eight or nine pitches. I didn't have to agonize very long. He got it over with in a hurry." In addition to good control, he had a great will to win. "Some people looked at him and thought he was a 'pretty boy' type of guy," La Russa said. "But he was one tough SOB."

John Smoltz served as the Braves closer for only a little over three years, but his save success percentage of .917 is the best of all the candidates. Before moving to the bullpen during the 2001 season, he was among the best starters in the league year after year. In his signature season as a starter, 1996, he won the Cy Young Award. In his four best years as a starter he went 71-35 with a 2.93 ERA. As a closer, he saved 154 games in almost four full years. During his three-plus years in the bullpen, he failed only 14 times, only about four blown saves per year. He was the Rolaids Reliever of the Year in 2002 and finished third in the Cy Young voting. If I were selecting a staff, he would be the first pitcher I would choose—not because he is the best pitcher I have seen but because he is one of the best and *the most* versatile.

John Smoltz is on My Team and I'm glad we don't have to face him. I still remember the game he pitched against us in the 1997 division series. We had our backs to the wall, trailing the

Braves two games to none, but we felt like we still had a chance when the best of five series moved to the Astrodome. Fat chance. In game three, Smoltz went the distance, winning 4–1 and striking out 11 batters. The thing that I remember most is that he didn't throw anything but his fastball for the first three frames. He moved the ball from one corner to the other, hitting 95 and 96 on the radar gun. He didn't throw a single pitch over the middle of the plate. The first time through the lineup, we had nary a hit. It was three up and three down three times before we even saw his nasty breaking stuff.

"I remember that game," his pitching coach Leo Mazzone said. "Bobby (Cox) turned to me and said, 'What is this, a fastball game?'"

It was frustrating to get swept after fighting all year to make the playoffs, but we weren't the only team Smoltz dominated. He has one of the most distinguished postseason records in the history of baseball. Though he was only 12-11, his combined ERA is a paltry 2.70. He was the NLCS MVP in 1992. His World Series ERA is just 2.49. He has struck out more batters in the postseason than any pitcher in the history of the game. In 1991, he pitched game seven of the World Series against Jack Morris of the Twins. "I couldn't believe it," Mazzone said, "He threw for about six minutes and didn't even throw a breaking ball. And then he said that's enough, the only thing that matters is out there, and he pointed to the mound. Then he went out and pitched a helluva game against the Twins. But Jack Morris was even better." An added benefit to having Smoltz on My Team is that he is a good hitter, which might help if he pitched the last three innings of the game and had an at-bat.

The Oakland A's of the early seventies had many great players like Reggie Jackson, Vida Blue, Catfish Hunter, Bert Campaneris, Sal Bando, Joe Rudi, and Rollie Fingers. Fingers probably embodied the A's spirit more than any of the others. They all went with the hirsute look, but Rollie's well-waxed handlebar mustache was the most stylish. With his swashbuckling manner, he attacked and pillaged opponents like a pirate. "He was powered by passion," Phil Garner recalled. "If he lost a game, he might throw his hat into the crowd. When he won it or saved it, he might take the whole team out to celebrate. And rag on guys, he was the best. One time he announced to the team that I played handball off the curb of the street. It was his way of saying I wasn't very tall. He was a great teammate in every way and a helluva pitcher."

After nine years with the A's, Fingers moved on to San Diego and Milwaukee and continued to be one of the most durable and consistent relief pitchers of his day. Rollie's signature pitch was the slider. It was a sharp, late-breaking pitch that usually got him an infield ground ball or a strikeout. "It was a bigger slider than most guys throw," Mike Cubbage told me. "It was nasty on right-handed hitters and it was tough for lefties, too. I hit left-handed and he was tough on me. And, don't forget, he was a hard thrower. There was nothing wrong with his fastball." His fastball had good sinking action, which is why he didn't allow many home runs. He didn't issue many free passes either. Fingers could pitch often—about 65 appearances in a typical season. And, like Eckersley and Smoltz, he could work more than an inning at a time. In fact, his average appearance was closer to two innings than one. He already had about 70 saves before they started counting save opportunities so it is impossible to get an accurate number for his save ratio, but he ended up with 341 saves. His success rate between 1974 and 1985 when his career ended was only about 80 percent, which is well below the ratios of the modern closers. Of course, the modern closers didn't work as many innings as he did. Robin Yount doesn't remember the failures. "During the whole twenty years I was with the Brewers, I never felt more comfortable than with him on the mound. When we had a lead and he came in, I knew we were going to win."

Fingers was the best in the business for a few years, but I

don't think he was as good as Eckersley or Smoltz. They had better stuff and better control, too. If we went up against the Dogs and Rollie came in to protect a one-run lead in the ninth, I know he would be successful most of the time. Still, I would rather face him than Eckersley or Smoltz.

The only other way I could approach the issue of long relief is to include a knuckleball pitcher, like Phil Niekro or Hoyt Wilhelm. I thought about this long and hard, but just couldn't justify having only one closer. I might need an emergency starter. But it is much more likely that I would need an extra closer in the event that one of them had to work two days in a row. If I did face a double-header situation, I could call on Eckersley or Smoltz to start a game.

Having selected two long relievers who can save games, I turn my attention to the ninth-inning-only guys. In order to identify all the candidates, I looked in the record books and found Lee Smith on top of the list with John Franco running second in saves. Big Lee is the most imposing pitcher in the group at six-foot-six and 270 pounds, but he wasn't mean at all. In his early years as a closer, he really didn't need much more than a fastball. He was doing you a favor if he threw you a slider. About halfway through his relentless march of 15 years' worth of ninth innings, he came up with a better slider. Toward the end, his slider was as good, if not better, than his fastball. Like the others, Lee threw strikes. He challenged all hitters, large and small, and once in a while they met the challenge. His save conversion rate was 85 percent during his best eight seasons. "I know he saved at least ten games for me in Boston," said teammate Roger Clemens. "I would go up to the clubhouse between innings occasionally. Lee would start getting warmed up and stretched about the sixth inning. If I had a short lead, I would ask him: 'Do you want some more points (Rolaids relief points),' and he would say, 'I think I would like that.' I could have finished some of those games, but I was confident that he could close it out as well as I could."

Franco was just about as durable as Smith. While Lee was retiring hitters with power, John was doing the opposite. John threw pretty hard, 90 mph or so, but it was his changeup and his control that made him so tough. Like most good pitchers, he did it with different pitches that all looked like the same pitch. When he was at his best, he could spot the fastball low and away from a right-handed hitter at will. He could also throw the changeup to the same location. If you tried to wait for the change, the fastball would zip by for a called strike. If you swung at the fastball and got the change, the pitch would die like a badminton birdie and fade away. You would look foolish, swinging way out in front of it. Franco's changeup didn't work as well on left-handed hitters. He had a slider to use on them, but since his fastball/changeup combo was his bread and butter, he was actually more effective against right-handed hitters.

The first year I managed the Astros, we had a left-handed relief pitcher by the name of Mike Magnante. Mike's best pitch was a screwball that worked a lot like Franco's changeup. I often brought him into the game to face a left-handed hitter. Since Mike had just come over from the American League, most National League managers didn't know much about him. I had to laugh when they pulled a good left-handed hitter out of the game and pinch-hit with a right-handed hitter. About halfway through the year, they figured him out and stopped pinch-hitting. Magnante helped us a lot, but he was no John Franco. He didn't have as good a fastball or slider, didn't hit corners as often, and he wasn't able to pitch day after day like Franco.

During his best eight years, Franco saved 257 games in 309 chances for a success rate of 83 percent. He also saved a lot of games in the other seasons, finishing his career with 424 saves. If I go with Franco, it will not be to use him as a lefty in the bullpen. I will use him just as I would use Lee Smith— against all hitters.

Actually the first guy that came to mind when I started thinking about a bullpen is Mariano Rivera, who was working in the Bronx while Franco was hurling in Queens. "Rivera is the best I've ever seen," said Joe Torre. "In '96, he was the set-up man for John Wetteland and it seemed like he pitched the seventh and eighth inning every day. I had no doubt he could close. I was right. Even with the pressure of New York, he maintains his poise and pitches with courage day in and day out. I still remember the All-Star Game in 2000 at Atlanta. I like to use all my players when I manage the All-Star Game. To do this, I had to pinch-hit with Edgar Martinez and close with Mariano. He was my last pitcher and we only had a one-run lead. I guess Darin Erstad overheard me talking about it. He came over and said, 'You don't need more than one run with that guy on the mound.'" Rivera's fastball usually has cut action. It runs away from right-handed hitters and in on lefties. He throws it so hard (mid-nineties) that it is almost impossible to adjust to the movement. He overpowered the best teams in the National League in the World Series, mowed them down as if they were Little Leaguers. His breaking ball is halfway between a curve and a slider, a pitch that is sometimes called a *slurve*. It is above average, but he doesn't use it very much. He doesn't have to, because he can spot his fastball so well. A couple of years ago, he started throwing a fastball that has sinking and tailing action—just the opposite movement that his cutter has. When he throws a fastball that is headed for the middle of the strike zone, the hitter can almost bet that it will end up on one corner or the other. There isn't much he can do except gear up for 95 mph and hope to get lucky. "He's simply the best I've ever seen," Clemens said. "He's a quiet guy, but he has a sense of humor once you get to know him. He has a great routine for preparing himself for the game. And he's so deceptive. He's not a big guy and his delivery is so fluid that the hitters don't expect the ball to get on them so quick, but it does. If you counted

broken bats per inning, he would probably come out on top."
Mariano has a deathly presence on the mound. Slim, with
his uniform neatly tailored, he doesn't show his emotions any
more than a snake would. The Astros used to call Danny Darwin "Dr. Death." Rivera could assume the same moniker. In
fact, his features are so tightly wrapped around his facial bones
that it almost looks like a skull. He is not intimidating like Lee
Smith or Goose Gossage; he doesn't hit many batters, or even
throw many pitches out of the strike zone. But he still has a
commanding air about him. The numbers bear this out. In his
eight years as a closer, his success rate is over 88 percent.

The closer who Mariano replaced in the Yankees bullpen
was John Wetteland. Wetteland himself is a candidate, as he
continued to save games after leaving the Yankees and going to
the Rangers. In his best eight years, he saved 295 games in 348
tries, for an 85 percent conversion rate. He featured a high-
velocity riding fastball and a sharp breaking ball, either a big
slider or a hard curve, a pitch that is similar to the one John
Smoltz throws. The combination was usually overpowering as
he averaged over a strikeout per inning for his entire career.
Wetteland's career was relatively short, but he does have eight
superior seasons and the quality of his work puts him right up
there with the best of them.

Trevor Hoffman was not the second guy that came to mind. I
must admit that even though I knew he was a good closer, I
didn't realize just how good he was until I looked at his record
closely. Outside of Smoltz, who has eight great seasons but not
all as a closer, Trevor is the only guy on the list that has suc-
ceeded in over 90 percent of his save opportunities. He carves
up hitters like a Thanksgiving turkey. Like Rivera, he doesn't
waste a lot of energy running deep counts. He throws a lot of
strikes and seldom pitches inside of the inside corner. He does
pitch on that corner and the other one, too. He is simply masterful with his fastball, and his changeup is the best in the busi-

ness. Every hitter is aware of this pitch and yet none of them can wait for it. It is so deceptive that he could tell them when he was going to throw it, and they still couldn't hit it hard very often.

I can relate, from a hitter's point of view. When I was pitching, I started four or five games against Rick Reuschel. The first time I batted against him he struck me out with three sliders. The next time he did the same. I decided that I wouldn't swing at a slider the next time, but every pitch looked like a fastball to me. I kept swinging and he kept throwing sliders and I don't know if I ever put the ball in play. The point is that every pitch he threw looked like a fastball. I couldn't make myself stop swinging. The same thing works for Trevor. The hitters tell themselves not to swing at the changeup early in the count and end up swinging anyway. One of the reasons is that he throws as many fastballs as changeups. His fastball is only average in terms of velocity, so that's the pitch they want to hit. The problem is that he always throws it on the corner. The hitters try to wait for a fastball in the hitting zone, but it's almost always too far in or out to hit well. When they see it coming down the middle, they take a mighty cut, only to learn that it is a changeup. He also throws a get-ahead curveball now and then for a bit of window dressing, and he gets it over for a called strike most of the time.

On top of all that, he doesn't need much time to get ready. In fact, I remember one game at Minute Maid Park when I couldn't believe he wasn't warming up. It was the ninth inning and we had the tying run on base. Padres manager Bruce Bochy got Trevor up and strolled to the mound. He wasted a minute or two talking to the pitcher and catcher and when the umpire came out to break it up, Bochy summoned him from the bullpen. I would guess that Trevor threw no more than ten or fifteen pitches warming up. "That's the only thing that bothers me," Bochy admitted. "He doesn't throw many warm-up pitches so when the game gets tight and he's not warming up, people notice. They think I've fallen asleep in the dugout. But I can't complain. He's made me a lot smarter than I really am. He almost never fails, and the reason is that he has more confidence than any pitcher I've ever seen. And he is a consummate pro. He does his warming up in the trainer's room. Every night, about the seventh or eighth inning, he gets his arm stretched to shorten his warm-up time. He has his rituals, like most of us, and I haven't been tempted to change them."

In that game in Houston, he came in and it looked like he was throwing pus up there. But he got us out and saved yet another game. One of the reasons Hoffman doesn't throw many warm-up pitches is that he has had arm surgery and doesn't want to throw anymore than he has to. "Maybe I took him for granted because he was so reliable," Bochy said. "Then, when he had arm problems, I learned what it was like to be without him. I know I'm prejudiced, but I think he is the best in the business."

In addition to being the most important pitcher on the team, Hoffman possesses leadership qualities. I asked if he was quiet because that's the way he always seemed to me, but Bochy just laughed. "No, he's not quiet." I asked him to explain. "Well, let's just say that when one of our players messes up, I don't have to say anything because Trevor will say something first."

Mariano Rivera is more impressive than Hoffman, but Trevor has a slightly better conversion rate on saves. I am going to go with Hoffman, and I will probably end up with Rivera, too. But first, let's look at the rest of the options.

Selecting a left-handed reliever is difficult for me because there are no clear-cut candidates among left-handed closers. I saw Billy Wagner up close and personal for six years and it is hard for me to leave him off My Team because his save rate is just a little less than Rivera's. The only thing that works against him is that, like Franco, he is not a specialist. He gets both left- and right-handed hitters out with his 99 mph fastball, which he can usually spot on either corner. He also has a good slider but doesn't have great command of that pitch. For that reason, left-handed hitters have just about as good a chance against him as right-handers. At this juncture, I am wavering. I want to pick Wagner, but when I play devil's advocate and ask myself, who would you rather face, Rivera, Hoffman, or Wagner, I think I would have a slightly better chance with Wagner on the hill. The numbers bear that out. I am ambivalent because I don't want the Dogs to have Billy, but they are going to get him. I wasn't a left/right situation strategist like most skippers. If I wanted a left-handed specialist for My Team, I would take a guy with a great breaking ball like Sparky Lyle or Jesse Orosco. But Sparky and Jesse just weren't quite as good against right-handed hitters. With only nine pitchers on my staff, I am not inclined to select one of them to pitch only against left-handed hitters.

Speaking of left-handed hitters, who will ever forget George Brett's pine-tar home run off Goose Gossage? Gossage was nasty. He threw very hard and his delivery had some deception, too. He almost turned his back on the hitter and then slung the ball from a low three-quarters-arm angle. Most pitchers who throw that way have sinking fastballs. But not Gossage. Sometimes his fastball would run in on right-handed hitters and sometimes it would just ride. When a pitcher has this kind of action on his fastball, he oftentimes throws one about waist high. If he gets a strike, he throws the next one a little higher and continues in that vein. It's called *going up the ladder*. When Billy Wagner was pitching for us, he often threw the first pitch high in the strike zone. I would look at my bench coach, Matt Galante, and one of us would say, "up the ladder, Billy boy."

Gossage's fastball was good enough to get most batters out, but he was especially tough on right-handed hitters because he had a wide, sweeping breaking ball. I've seen right-handed hitters bail out on breaking balls that were called strikes. The right-handed hitters he faced would probably have voted him public enemy number one. Like Eckersley and Smoltz, he was a starter at first, with the White Sox. He went 29-36 during his first five years as a starter for the White Sox. Although his arm strength was well known, the Sox gave up on him before trying him in the bullpen. Instead, they traded him to the Pirates, where he saved 26 games in 1977. After that, he got better.

Like most of the early closers, he often worked more than one inning at a time. He actually worked even more innings per appearance than Fingers and Sutter. Rollie did it with an ERA of 2.48, while the Goose came out number one in ERA with a 1.93 mark. His save percentage is a bit low, probably because he pitched more than one inning at a time. But I'm sure his managers and teammates felt like the game was in good hands when he came in with a lead. He was also a fun-loving guy and, like many closers, he was a little crazy. Madness is not a requirement for the job, but it helps.

No discussion about closers would be complete without a guy who changed baseball for good—Bruce Sutter. Sutter was a pitcher of middling talent until he came up with the split-fingered fastball. The pitch was so devastating that he immediately went from the bottom of the Cubs pecking order to the top. I remember when he came up with the split and am still amused about how he kept it secret. He told people that he spread his index and middle fingers and pushed the ball through them with his thumb, giving the ball a forward tumbling rotation. When I heard about that I started trying to throw it and couldn't even come close to getting the thumb action right. Actually, I didn't have to, but I didn't know it at the time. To this day, I don't know if Sutter felt like he was pushing it with his thumb or was merely trying to confuse everyone. A few years later, Tigers pitching coach Roger Craig encouraged his pitchers to try it without the thumb push. It worked. These days, you don't hear anything about the thumb and there are probably 100 pitchers in the major leagues that throw splitters. I still remember when Sutter first started throwing it. Hitting coaches would tell the hitters to lay off the knee-high pitch because it was destined to dive into the dirt. There were only two problems with that advice. First, if it wasn't a split, it wouldn't dive and would be a mediocre fastball at the knees. Second, if the split started thigh high, it would drop down to knee high and the hitters would still swing over it. I was amused when I saw clips of him pitching on the day he was voted into the Hall of Fame. All the pitches they showed were high fastballs. I thought they would show him throwing his signature pitch, but they did not.

It seemed like Sutter saved practically every game, but the statistics tell a different story. During his best eight years he saved 250 games in 325 save opportunities, or 76 percent conversion rate. These days, most good closers have a better success ratio. And, of course, many of them, and the starters as well, throw the split-fingered fastball. I wish I had known I didn't have to shove the ball through my fingers to make it work. It would have been great fun to watch the hitters swing at the good ones and take the bad ones, not to mention all the called fastball strikes at the knees. Bruce Sutter invented a new pitch and changed the game. If I were a hitter, I would hate him—both for getting me out and for the arrow that he and Roger Craig added to many pitchers' quivers. Sutter will not make My Team or the Dogs. But he certainly deserves an honorable mention.

The other pitchers I reviewed for this spot on the team are Rick Aguilera, Jeff Reardon, Randy Myers, Robb Nen, Tom Henke, Rod Beck, and Roberto Hernandez. It was hard to cut Henke, Nen, and Myers, but the rest of them didn't quite measure up. I also checked Todd Worrell and Jose Mesa. They had a lot of saves but didn't have eight good years. All of these guys had better-than-average velocity except for Beck, and his fastball wasn't bad. This position is so loaded with talent that it is almost impossible to sort things out. I have decided to go with

Relief Pitcher

Eckersley, Smoltz, Hoffman, and Rivera. I have a loaded bullpen—the Dogs do, too.

RELIEF PITCHER: ECKERSLEY, SMOLTZ, HOFFMAN, RIVERA.

My Team's Roster

SP Clemens, R. Johnson, Maddux, Seaver, and Gibson
C Bench and Piazza
1B Bagwell and Stargell
2B Morgan and Biggio
3B Schmidt and Brett
SS A. Rodriguez and Jeter
LF Bonds and F. Robinson
CF Mays and Mantle
RF Aaron and Griffey Jr.
RP Eckersley, Smoltz, Hoffman, and Rivera

1 1

The Underdogs

You can never have too much talent. Even
the 1927 Yankees didn't win every year.
——BUZZIE BAVASI, CALIFORNIA ANGELS
GENERAL MANAGER.

NOW THAT I have assembled My Team, I
need an opponent. My selection process
has been difficult, almost agonizingly so. For example, it was
hard for me to leave the best leadoff hitter in the history of the
game, Rickey Henderson, peeping through a knothole at Barry
Bonds and Frank Robinson. I wanted Rickey on My Team because the leadoff man is very important in my scheme of things.
However, I could make Bonds my leadoff hitter and then *he*
would be the greatest leadoff hitter in baseball history. You get
the idea. In many cases, it's like splitting hairs. A team of the
players I have cut from My Team would be far better than the
typical All-Star team. In fact, I'm not sure I would be comfortable facing them, even with My Team. See what you think.

201

Catcher

The Dogs regular catcher would be Pudge Rodriguez. He seems the equal of Johnny Bench in catching the pitch, blocking it, framing it, and throwing runners out. Several pitchers have said that Pudge doesn't call a good game. Some catchers are known for calling a good game and some are not. All I can say is that it shouldn't make a big difference because the pitcher has the last say. Most good pitchers know what they want to throw and, for that reason, they call their own games. It's easier to pitch when the catcher calls for the pitch you want to throw most of the time, but it's not an excuse for failure if he doesn't.

Sometimes, it seems, the catchers who are good fielders and poor hitters, like Brad Ausmus and Mike Matheny, are typecast as smart catchers. I don't think you have to be a bad hitter to be smart. I suspect that good-hitting catchers get a bad rap. Pitchers who don't pitch well sometimes say that a catcher like Bench, Rodriguez, or Mike Piazza only cares about his hitting. They can't say this about a catcher who doesn't hit well because he wouldn't even be in the major leagues if he weren't a good defensive player. Catchers of this ilk often solicit and get praise from the pitching staff. In my opinion, a pitcher should be responsible for the pitches he throws. If the catcher lets a lot of pitches get by him, or doesn't frame the pitches well for the umpire, or can't throw out an average runner, the pitcher has a beef.

A lot of runners challenge Mike Piazza's arm. It is no secret that you can run on him. I wouldn't mind that so much because he produces so many runs with the bat. As long as he could block the ball and frame pitches, I would be satisfied, and I know he can do those two things.

Bench and Rodriguez are two of the best-throwing catchers I have seen. Bench became a force with his RBI bat right away. After a few years of free swinging, Pudge became a more patient hitter and started putting up some impressive numbers of his own. If you look at them side by side with Bench, you may be surprised. I was.

PLAYERS	OBA	SLG	OBS	R/PA	RBI/AB	SB	CS
BENCH	.347	.493	.839	1/7.5	1/5.3	46	31
RODRIGUEZ	.351	.496	.847	1/6.9	1/6.6	86	41

I favor Gary Carter over Lance Parrish and Carlton Fisk as the Dogs' backup catcher, though making this distinction is like threading a needle with a pair of pliers. Since there is very little difference between them, I'm going to complicate matters and pick Tim McCarver. McCarver wasn't as good a hitter as the others, and he wasn't as good a catcher as Bench or Rodriguez, but he was a little bit better with the mitt than Piazza. In combination with Steve Carlton, McCarver was deadly.

What this amounts to is using McCarver on the Dogs in the same role that Piazza plays on My Team. Greg Maddux likes to pitch to his own personal catcher. In this case, it is Piazza. With a McCarver/Carlton entry, the Dogs would be hard to beat. From a defensive standpoint, I think Bench is a little better than Pudge, but only a little. I concede that the Dogs have the fielding advantage when Piazza is playing. He would only catch every fifth game and perhaps stay in the game after pinch-hitting once in a while. You may note that I am contradicting my introductory intention of selecting the best fielders for My Team instead of the best hitters. In this case, Piazza is *so much better* a hitter that I willingly contradict myself, breaking my own rule.

CATCHER: I. RODRIGUEZ, McCARVER.

First Base

When I was selecting My Team, I was debating as to whether to choose Keith Hernandez or Willie McCovey over Willie Stargell at first base. I still don't feel great about my own selection, because of my preference for good defense and because Stargell played more games in the outfield than at first base. In the end, Stargell's powerful RBI bat and sunny personality won me over. Still, I could see a tandem of Thome or McCovey and Eddie Murray or Frank Thomas standing strong against Jeff Bagwell and Stargell. Since Bagwell, like Bench, would play most of the time, I don't think I have strayed too far from the fielding emphasis on My Team. If the Dogs chose Hernandez they would beat me with the glove, but my guess is that most baseball professionals would go for offense and choose two of the others, Thome, McCovey, Eddie Murray, or Frank Thomas. I probably would have picked Hernandez to back up Bagwell if I hadn't chosen Stargell. In the Dogs' scenario, I think Keith would be left out again. All things considered, I am going with McCovey and Thomas. I know Willie "Stretch" McCovey doesn't quite measure up to Thome with the bat, but I think he would have if he had played in the slugging era of the 90's and early 00's. Looking at the numbers, My Team would have a significant defensive advantage at this position, but would have no edge at the plate.

PLAYERS	OBA	SLG	OBS	R/PA	RBI/AB	SB	CS
BAGWELL	.418	.572	.990	1/6.0	1/4.8	166	61
STARGELL	.373	.550	.923	1/7.0	1/5.0	6	8
MCCOVEY	.391	.554	.945	1/7.4	1/5.0	15	11
F. THOMAS	.438	.594	1.032	1/6.3	1/4.5	26	17

Many fans, even some experts, would include Murray on My Team and most of the rest would pick him for the Dogs. After all, he has scored more runs and driven in more teammates than any of the others. I tend to go for the players with the best OBS ratings, provided they are good fielders. Eddie was a good fielder but not a great one. He was a switch hitter, so there would be some advantage in not having to pinch-hit for him or in using him as a pinch hitter. Of course, Bagwell faced all the right-handed pitchers of his era, and Stargell faced all the lefties. It's really not a big deal with the great ones. They tend to hit just about everyone.

I keep coming back to Bagwell not because he is my friend or because I have seen him play a lot more than the others, but because of what he had to overcome playing in Houston. Playing virtually all his home games in the cavernous Astrodome, Bagwell has the third best OBS in the class, only slightly behind Thome and Thomas. Thome had the advantage of playing at Jacobs Field and hitting in the middle of a great lineup. In the end the best the Dogs can do is to go with McCovey and Thomas. One problem with this combination is that there would be no one to come in for defense. More on that issue later.

FIRST BASE: THOMAS, McCOVEY.

Second Base

Roberto Alomar. The simple sound of the name suggests grace and artistry. It is a public address announcer's dream—fluid, and a bit racy. Alomar burst upon the scene in San Diego in 1988. He had a winsome smile and was a natural, right from the start. He was only twenty years old, and I thought he became the best defensive second baseman in the league that same year. He made seemingly impossible plays look easy. He was nimble of foot and could throw accurately from all angles while on the run. And he could really run. He didn't hit with much power the first few years—the power came as he got older and stronger. He did, however, become a great base stealer right away. He did everything with style. For me, he was as fun to watch as anyone in the National League.

Now that more time has passed, I am less charmed with him. When he spit on umpire John Hirschbeck in Toronto at the end of the 1996 season it showed a side of his personality that I hadn't seen. Robbie continued to have good years until 2002, then inexplicably lost the spirit that had guided him gracefully through 14 years in the major leagues. He was only 34 years old.

I was sure he would come out on top of the second base rankings when I began this study. His arm allowed him to make plays Joe Morgan and Craig Biggio couldn't make. Jeff Kent had the arm to make the plays but didn't have Alomar's range. Robbie had a much better OBA than Ryne Sandberg and almost as good a slugging average. He got on base almost as much as Rod Carew and had more power. While his last few years were disappointing, Robbie still has the ten years of excellence required to make My Team. For ten years he had batting records that were equal to or better than the other second baseman on my list and he had more talent than any of them in the field. Why did he wear out his welcome everywhere he went? He lasted only three years in San Diego. He spent the next five in Toronto, then three with the Orioles and three with the Indians. All of the seasons from his Blue Jays years forward were productive.

For ten years, Alomar played All-Star caliber second base, but it may be that he wasn't quite as good as I thought he was. Kent and Sandberg had more power and they both had good hands. I believe Sandberg covered as much ground as Alomar and could also throw from any angle on the run. But Ryne struck out a lot; he was easier to pitch to than Alomar, who walked almost as often as he struck out. By the numbers, Jeff

Kent is the best hitter. His slugging profile more than makes up for his relative lack of speed. He didn't cover as much ground on the infield, but didn't make many throwing errors. Guys like Alomar, who can make incredible plays, sometimes make wild throws trying to make impossible plays.

Rod Carew was a cat burglar. He seemed to float effortlessly a millimeter above the field. He didn't get much limelight in Minneapolis or Anaheim, but he was visible enough to make the American League All-Star team 18 times. Rod had a magic wand for a bat, just like Tony Gwynn. He, too, walked as often as he struck out. Infielder Alan Bannister once said that Rodney was the only guy he knew who could go 4-for-3. He was inconspicuous by choice, not a rally-around-the-flag guy, not a leader, as such. But he was dependable day after day. If you didn't notice him when he was on third base, you might notice him a moment later in a cloud of dust around home plate. He stole home safely 17 times during his career. He also made a legitimate run at hitting .400, finishing at .388 and winning MVP honors in 1977.

Even the best left-handed pitchers had trouble with him. He got his first hit off Dave McNally and his three thousandth off Frank Viola. He won seven batting titles and was voted into the Hall of Fame on the first ballot. Most players who make it to Cooperstown do it with both bat and glove. Unlike Ozzie Smith, who made it mostly because of his glove, Carew made it mostly with his bat. Though he was fast, and pretty good with the glove, he was never regarded as a great fielder. During his prime years, the Gold Glove at second base went to Bobby Grich and Frank White, neither of whom hit quite well enough to make it with the Dogs.

Reviewing the contenders for the Dog team at second base, the difficulty of making a choice is clear. (See chart on next page.)

When you compare these numbers to those of Morgan and Biggio, you will see why I don't have a strong conviction

PLAYERS	OBA	SLG	OBS	R/PA	RBI/AB	SB	CS
ALOMAR	.386	.469	.855	1/6.5	1/7.2	355	83
CAREW	.404	.449	.853	1/7.2	1/8.6	264	128
KENT	.357	.519	.875	1/7.0	1/5.3	74	41
SANDBERG	.352	.472	.824	1/6.9	1/7.7	277	79

about my own team. Three of these fine second basemen, Morgan, Sandberg, and Kent won league MVP awards. Morgan won it twice. I am tempted to choose Sandberg and Kent, to avoid the possible chemistry problem with Alomar, but both of them are right-handed power hitters.

Considering the batting lineup, I have to drop Kent, only because he is a middle-of-the-lineup hitter and the Dogs will get plenty of power hitting from the other positions. I think the most versatile combination at second base is Alomar and Sandberg. But then going into the 2005 season, as I was writing this book, Alomar suddenly retired. This last red flag changed my mind. He was too young to quit, which suggests that he could not overcome adversity. If I selected Robbie, the Dogs would have a slight defensive improvement over My Team's second sackers, Joe Morgan and Craig Biggio. But I am choosing Rod Carew, replacing Alomar as the top of the lineup hitter. I don't think I am losing any offense this way but concede that I am giving up some defense. I know I could be over-reacting to the chemistry issue, but if I am, the Padres, Blue Jays, Orioles, Indians, and Mets did, too.

With Biggio and Morgan I think I am gaining in the attitude department. I view Sandberg and Carew as neutral in terms of chemistry. I think Biggio and Morgan may be more difficult to manage because they are driven men who expect as much from their teammates, and seldom get it. As a manager, however, I would rather have too much hard-nosed leadership from the players than not enough. On My Team, my second basemen would get what they expect from their teammates, which would obviate the concern about them stepping on toes.

SECOND BASE: CAREW, SANDBERG.

Third Base

Making a choice at this position isn't easy either. Chipper Jones and Eddie Mathews have a slight edge on George Brett in hitting. They are only slightly below Mike Schmidt. Chipper was the first selection in the 1990 June draft. He was a shortstop at the time. Like Schmidt, he reminds me of Honus Wagner, because he has played several positions and played them all well. At shortstop and in the outfield he was pretty good. At third base, he is superb. Mathews was a tough guy. If I were managing the Dogs, I would depend on him to provide leadership, both by example and with words. Eddie played his home games in parks that favored power hitting. Still, his power hitting was so strong that he would likely have been nearly as good a hitter in a big park. Though he posted a high on-base average, he would be paid for his slugging and would hit somewhere in the middle of the lineup.

The backup third baseman should be a right-handed hitter to provide balance. That leaves out Wade Boggs, who had better offensive numbers than all but Schmidt, Brett, Jones, and Mathews. Ron Santo was more productive with the bat than Brooks Robinson. Jones is the most versatile of the candidates. He is a switch hitter and can play a lot of different positions. The only thing that gives me pause is that he has more power from the left side of the plate. As a right-handed hitter he is not quite as productive as Ron Santo, especially when you consider that Ron was playing when the pitching was better, in the sixties and early seventies. Both Santo and Jones would fit neatly in the lineup in place of Mathews. Robinson and Jones played on a lot of championship teams, but Santo never made it to the postseason. I know many people believe that players who have been on championship teams know how to win. I am not among them and I'm sure Santo and Ernie Banks are on my side.

In fact, I still remember getting irritated over this with Gene Tenace, who was an Astros coach in 1986. We were in St. Louis at the time, about halfway through the year, cooling off with a beer after losing a ball game. Gene was complaining about the way the team was playing and said something about our players not knowing how to win. Since he had played on winning teams in Oakland and San Diego, he thought of himself as a winner. I thought of him as lucky. He was a good ballplayer, but I don't think he knew any more about winning than Santo or Banks. He just happened to be one of 25 guys who played on a winning team, and he did it several times. I told him that I didn't agree with him. "That makes me look like a loser," I said. "And I'm not a loser. I would have been a starting pitcher on any playoff team I can think of. I don't think our guys are losers either. They just need to be on a team where all the parts fit together."

Well, what do you know, the same guys that lost in St. Louis that night won quite a few games during the second half of that year, running away with the division title and barely losing to the Mets in the playoffs. For this reason, I do not blame Santo for the Cubs failures. Ronnie was clearly a better hitter than Brooks and although he wasn't as good at the hot corner, he was above average with the glove. If his offensive superiority were slight, I would be happy with Brooks. But Santo's advantage at bat was significant. In the final analysis, I am going to go with Jones to complement Mathews, even though I may not have quite as good a lineup against left-handed pitchers. I hate to shun Santo because the Hall of Fame committee has done the same. He should be in the shrine at Cooperstown, but is not. He should be in my top four but he isn't. If all I had to consider were hitting and fielding, Ron would make it, but Jones is an even better fielder, however, almost on a par with Robinson and Schmidt. The fact that he may not be as good in the lineup hitting right-handed is offset in my scheme of things by the many different ways the Dogs could use him. As a pinch hitter, he would make me squirm trying to decide whether to change pitchers to make him hit right-handed. If the Dogs had a fly-ball pitcher going, they could start Jones at shortstop or right field to get another left-handed bat in the lineup.

PLAYERS	OBA	SLG	OBS	R/PA	RBI/AB	SB	CS
MATHEWS	.384	.539	.923	1/6.3	1/5.5	44	21
BOGGS	.428	.463	.891	1/6.8	1/9.1	15	27
JONES	.399	.535	.934	1/6.4	1/5.4	118	40
ROBINSON	.341	.438	.780	1/8.6	1/7.1	16	13
SANTO	.378	.497	.875	1/7.7	1/5.8	24	31

Many fans would take issue with these choices—I can make a strong case for Boggs, Santo, and Robinson myself. I also considered Graig Nettles, Bill Madlock, and Buddy Bell, but they didn't quite measure up. Looking ahead to the lineup and bench players for any given day, I think I am better off with an RBI man at third base.

THIRD BASE: MATHEWS, JONES.

Shortstop

I feel like My Team has a significant advantage at this position because of Alex Rodriguez. His defense at short is above average, even at a position where most teams have a good fielder. And his offense? Well, it is the best in the field of candidates by a wide margin, even better than Honus Wagner's. The old golfer Walter Hagen once described showmanship this way: "Make the easy ones look hard and the hard ones look easy." A-Rod makes them all look easy—at the plate and in the field. His eminence is not obvious the first time you see him, because he is so graceful that his actions look effortless. He is relatively tall and runs with long, loping strides. He never really looks like he is running full speed. You don't realize how fast he is until you see him steal a few bases, or how powerful he is until you see him hit a few home runs. You can usually see both speed and power in one three-game series. If ever there was a player who justified being the first player selected in the June draft, it was Alex Rodriguez.

After A-Rod, there are several players who were well above average—enough that a few of them are in the Hall of Fame and a few more are on the way. Banks, Ozzie Smith, and Robin Yount are already in, Ernie for his bat, Ozzie for his glove, and Yount was excellent both ways. Cal Ripken Jr. will make it to Cooperstown as will A-Rod, Derek Jeter, and possibly Miguel Tejada and Nomar Garciaparra. I think Barry Larkin was as good as any of them when he was healthy, but his offensive totals aren't what they could have been if he hadn't been hurt so often. I'm not sure if the Hall of Fame voters will acknowledge the excellence of his fielding, but I think he was as good or better than all of them but Ozzie. He also was able to hit with midrange power while walking more than he struck out. I think he should make the Hall of Fame, but I don't have a vote.

The Dogs will be well represented at this position. If not for A-Rod, it would be hard to pick the best four and put them in order. It is hard enough to pick three more because a couple of guys who are worthy won't make either team.

Tony Fernandez was a terrific shortstop. I think he was the equal of Larkin with the glove, and he was a good hitter, too, but not quite good enough to make the grade. Cal Ripken Jr. is like Jeff Kent—good hands, good accurate arm, good RBI man. His durability was unbelievable, especially when you consider that he was a shortstop. Outside of catcher, I can't think of another position where the possibility of getting hurt is greater. Just ask Larkin.

I don't think Cal's consecutive game streak will ever be broken. The one area where he falls short (not of Cooperstown but of My Team and the Dogs) is in foot speed. He was fast enough to play short, but not a step faster. All of the other candidates could outrun him. This wouldn't be a factor in most games, but in the course of 162 games, it would make a difference. Ernie Banks won a Gold Glove and led the league in fielding percentage three times at short, but he couldn't run any faster than Ripken. After nine years at short, Ernie moved to first base. The same thing happened to Yount, but with Robin it wasn't a speed issue. Robin moved from shortstop to a position that requires even more speed—center field. Most of the shortstops could hit at the top of the batting order and some could hit in the middle. Because their on-base averages were comparatively low, Banks and Ripken would have to hit sixth or seventh in the lineup and, for that reason, they might not make either of my squads.

Alan Trammell is another fine shortstop who falls a little short. His offense was good enough for Hall of Fame consideration, but his defense, though excellent, was not in a class with Smith or Larkin because his range, though good, was not great. He was, however, good enough to attract Tony La Russa's attention. "I used to go down to the dugout early when we were in Detroit," he said. "He gathered the ball in so smoothly it was a joy just to watch him. And, the throws. He hit the first baseman in the chest every time. Plus, he was so versatile with the bat. When they hit him at the top of the lineup, he scored a hundred runs; when they hit him cleanup, he drove in a hundred runs. I don't know why he doesn't get more support for the Hall of Fame."

PLAYERS	OBA	SLG	OBS	R/PA	RBI/AB	SB	CS
RIPKEN JR.	.350	.468	.818	1/7.3	1/6.7	28	24
YOUNT	.364	.482	.845	1/6.7	1/6.9	160	47
SMITH	.354	.348	.702	1/8.4	1/10.6	356	79
TRAMMELL	.361	.441	.802	1/7.2	1/7.6	176	90
BANKS	.344	.538	.882	1/7.1	1/5.4	40	37

Robin Yount got all the support he needed to make the Hall of Fame. I favor him over Trammell and Ripken and Smith by an eyelash. Now, I have to pick one of them to back up Yount at short. There is no doubt Ozzie was the better fielder and both Alan and Cal were better hitters than Ozzie. Which of them would help the most, starting occasionally and coming off the bench? The best way to answer that question may be to decide whether you would rather have another RBI bat on the bench or a defensive replacement at shortstop. If I were managing the Dogs, I would not be inclined to bring Ozzie into the game as a defensive replacement for Yount. The Dogs will have better power hitters than Trammell and Ripken on the bench. For me, there is just something fundamentally wrong in having Ripken on the bench. Having Trammell on the bench wouldn't be an advantage in very many games. I could use either of them to pinch-run, but I think Ozzie would be a little better in that regard. What if I wanted to give the starter a break once in a while? In that case, I would favor starting Ozzie and hitting him second in the lineup. Trammell could hit second, too. His on-base average for ten years is a little better than Ozzie's, but he wasn't quite as good a base stealer or bunter. I would likely hit Alan down in the order if I started him, but I already have guys who can hit down there. If I were looking for a number-eight hitter, I would take Alan, but I would favor a number-two hitter who can play an important defensive position as well as it can possibly be played. So Ozzie it is.

SHORTSTOP: YOUNT, O. SMITH.

Left Field

Catching a fly ball is a pleasure. Knowing what to do with it after you catch it is a business.

——TOMMY HENRICH, NEW YORK YANKEES

As with most of the positions, there are Hall of Fame players who were left fielders and still didn't make My Team. In left, I can choose among Billy Williams, Rickey Henderson, Lou Brock, Carl Yastrzemski, Tim Raines, or Dave Winfield. Brock is in the Hall of Fame, but his offensive numbers aren't nearly as good as Henderson's. Winfield is also in the Hall of Fame but was not a leadoff hitter. I would choose Henderson as my starter and leadoff hitter. Since Rickey was a right-handed hitter, I am inclined to pick a left-handed hitter to go with him. The problem is that the two best are Yastrzemski and Williams, and they don't fit into the lineup as leadoff hitters either. Al Oliver is another worthy candidate and left-handed hitter, but was not the best outfielder and did not post offensive numbers that were better than the others. I could go with Brock or switch hitter Tim Raines because they are both left-handed hitters who would be tough on right-handed pitchers and who could hit first in the lineup. Raines's 10-year numbers are even better than Brock's, though he is not in the Hall of Fame. If I were the manager of this team, I would likely take Raines, even though I know he was not as good a hitter as Yastrzemski or Williams. The fit in left field is perfect with Henderson and Raines because they do the same things offensively—hit first, get on base a lot, steal bases, and show occasional power.

PLAYERS	OBA	SLG	OBS	R/PA	RBI/AB	SB	CS
RAINES	.391	.435	.826	1/6.6	1/9.5	581	96
YASTRZEMSKI	.397	.503	.900	1/7.1	1/5.9	113	70
WILLIAMS	.367	.514	.881	1/7.0	1/6.2	60	27

During the course of the game, I wouldn't have many reasons to pinch-hit because of the quality of the lineup, but I might need a pinch runner who can steal a base late in the game. This proved to be of considerable value to the Astros in 1986 after they obtained Davey Lopes in a trade. I would guess that he stole six or seven bases as a pinch runner during the second half of that season. Lopes played outfield occasionally but his hitting numbers, though good, do not match up with those of Henderson or Raines. Raines, like Henderson and Brock, could cover a lot of ground in the outfield, but was not a Gold Glove caliber outfielder.

I'm sure there are some who would choose Manny Ramirez over all of them. His hitting numbers are a little better than Frank Robinson's, but they are not enough to offset his sour disposition. His indifference to playing the outfield and running the bases takes him off my list. Going with Henderson and Raines gives the Dogs a good leadoff situation, but My Team is significantly better in left field. I wouldn't hit Frank Robinson first in the order but Bonds would be a great leadoff man. If I hit Bonds third, I can use Willie Mays as a leadoff hitter, and he would be better than Henderson and Raines. I think My Team has a big advantage in left field. I also think many experts would say I am crazy for not selecting Yastrzemski or Williams. Williams didn't play as long as Yaz, but his 10-year numbers are comparable. I would probably pick Yastrzemski if I had only one pick for an everyday player. If I only had one second pick, I would select Williams. In the context of a Dogs lineup and versatility of the bench players, however, I think Raines and Henderson, and even Brock, would be better.

LEFT FIELD: HENDERSON, RAINES.

Center Field

My Team has an advantage in center field, too. Actually, Mays and Mantle have a smaller, but still significant edge over Jim Edmonds and Bernie Williams. I looked at Kirby Puckett, Cesar Cedeno, Fred Lynn, Dale Murphy, Andy Van Slyke, and a few others, but couldn't find anyone who could compare with Williams or Edmonds, let alone Mays or Mantle. With Edmonds and Williams, the Dogs can hold their own defensively, but fall short in both on-base average and slugging percentage.

PLAYERS	OBA	SLG	OBS	R/PA	RBI/AB	SB	CS
WILLIAMS	.398	.510	.908	1/6.2	1/5.7	102	56
EDMONDS	.389	.561	.951	1/5.9	1/5.4	50	38
MAYS	.396	.612	1.008	1/5.5	1/5.2	217	68

In 1996, when I got the manager's job in Houston, we had a chance to trade for Edmonds. Our scouts warned us that he might be a problem in the clubhouse. He had also been injured a lot. This was a red flag because some great players like Barry Larkin seem to get hurt a lot for no apparent reason. I wish we had pursued the Edmonds deal. He killed us when we played the Cardinals. And he was never hurt. The concern that he might be a prima donna or a clubhouse lawyer concerned Tony La Russa at first. After a few years, he wasn't worried at all. "I think a lot of people get the wrong impression of him," Tony said. "He's got that blasé California attitude and sometimes people took that to mean he didn't care. He seemed aloof at first, but that first spring training I saw him spraying line drives all over the ballpark in batting practice. I knew he had the talent. Then one day, he got a bad jump on a fly ball and it fell for a double. When he came back to the dugout, he asked me, 'Does this guy (I can't remember who the pitcher was) hang his slider often?' I said, 'What do you mean?' 'Well,' he said, 'I was leaning toward left center and when he hung the slider the hitter took it the other way and I got a bad jump.' Right then and there," Tony said, "I knew he had his head in the game. He's an amazing outfielder."

Bernie Williams is just as good in the field. "He has everything but a strong arm," Roger Clemens said. "He gets to balls you don't think he has a chance at, and he does it effortlessly." He also adds a dash of levity to the chemistry of the team. "He is one of those carefree guys," Clemens said. "Nothing bothers him.

"One time we were playing in Oakland, and he thought ball three was ball four. He started jogging to first and was about halfway down the line when he realized what he had done. Most guys would be so embarrassed they wouldn't be able to concentrate when they got back in the box. Not Bernie. He just casually stepped back in there and hit the ball about 400 feet. The pitcher would have been better off walking him!

"The first day, when we were in Arizona during the 2001 World Series, he missed a few buses. He missed the early bus for guys who needed treatment. He missed the early players' bus. He missed the regular players' bus, too, and guys started getting worried. Well Bernie wasn't worried. He got mixed up on the time change, and came out on the first family bus about an hour before the game. Most guys would have been sheepish about that, but not Bernie. He went out and had a great game."

Willie Randolph echoes the same sentiment. "He's almost too mellow," Willie said. "That's probably why he has been underrated. There is a serenity about him. And I think that's why he gets so many big hits." If Edmonds were playing and a left-handed reliever came into the game, I could use Bernie to pinch-hit.

There are a couple of modern players who may challenge for one of these two teams before they are finished, but they don't have the requisite 10 years yet. They are Carlos Beltran and Andruw Jones.

CENTER FIELD: EDMONDS, B. WILLIAMS.

Right Field

By taking Ken Griffey Jr. as My Team's back-up right fielder, I have really delivered a body blow to the Dogs. Still, they have two guys who many would pick over Griffey (though perhaps not Aaron). These are two of the most storied right fielders of all time. They could do it all: hit for average, hit with power, run fast, and throw hard. Neither could match Aaron and Griffey at the plate, but they were both good outfielders, probably better than the guys on My Team, and they were both good enough with the bat to make the Hall of Fame. They are, of course, Al Kaline and Roberto Clemente.

"People used to criticize Roberto for not playing hurt," teammate Dave Giusti recalls. "But he was a team player. He didn't want to play if he couldn't go all out, one hundred per-cent. He wasn't as vocal as Willie Stargell, but he was a leader. All you had to do was watch him play and you immediately knew how the game should be played." Roberto wasn't hurt all that often. You can't collect three thousand hits sitting on the bench. I suppose it is fitting that he got his last base hit, num-ber three thousand, on the last day of the 1972 season. He died a hero in a plane crash that winter, taking emergency supplies to earthquake-ravaged Nicaragua.

I remember facing Kaline only once. It was during a game at the Astrodome, just before the start of the season. I threw him a good, hard slider, low and away—a pitch that very few hitters could hit well. One of the few was Kaline. He singled sharply up the middle. Clemente and Kaline could hit all the pitchers on My Team and the Dogs. So could Aaron and Griffey Jr.

There is no question Clemente and Kaline could throw better than Aaron. I think they could throw better than Griffey, too, but Junior has a good arm. There is also no question that Tony Gwynn, a future Hall of Famer, could hit for a higher average than any of them. One of the reasons Tony didn't do even more damage was that he didn't walk much so his on-base average was good but not great. His batting average was the best of his era, but the guy who had the second-best average, Wade Boggs, had a much higher OBA. Tony got a lot of doubles but did not hit very many home runs. As a result, the guy who many would consider the best hitter of his era did not produce as many runs as one might expect. Like the others, he was a good outfielder, probably about like Aaron or Frank Robinson, but not as good as Clemente, Kaline, or Griffey.

PLAYERS	OBA	SLG	OBS	R/PA	RBI/AB	SB	CS
CLEMENTE	.376	.502	.879	1/6.7	1/6.4	60	23
KALINE	.385	.513	.898	1/6.6	1/5.9	75	40
GWYNN	.397	.473	.871	1/7.1	1/8.1	226	77

Reggie Jackson has some impressive hitting numbers as well, but no better than the others. There must have been a reason he wore a batting helmet when he was playing right field. Actually, he wasn't that bad, but he certainly couldn't play defense with the guys in this group. Andre Dawson, Winfield, Jim Rice, and Reggie Smith deserve a mention here, but they fall a little short of the others offensively. Like Dale Murphy, Roger Maris was the MVP of his league twice, but he did not have ten superior seasons.

RIGHT FIELD: CLEMENTE, KALINE.

Starting Pitchers

One might think that I would be better able to select pitchers than position players, but I am not. First of all, when I selected My Team, I had to admit that I could pick five different pitchers who would be just as good. Now, it's time to make those choices.

I agonized over leaving Pedro Martinez off My Team, but finally decided to do it because he has not been quite as durable as the five I chose. I cannot leave him off again. His ERA relative to his contemporaries is the best of any pitcher on the list, and he pitched a lot of those innings in the American League, where he had to face nine hitters instead of eight hitters and a pitcher. The lack of durability shows in the 10-year averages. He hasn't been able to pitch as many innings as the others have, but the quality of his work exceeds all the others. With his various pitches, he has a way to get left-handed hitters out as well as right-handers. About the only area where a few of these guys have him beat is in the hitting. Who knows, after a few years back in the National League, he may become a good hitter, too.

Next up is Nolan Ryan. The best hope I have for My Team in this matchup is that I have a lot of guys who draw walks. I don't think we could score much against Nolan without a few walks. In fact, when he was really on (seven no-hitters) nobody could hit him. He could pitch a no-hitter against My Team and it is not likely that any of my pitchers would be able to no-hit the Dogs. Nolan came up with a great changeup late in his career. If he had had that changeup in his prime seasons, he would likely be the opening-day starter on My Team. The guy who held the no-hitter record (four) before Ryan, Sandy Koufax, was what one hitter called a "comfortable 0-4". I doubt anyone would say that about Nolan. He pitched inside aggressively throughout his career.

Giving the nod to Randy Johnson over Steve Carlton wasn't easy either. Randy has a slightly better ERA and the second lowest ERA versus the league ERA. His winning percentage is better than Carlton's, too. Carlton was much more likely to pitch a complete game, and he was a far better hitter than Johnson. He also had a better pickoff move (but was called for quite a few balks). His durability was almost as good as Ryan's and Clemens's, as he pitched until he was 44 years old. He did not, however, pitch nearly as well after age forty as the two Texas fireballers. For that matter, he didn't pitch as well as old Gaylord Perry, who won his second Cy Young Award at age forty and won 64 games thereafter.

Carlton ended up with 329 wins. Among modern pitchers only Warren Spahn and Clemens have won more. Only Ryan, Clemens, and Randy Johnson have struck out more batters.

If for no other reason than to watch him pitch, I favor Juan Marichal over Niekro, Sutton, Jenkins, and Perry. When Juan was on the mound, fans were treated to two performances for the price of one. First there was the ball game. Then there was the ballet, with Marichal taking center stage.

On July 2, 1963, in a night game at Candlestick Park, Juan got into a scoreless duel with Warren Spahn. Marichal was a 25-year-old kid at the time, while Spahnny was forty-two. After the game went into extra innings, Giants manager Alvin Dark asked Juan if he had had enough. Juan said that if the old man in the other dugout could continue, he could, too. And he did. Willie Mays won the game for him in the bottom of the 16th with a solo homer off Spahn. Can you imagine a pitcher going 16 innings these days? (Can you imagine pitching in eight All-Star games, working 18 innings, and giving up only one earned run? Juan did that, too!)

To successfully navigate 16 innings, it is necessary to retire the other team's best hitters seven or eight times. If you don't have enough different pitches to show them, they will eventually make an adjustment to what they have seen in previous at-bats. With Spahn and Marichal, that would be hard to do because they both threw five or more different pitches.

Last, but certainly not least, is Jim Palmer. Palmer's numbers look a little better than Bob Gibson's and at first I had him on My Team. After talking with a lot of their teammates, I switched to Gibby. Palmer got rave reviews all around, but Gibson did, too. The difference is that Gibby's teammates seemed in awe of him, even after all these years. I can also argue that I think the National League had more talent when they were both pitching (after all, Gibson lost nine games in the year when he posted an ERA of 1.12). Over the course of their long careers, Palmer had more good teams behind him. Another reason for my flip-flop is that Gibby was an N.L. pitcher all the way. He was the best fielder and hitter among the pitchers of his generation. For that matter, he was better in the batter's box than any of the modern pitchers. Because we will be playing on natural grass in a league without a DH, Gibson gets another slight advantage.

Giving the Dogs Pedro Martinez, Nolan Ryan, Steve Carlton, Juan Marichal, and Jim Palmer would make it very difficult for My Team to score. Of course, the Dogs would have a tough time scoring, too. I imagine there would be a lot of games played in less than two hours.

STARTING PITCHER: MARTINEZ, RYAN, CARLTON, MARICHAL, PALMER.

Relief Pitchers

When I was selecting My Team's bullpen, I seriously con-sidered using Phil Niekro as a swing man—a guy who could pitch long relief or start a game if needed. The knuckleball is an enigmatic pitch. It often eludes not only the bat, but the catcher's mitt, allowing runners to advance. But it is so hard to hit squarely that even the best hitters sometimes seem helpless. Having a knuckleball pitcher on a team can be a real asset in emergency situations, such as doubleheaders and extra-inning games when you need someone who can pitch a lot of innings on short rest. Hoyt Wilhelm had a great knuckler, too, and he saved a lot more games than Niekro, but he didn't win nearly as many, and he wasn't as good a hitter and fielder as Niekro. Since I didn't pick Knucksie as a starter, I am picking him now, the same way I picked Ken Griffey Jr.—in a slightly different role than he normally played. I know the guys on My Team wouldn't be eager to face him. Of course, few of the hitters on either team would be eager to face any of the pitchers. Johnny Bench killed Steve Carlton, but I doubt there are many other lopsided matchups among this group of players.

Rollie Fingers is another guy who almost made My Team. I left him off because I thought Dennis Eckersley and John Smoltz would be better in long relief. Tug McGraw would be good in this role, too, and also give the Dogs a lefty reliever. McGraw didn't approach the save numbers of the other reliev-ers, mostly because he was used as a long man in the bullpen many times. In fact, he averaged more than two innings per ap-pearance during his requisite eight years. He was also used as an emergency starter 14 times. He was a starter for two years before moving to the bullpen, and his 96 wins are exceeded only by Eckersley, Smoltz, and Fingers.

John Franco saved more games than any other left-handed pitcher. He is third on the all-time-saves list. Although Franco is left-handed, he actually pitched better against right-handed hitters throughout most of his career. Franco specialized in hitting corners with his fastball and throwing a maddening changeup that even the best right-handed hitters had trouble with. He also had a nice little slider that he could use on left-handed hitters, and was one of the most durable pitchers in the history of the game. I believe he could pitch two or three innings if necessary. Still, I am inclined to go with Fingers. He was tough on both left- and right-handed hitters, and could pitch more innings than Franco. If Steve Carlton started for the Dogs and had to be removed for a pinch hitter in the seventh inning, Rollie would be the perfect reliever because most of the hitters he would face would be right-handed.

I cannot ignore Lee Smith, the top save artist in the history of the sport. His save success ratio isn't as impressive (85 percent) as some of the others but, in his prime, he was one of the most dominant pitchers I have ever seen. At first he did it mostly with a fastball that sometimes reached 100 mph. Later, when his velocity dropped in the mid to low nineties, he came up with a good hard slider. Like all of the pitchers in this book, he had good command of both corners with his fastball and a good secondary pitch. What's more, it was scary just to face him. He actually didn't hit very many batters (and didn't walk many, either). But his visage was still fearsome. He could dominate you by staring in at the catcher for the sign. Lee ended up pitching in over 1000 games and saving 478. He was a likable guy and a great teammate.

Lee Smith is my first closer. The last spot is the one concession I will make to having a left-handed specialist; in a sense, it is not a major concession. Sparky Lyle or Jesse Orosco would be great against left-handed hitters, but with two players at every position, I could pinch-hit with a right-handed hitter at the same defensive position most of the time. Lyle and Orosco might end up facing Craig Biggio and Frank Robinson if Joe Morgan and Ken Griffey were in my lineup. They would also face Bench, Bagwell, A-Rod, Schmidt, Bonds, Mays, or Mantle, and Aaron. Given this set of circumstances, I think the Dogs would be be better off with Randy Myers or Billy Wagner. Myers and Wagner would bring it up there at velocities of 95–100 mph. I think they would have a better chance to get my right-handed hitters out than Lyle or Orosco. Bonds hit a home run off Wagner in San Francisco, but Wagner has retired him most of the time. He has also retired just about every hitter in the National League most of the time. Because Wagner's save percentage is slightly better than Myers's, I am selecting Wagner to team with Lee Smith to pitch the ninth inning.

The closers that didn't make either team were just about as good. In fact, I'm sure many managers would have selected one or more of these guys if they were choosing. McGraw had versatility, Lyle dominated left-handed hitters, Sutter's split-fingered fastball was just as good against lefties and righties, and Wetteland and Henke had great save percentages. Franco could get lefties and righties out. Gossage was nasty and a great guy to have on a team. But I think the Dogs have a great bullpen.

RELIEF PITCHER: FINGERS, P. NIEKRO, L. SMITH, AND B. WAGNER.

Dogs Roster

SP Martinez, Ryan, Carlton, Marichal, and Palmer
C I. Rodriguez and McCarver
1B Thomas and McCovey
2B Carew and Sandberg
3B Mathews and Jones
SS Yount and Smith
LF Henderson and Raines
CF Edmonds and B. Williams
RF Clemente and Kaline
RP Fingers, P. Niekro, L. Smith, and B. Wagner

12

Lineups

Theory

BACK WHEN BALLPLAYERS traveled on trolleys and trains, managers tried to align their batting orders to get the maximum production from the same eight guys (before the DH and on My Team and the Dogs). It didn't take long for a theory to evolve that even today, with statistical analysis, seems to make sense. The first two hitters are typically guys who can get on base a lot and run fast. The first batter should be able to steal bases. The second hitter should also be able to steal a few bags and also be a guy who can bunt and execute the hit-and-run. The third hitter should be the best hitter on the team. He should be able to hit for average and with power and also draw walks and be fast enough to score from first base on a double. The fourth hitter is generally the most powerful hitter in the lineup and the fifth batter should also be a good RBI man. The sixth hitter on a good team is a second-tier RBI man, who doesn't have a great OBS but does have some power. The seventh, eighth, and ninth hitters are the weakest hitters on the team. It helps if the eighth hitter is fast enough to advance on a decent bunt. These characteristics were recognized and employed by managers long before modern statistical analysts like Bill James, Pete Palmer, Gary Gillette, Steve Mann, and others started addressing the subject.

Actually the first person to produce a thoughtful study of batting order was Earnshaw Cook in his book *Percentage Baseball,* published in 1964. Cook's conclusion was that batting orders such as the one I have described are not the best because, over the course of the season, the most productive hitters would hit in the middle of the lineup, thereby getting fewer at-bats than lesser hitters who usually batted first or second. He believed the standard lineup put the cart before the horse. Cook's theory seems to make sense, but it does not account for opportunity. The traditional lineup allows the first hitter more chances to get on base and use his speed to score. The second batter has the opportunity to move the first hitter forward, even if he makes an out doing it. The middle of the lineup hitters are thereby presented with more opportunities to hit with men in scoring position. For example, John Thorn and Pete Palmer, who collaborated on one of the best books on baseball statistics, *The Hidden Game of Baseball,* discovered that the typical value of a home run for all hitters from 1969 through 1971 was 1.40 runs. The home-run value of a home run from a leadoff hitter during the same time frame was 1.28. Obviously, with the weak hitters at the end of the lineup, the leadoff man did not come up with men on base as often. If the best hitter, who hit third in the lineup, played a full season and hit leadoff, he would go to the plate approximately 36 more times than he would hitting third. His runs scored might improve slightly in that scenario, but his runs batted in would decline.

Surprisingly, it doesn't make very much difference whether a team hit in Cook's suggested batting order or the traditional one. Using the same three years, Thorn and Palmer's computer-generated comparison showed the Cook order producing 4.130 runs per game, while the traditional order scored 4.154. Even more startling is the computation for a lineup that started with the pitcher and proceeded in descending order based on ability with the best hitter hitting last. That lineup produced 4.026 runs per game. Palmer was the American League's official statistician at the time of the study. It is likely that his calculations were accurate. This being the case, the quality of specific players who inhabit the lineup is much more important than the way they are aligned. In short, the intuitive lineup theory is a little bit better than any other lineup consisting of the same players. Legendary Yankees skipper of the Babe Ruth era, Miller Huggins, was forty years and .024 runs ahead of Earnshaw Cook working on instinct alone.

Still, an advantage is an advantage, even when it is slight—but that is a statistical advantage. Over the course of 162 games the difference could amount to an extra win or two. You could point this out to all the players in the major leagues and they would be unimpressed. They are always thinking about the batting order and are often most critical of their manager for using the supposed wrong lineup when the team is struggling to score runs. Like most fans, they think the way the lineup is structured is much more important than it really is. The point is: If they think it is important, it is important. Psychological considerations can greatly offset statistical analysis. I didn't realize that when I was pitching. I knew I was the worst hitter in the lineup and wasn't responsible for the other eight guys. When I started managing, things changed.

Beyond Theory

One of the things I found to be different when I came down from the broadcast booth to manage the Astros was that the players showed up at the ballpark much earlier than the players of my era. The first items on a team's agenda each day are stretching and taking batting practice. Batting practice starts at about 5:00 P.M. for a 7:00 P.M. night game. We used to get to the ballpark an hour before BP, or about 4:00 P.M., unless we needed to arrive early to treat an injury. Now, in most cases, players arrive at 2:00 P.M. or a little later but, in all cases, much earlier than we did. Back then, a few guys came out an hour early or so on the road and the rest came on the team bus, which arrived at about 4:15. As a manager, I didn't have enough to do between 2:00 P.M. and game time (except when we played a team we hadn't seen for a while) so I worked crossword puzzles, like I did on the days I pitched, to pass the time. Last year, Tony La Russa asked me how I liked life outside the foxhole and I told him that while I enjoyed the competition in the dugout, I was glad to be free of the "dead time." "I haven't worked five crosswords since I left the dugout," I said. "When I was managing, I worked one every day."

As a manager, I felt I had to be at the ballpark when the first players arrived, mostly because they wanted to know who was in the lineup. Some managers change the lineup a lot from day to day. I did that at first but, as we improved, the lineup stayed pretty much the same. Like most managers, I allotted playing time to the reserve players when we had a day game after a night game or when we had to fill in for an injured player. Even though the players knew who was going to be in the lineup each day, they still wanted to see it posted on the clubhouse wall.

Jeff Bagwell hit in the three hole for the Astros almost exclusively during my five years in the dugout. Still, he was there early every day just to make sure. Johnny Bench hit in the clean up spot for the Reds for practically his whole career. But when I post the lineup for My Team, a lot of guys, like Bagwell and Bench, who are or were used to hitting in the middle of the lineup, will be hitting elsewhere. Bench is a pretty bright guy, and I think he would understand why he was hitting eighth in-

stead of fourth, and Bagwell would be happy for the RBI opportunities he would get hitting seventh. The lineups that follow for My Team and the Dogs are just a starting point. I would
look at each player's hitting tendencies, and place him in the
lineup accordingly. This alignment would have to change during a typical season because there are always injuries. The lineups might also change if I thought I could get more production
by moving some players up or down in the order. With so
many stars, I would probably change the lineup more on My
Team than I did with the Astros.

I have heard that some managers have picked the lineup
out of a hat when their teams were slumping, though I never
saw one do it and did not do it myself. If I did this with My
Team, I would still come up with a potent lineup—even if the
pitcher were hitting third! But I'm not going for the hat trick;
I'm going for the jugular vein. These are what I consider my
best starting lineups, based both on statistics and characteristics
of the hitters.

My Team Lineup

1. WILLIE MAYS/MICKEY MANTLE. Willie could bunt, steal, or
hit a home run. There are a couple of guys on My Team who
have better OBAs than Willie, but none that were more disruptive. Besides, with good hitters in the seven and eight holes,
Willie would come up with men on base often enough to drive
in a lot of runs. I diverge slightly from both Palmer and Cook,
because I favor a leadoff hitter who has some home-run power.
As a pitcher, I sometimes had men on base when the bottom of
the order was coming up. If the leadoff man had no power, I
had to consider that when pitching to the seventh and eighth
hitters. Many times, I decided that I would not give those hitters
anything good to hit, because I preferred to walk them than to
let them hit a fat pitch. I thought I could escape without allowing a run by getting the pitcher and the leadoff man out. If

Willie Mays were leading off, I would be more likely to challenge the seven and eight hitter and try to end the inning with the pitcher. I like a leadoff man who can drive in runs. Mickey Mantle would be just like Mays in that regard and would probably steal more than he did for the Yankees.

2. JOE MORGAN/CRAIG BIGGIO/DEREK JETER. Joe was another disruptive player and a good RBI man. The reason I am hitting him second instead of first is that he was a left-handed pull hitter. With Mays on first base, Joe could pull a ground ball through the hole on the right side of the infield. He could do this as well as any player I have ever seen. Once on first, he would be a threat to steal. How would you like to try holding Morgan on first while pitching to Barry Bonds? I wouldn't want any part of that. I wouldn't want to face Biggio or Jeter in that situation either.

3. BARRY BONDS/ALEX RODRIGUEZ. On most teams, the best hitter hits third in the lineup. My Team is no exception. The only time Barry would not hit third is when he wasn't playing. If I had Frank Robinson in the lineup on a given day, I would hit Frank further down and go with a three hitter with more speed and a higher on-base average, like Alex Rodriguez, in the three hole. Ted Williams once said: "They didn't know whether to pitch me high or pitch me low. They didn't know what to do." Barry Bonds could say the same thing.

4. HENRY AARON/KEN GRIFFEY JR. Aaron would have a great time driving all these guys in. His numbers are similar to those of Mays, but Henry didn't bunt and didn't steal as often as Willie. In addition to his home-run hitting, he was also a good on-base hitter. He could steal a base occasionally because he had good speed and good instincts. With fast players in front of him and fast players behind him, he might not try to steal much at all, but he could run fast enough to advance more than one

base on a hit, allowing Alex Rodriguez or Mike Schmidt to advance behind him. Griffey Jr. has almost the same hitting profile as Aaron.

5. ALEX RODRIGUEZ/FRANK ROBINSON. A-Rod would continue the theme of home-run hitters with base-stealing speed. He would have ample opportunity to drive in the guys ahead of him, and with Mike Schmidt hitting behind him, it would be hard to pitch around him. (If Frank Robinson were playing instead of Bonds, I would hit A-Rod third and Robbie fifth.)

I don't put as much faith in left/right matchups as many managers, but I did try to go left-right-left when I constructed my Astros' lineups because that order makes pitching decisions more difficult for the opposing manager. He has to either let a left-handed pitcher pitch to a right-handed hitter or he has to make two or three pitching changes to avoid doing so. I think most of the relievers on My Team (and on the Dogs) could pitch effectively to both left- and right-handed hitters, which is why I have so many right-handed hitters in a row. As a manager, I didn't like to change my lineup very often. But if, after a long trial and much deliberation, I thought I could improve it by putting A-Rod between Morgan and Bonds and pushing Aaron back to the five hole, I would do it. If it came to that, I would call all of them into my office and tell them why I was doing it. When I was playing, managers seldom explained their thinking, but players are not soldiers or pieces on a chessboard. These days, they want to know both what and why. I wouldn't mind sharing my thoughts with them, anyway.

6. MIKE SCHMIDT/GEORGE BRETT/FRANK ROBINSON. Schmidt won the home-run title eight times with the Phillies. He was also named the league MVP three times. Looking at the players who hit ahead of him on My Team, it seems like he could be the MVP on a team full of MVPs. If this happened, he

might be the only player in history to win the award out of the sixth slot in the batting order. And, since he walked so often, he would be on base for Jeff Bagwell, who drove in a run for every 4.8 at-bats during his ten prime years. If George Brett were playing, I would hit him sixth, too. Robinson would fit well in the six hole as well.

7. JEFF BAGWELL/WILLIE STARGELL/JOHNNY BENCH/MIKE PIAZZA. Jeff's best ten hitting years were meteoric, and would be even more glittering if Barry Bonds hadn't eclipsed him practically every season. Because Jeff got on base 42 percent of the time, he would be cued up for Johnny Bench, one of the best RBI hitters of his time. With A-Rod and Schmidt in front of him, Bagwell could win the MVP award out of the seven hole. If a hitter has an OBS over 1.000, his average at-bat is better than a walk. Jeff fell just barely short of this mark during his ten years; it is all the more amazing since he played almost half his games in the Astrodome. However, there were a few pitchers who gave him a lot of trouble over the years, and I would play Willie Stargell at first base when those guys were pitching. If I had Derek Jeter in the lineup when Morgan was playing, I would leave Morgan in the two hole and leadoff with Jeter.

The most difficult thing about managing this team is that with so many great players it would be hard to go with a set lineup. Everyone would need to play often enough to stay sharp. This could be quite a juggling act and there would be some griping about who I played from day to day. I found that my premier players never wanted a day off. If I gave them one because they had trouble with the other team's starting pitcher, they wanted the challenge of turning the tables on him. If they were in a slump, they asked me how they could get out of it while sitting on the bench. If I wanted to get them some rest in a day game that followed a night game, they would have another reason such as: "I always hit good in this ballpark." Or "I'm just starting to get my timing down again and I don't want to take a break now." Or "I feel great. I'm not tired at all." Great players never buy the idea that they could use a rest. They never buy the idea that they are important strategically, even when they are on the bench. About the only thing they will concede is that the guy behind them needs to get some at-bats. When they look at the guy behind them on this team, they might understand why they weren't in the lineup every day.

8. JOHNNY BENCH/MIKE PIAZZA. It's a windfall to have a catcher who is a good fielder and a good hitter. Bench didn't walk as much as some of the other players in this lineup and he is certainly the slowest runner. That's why he finds himself hitting in front of the pitcher. But when you consider the players who hit in front of him, he would probably drive in 100 or more runs anyway. And, he wasn't deadly slow. It wouldn't be that hard for the pitchers to bunt him up to second or third base for Willie Mays. One thing I remember about Bench is that he couldn't hit Rick Reuschel. If that type of matchup came about, I would probably play Piazza, even if Greg Maddux wasn't pitching.

Although the guys listed first would comprise what I might call my standard lineup, if we played the Dogs for a whole season, I would learn which players to use against the various pitchers. The Dogs manager would learn the same things about My Team.

I would change the lineup against a tough right-handed pitcher more than I would for a left-handed pitcher. If a sidearm pitcher like Don Drysdale, Jim Bunning, or a guy with a nasty slider like Bob Gibson or Pedro Martinez were pitching against us, I would work Mantle, Brett, Stargell, and Griffey into the lineup. The only big problem I can foresee is getting enough playing time for Frank Robinson because he would be playing in place of Barry Bonds. I might have to split his time between right and left field to get him enough at-bats to stay sharp. I *think* Griffey Jr. could play right field, but I *know* Robinson can, because he did.

On days when Greg Maddux was pitching, I would play Mike Piazza behind the plate. This strategy has several advantages. It gives Bench a day off each time through the rotation. It gives Maddux his personal catcher, which is the way he likes it. And it gets Piazza consistent at-bats so he can be sharp when he comes up as a pinch hitter. I would hit Piazza eighth, like Bench, because his slugging is better than his on-base hitting and he is not a fast runner. The only time I would move the catchers out of the eighth spot would be when Biggio and Jeter were both in the lineup, which wouldn't be often unless A-Rod or Morgan were injured. If they were both in the lineup, I would hit one of them second and the other eighth. Another advantage of having the catcher hitting eighth is that he doesn't get as many at-bats as a player further up in the order. This would help Bench keep his legs fresh if he caught four out of every five games.

If Steve Carlton were pitching against us, I might start Biggio over Morgan or Robinson over Bonds, but I would do it only against the tough sidearm to three-quarters delivery lefties who have good breaking stuff. Morgan used to hit Sandy Koufax pretty well, but I doubt he had much success against John Candelaria.

Against the wicked right-handers I would lead off with Mantle (he was a good bunter and walked a lot) instead of Mays. I would follow with Morgan and Bonds. I would hit Griffey fourth, A-Rod fifth, Brett sixth, Stargell seventh, and Bench or Piazza eighth. Mays, Aaron, Schmidt, Biggio, Robinson, and Bagwell would be on the bench as pinch hitters. That might prevent the opposing manager from bringing in a left-handed reliever to face Morgan, Bonds, Griffey, Brett, or Stargell. In view of the Dogs excellent starting pitchers, I would likely use the left-handed hitting lineup often enough that it would be hard to call any of the variations an every-day lineup.

Of course, there are numerous combinations that could be used. As I said, picking them out of a hat would yield a good team and a good lineup. I would switch it around some, but I would try to find three or four standard lineups so that the players could get comfortable with their roles. One thing you might notice is that no matter which lineup I use, I always have a player on the bench who can steal a base. I was lucky enough to have this luxury when I managed the Astros, and it yielded an extra win or two each year.

The idea of roles is something I have heard more about in recent years. It came up several times when I was managing. The first time was in Kansas City, about halfway through my first year as manager of the Astros. We were at or near the top of our division at the time, but were in a slump. I sensed some discontent and it exploded in a meeting before the first game of the series. We were discussing the positioning of our fielders, but Derek Bell changed the subject. He said that he didn't even know his role on the team because I had him batting in several different places in the lineup. I had been doing a lot of lineup juggling that year based on match-up statistics. I kept Biggio in the leadoff spot because he was one of the best in the business. After Biggio, I used several number-two hitters, hit Bagwell third, and used various players in the remaining slots, moving them forward when they had good numbers against the other team's starting pitcher and vice versa. Derek seemed to strike a nerve and several other players chimed in. Bill Virdon was my bench coach that season and he blew his stack. "Just do your own job and don't worry about the manager," he said. "Your role is to help the team win. His role is the same. He can do his job a lot better if you do yours."

I really appreciated what Bill said because I couldn't have said it any better. And with 15 years of managerial experience, his words carried more weight than mine would have anyway. I could see the veins pulsing in Bill's forehead. He really had "the ass" (short for The Red Ass). I considered Derek's point and thought about it a lot afterward. Even though I didn't say much about it, I did try to find a comfortable spot for the everyday players in the lineup and stick with it. It wasn't long before we started playing better. We were due to start playing better anyway, but the meeting influenced the way I managed thereafter.

The next year, Derek was usually in the number-five hole in the lineup. He kept telling me that he didn't like to hit fifth because the other team's pitchers kept pitching around him because he was our last power threat. He wanted to hit second, in front of Jeff Bagwell. There was some truth in what he said, but there was no way I could produce another power hitter for the five hole or the six hole and Derek didn't fit the description of a number-two hitter at all. He didn't bunt, didn't walk, and didn't like to hit with the runner breaking from first. One day in New York, near the start of the season, I had to scratch Bill Spiers just before game time because he hurt himself during batting practice. I had had him hitting second, and I changed the lineup, moving Derek up to the second spot. He hit the first pitch thrown to him that day over the center-field fence at Shea Stadium, a titanic blast. He got a couple more hits that day and we won easily. The next day, I kept him in that spot and then the next day and then the rest of the year. He ended up having his best year, hitting .314 with 108 RBI and 111 runs scored. Neither Pete Palmer nor Earnshaw Cook could make any sense of hitting Bell second, but it worked. Because he walked only 51 times, his OBA was less than you would like at the top of the order, but hitting behind Biggio and in front of Bagwell gave him confidence. With Biggio on base, and the opposing pitcher worrying about him stealing second, Derek assumed he would get a fastball to hit. When Biggio wasn't on base, and Derek was ahead in the count, he assumed that the pitcher would throw him a fastball because he wouldn't want to walk him with Bagwell coming up. All year long he looked for the fastball and we ended up winning 102 games, the highest total in team history.

When the Pirates were a top team in 1990-92, Jimmy Leyland used Barry Bonds as his leadoff man, which made perfect sense because Barry had a high on-base average, was a good base stealer, and had not yet become a prolific home-run hitter. Leyland hit Jay Bell second, which made no sense at all. Bell was a medium-range power hitter, and, like Derek Bell, he seldom walked and he struck out a lot. The only reason he hit second was that he was a good bunter. Leyland was a manager who put a lot of faith in the conventional strategy of trying to score first. Since he had two excellent hitters to follow Bell, Andy Van Slyke and Bobby Bonilla, he got a run in the first inning quite often. Most of the time, when Bell bunted, I thought Bonds could have stolen second base. Bell was not a good on-base hitter, so when Bonds didn't get on base, and there was no reason to bunt, the Bucs had a guy who was a better RBI man hitting with one out and nobody on base. Bell's hitting tendencies fit better in the six or seven hole. But who could question the lineup when the Pirates were winning a lot more games than they were losing? It was the same scenario we had with our Bell hitting second. If it's not broken, don't fix it!

Since then, I've noticed several successful managers juggling the order from one day to the next and wondered how the players felt about it. If you are winning, it probably isn't a problem. If you are not, it can be used as an excuse. I always wondered what the Cardinals' players thought in '98 when Tony La Russa batted the starting pitcher eighth instead of ninth. I think his goal was to get as many men on base in front of Mark McGwire as possible, because Big Mac was the best hitter in the league that year. But Tony was a veteran manager and although he was criticized some in the media, his team started playing better. That pretty well silenced the critics. I'm not sure what the players thought. And I'm not sure Tony cared what they thought. The point is that, over the course of a season, a team can develop a gestalt that seems to defy logic, but it still works. Things happen during the epic journey of a baseball season that define a team—even My Team. To be perfectly honest, I can't project what would happen to the lineup in the course of 162 games, I would start with the basic lineup theory, but I would not become a slave to it.

In 2000, the Astros had a disastrous season, starting slowly and getting progressively worse as the All-Star Game approached. Pitching was our biggest problem. As you might expect, the trouble started in the first inning. Our starters seemed psyched out at our new ballpark, Enron Field. They tried to catch a corner on every pitch, fearing a cheap home run. As a result, they walked more batters than they had when they pitched in the Astrodome. That led to high pitch counts, which led to early exits, which led to more work for the relievers, none of whom was very effective. Even Billy Wagner had problems and had to have elbow surgery midway through the year.

One night, after a game in Milwaukee, I spoke with our general manager, Gerry Hunsicker, at some length. Gerry's concern was with the roles of the guys in the bullpen. "One day you use [Joe] Slusarski as a long man and the next time you use him it's in a tight game in the eighth inning," he said. "How does he know if he's the long man or the set-up man?" I explained that I was trying to use the guy I thought had the best chance of succeeding in each situation. For example, Slusarski had been a starting pitcher and could go three or four innings if necessary. But he also had a good sinker, slider, and forkball combination, and usually kept the ball low. If we were playing on a grass field, and a good high-ball hitter was coming up with a man on first, I sometimes used Slu late in the game, hoping to get a double play or, at least, avoid an extra-base hit. "All I can say," I said, "is that I'm trying to get the guys into situations where I think they have the best chance. I wish they all had roles, but, at this point, they just don't." The conversation went on for half an hour or so and

I could only observe that none of the pitchers had performed consistently enough to earn a set-up role. We decided to call them in, one by one, and give them roles, hoping they could rise to the challenge. They did not.

After about two weeks of role-playing, it was obvious that we weren't getting any better. I think Gerry understood that I was trying to manage the pitching as well as I could, and after those two weeks, I think he was as frustrated as I was. One day he said, "Just go with your gut, or matchups, or anything you think might work. These guys just aren't getting the job done."

On most winning teams, players acquire roles either from past performance if they are veterans, or good work in specific jobs if they are young players. A team with talented players who are comfortable with their roles is much easier to manage, and I was fortunate to have that type of team in three of my five years at the helm.

On the offensive side of the game, I prefer to go left, right, left, if I can. I couldn't do it often in Houston because almost all of our good hitters were right-handed. This is one of the reasons we had trouble against the tough right-handed pitchers. It's no secret that the standard strategy is to throw fastballs up and in, and low and away, and to throw breaking pitches low and away. But up and in to a right-handed hitter is up and away to a lefty and the off-speed pitches that were low and away to a right-handed hitter, would be down and in to a lefty, which is a power-hitting zone. In a lineup full of right-handed hitters, the pitcher only has to master two spots with his fastball and can get into a groove with the low and away breaking ball. But if you go left, right, left at-bat, he has to master all four corners of the strike zone with his fastball and has to throw his breaking ball to both sides of the plate, too. My experience as a pitcher told me loud and clear that it was much tougher to face a team with left- and right-handed hitters scattered throughout the lineup. This is what bothers me a bit about the standard lineup for My Team. I think I might end up using the left-handed hitters more and placing less emphasis on the statistics. In other words, the lineups in this chapter would be subject to change. I would try to find slots in the lineup and roles for the bench players and relief pitchers as quickly as possible. Obviously, the lineups in this chapter would just be a place to start.

In the bullpen, I would only have four pitchers, which could be a problem if our starters failed early two or three days in a row. With My Team's rotation, I doubt this would happen more than once or twice in a month. In a way, Eckersley and Smoltz made it easy for me to pick my bullpen. Since both of them were starters in the first half of their careers, I know that each of them could pitch more than one inning at a time. Their records as closers are so good that it would be hard not to use them in that role, but it's hard to justify having two closers on a team, let alone four. I would stretch Eckersley and Smoltz out to six innings at spring training to get them ready for long relief, but I could use them to close a game too if the matchups were favorable. Because they are both accustomed to closing, I could let them finish the game if they came into it in the seventh inning and hold Mariano Rivera and Trevor Hoffman in reserve.

Although I could use all four pitchers to close out a game, I would probably give most of the work to Rivera and Hoffman. Hoffman, with his almost impeccable control and paralyzing changeup, can get both left-handed and right-handed hitters out. With his darting fastball Rivera can do the same. I was thinking of using Tug McGraw, John Franco, or Sparky Lyle as the left-hander in the bullpen because of their good records and their personalities. They were all loose cannons who could keep things on the light side even while pitching in the heavy atmosphere of the ninth inning. Rivera and Hoffman aren't as wacky as the lefties, but they are great guys to have on a team—good professional pitchers who are easy to manage and friendly with both their teammates and the media. Winning, in the end, is better for the chemistry of a team than practical jokes.

Lineups

I could draw my starting rotation out of a hat, too, but someone has to start the opening game and four others have to be cued up behind him. One thing that made the Astros rotation so tough in 1980 was diversity. First, you would have to face Nolan Ryan. The next day you would face Joe Niekro—quite a contrast from a 100 mph fastball to a 75 mph knuckle ball. Nolan's breaking ball was a curve that broke almost straight down. Niekro's was a slider that broke sideways. Niekro could throw a little harder than his brother Phil. When he made it to the major leagues with the Cubs in 1967, he didn't even throw the knuckler. Joe won 25 or 30 games as a conventional pitcher before he gave his heart and soul to the capricious pitch his brother, Hoyt Wilhelm, and a few others had used before him. It was no fun hitting against Ryan and sometimes it could be downright embarrassing to try hitting the knuckler. The next pitcher in the rotation was J. R. Richard, a six-foot-eight inch flamethrower with a nasty slider. If he had pitched for 10 years, I would have had to consider him for My Team. J. R. is the most intimidating right-hander I have ever seen. And he had a much higher release point than Ryan or Niekro. Ken Forsch was next in line and he was a hard-throwing sinker/slider pitcher with excellent control. Unlike the others, he worked fast. Opposing hitters had to be ready when he was pitching because he would start his delivery shortly after they got into the batter's box.

In the middle of the 1980 season, J. R. went down with a stroke and Vern Ruhle replaced him. He went 12-4 with a couple of shutouts. Vern didn't throw quite as hard as the others, but had better control than any of them except Forsch. Vern threw only a little bit harder than Niekro, but he had such a wide assortment of breaking balls and off-speed pitches that it was almost impossible for a hitter to guess what he would throw. The point is that from one game to the next, opposing hitters would have to face pitchers with dramatically different styles. I will arrange My Team's rotation the same way.

Because he has won more Cy Young Awards than the others, Roger Clemens would get the opening day assignment. I would follow him with Randy Johnson, another strong-armed, flamethrower, and a left-handed one at that. The only similarity between these two fine pitchers is that they both throw hard. Randy doesn't throw as many different pitches as Roger and has a much higher release point. I will go to Tom Seaver next. How's that for a change in style? First you get left-handed gas, from a high and wide angle, then you get right-handed heat from a low release point. I would follow Seaver with Maddux, the master of finesse and late moving, but not particularly fast, pitches. Maddux is a ground ball pitcher and Tom Seaver was mostly a fly ball and strikeout pitcher. Maddux would hand the ball over to Bob Gibson for the fifth game. Gibson worked fast and threw hard. Seaver threw mostly four-seam fastballs that did not have lateral movement. Gibson was the opposite. He threw fastballs that sometimes sailed and sometime tailed. His breaking ball was a slider and it was a big-breaking, high-velocity pitch that broke down and away from right-handed hitters. He could also bring it in the back door (third base side of the plate) to left-handed hitters. There was no one better in a big game, as he proved in the postseason. Actually, I could line these guys up by drawing their names out of a hat, because they are all big-game pitchers and they all have different styles.

I don't have a knuckleballer to offer the greatest variety. I was sorely tempted to pick Phil Niekro or Hoyt Wilhelm to give My Team more versatility, but to do that I would have to leave off Gibson, Eckersley, or Smoltz, and I couldn't justify doing that. I suppose there were hitters who would rather face Seaver than Phil Niekro, but I doubt there were many hitters who liked hitting against any of the guys in my rotation.

As good as My Team is, the one I have fashioned for the Underdogs is just about as good. In some ways, it is better. The Dogs have more options for long relief and spot-starting. They also have a bit more speed. The defense is about equal, with both teams having slight edges at some positions. The Dogs are formidable as you can see.

1. RICKEY HENDERSON/TIM RAINES. Rickey is generally acknowledged to be the best leadoff hitter of all time. His OBA is excellent; he is the best base stealer in the history of the game; he scored more runs than anyone in baseball history. Like the player he surpassed in stolen bases, Lou Brock, Rickey could cover a lot of ground in the outfield, but was not considered to be a great outfielder. Good, but not great. What impressed me most was his defiant attitude. He stood up close to the plate in a crouch with his feet slightly open. When he leaned in just before the pitch, his head was almost in the strike zone. I wouldn't have liked that and may have been motivated to throw a pitch in that area even though I never intentionally threw at a batter's head. Of course, I can't think of any other batter whose head was that close to the strike zone. I'm sure many pitchers tried this strategy, but the numbers suggest that it didn't work too well. I would lead off with Rickey but I still think My Team's leadoff man, Willie Mays, would be better, both in the field and at the plate. I have decided to use Tim Raines as my backup left fielder, over Carl Yastrzemski or Billy Williams. I might get death threats from Boston and Chicago, but Raines would fit neatly into the leadoff spot, and Yaz and Billy would not. My Team's backup leadoff man would be Mickey Mantle. Raines and Mantle were both switch hitters and fast runners. Mantle had a lot more power.

2. ROD CAREW/BERNIE WILLIAMS/JIM EDMONDS/OZZIE SMITH. Like Henderson, Rod Carew had good speed and a good OBA. He was an excellent bunter and, like Tony Gwynn, he was as close as you can come to a place hitter on the hit-and-run play. Rodney didn't hit many home runs, but a lot of his 3053 career hits went for extra bases. He is perhaps the

penultimate number-two hitter behind the ultimate—Joe Morgan. Joe did everything that Carew did, but with more home runs and more stolen bases. He was as fierce a competitor as anyone I've seen. Rod was smoother, a more natural hitter than Joe. He did not, however, win any Gold Gloves; Morgan won five. The Morgan/Biggio tandem would fit more neatly into a lineup than the Carew/Sandberg entry. Both Morgan and Biggio would hit second. If I were making up a lineup for the Dogs, I would have Ryne Sandberg, my back-up second baseman, hit seventh or eighth because he was more a power hitter than an on-base hitter. He was fast, though, and stole a lot of bases, despite playing more than half of his games on dirt infields. I would probably start Ozzie Smith when Sandberg was playing second base. I would hit Ozzie second, which would compromise the offense slightly. But with Sandberg and Smith in the lineup, the Dogs would have better infield defense than My Team. Smith could bunt and steal. Sandberg would provide the same type of offense as Yount and he was a better base stealer. If Yount and Sandberg were playing at the same time, I would move Bernie Williams and Jim Edmonds up a notch and move the rest of the lineup down one, too.

3. JIM EDMONDS/B. WILLIAMS/CLEMENTE/KALINE. Though Edmonds barely has the ten years necessary to be selected for either of these teams, he has the numbers. He is well behind my three hitter, Barry Bonds, but so is everyone else. Edmonds hits with power, has a good on-base percentage and is a Gold Glove center fielder. He does not, however, steal many bases— more than my backup center fielder Mickey Mantle, but far fewer than Willie Mays. Edmonds's power hitting is even more impressive when you consider that his home ballparks in both Anaheim and St. Louis favor pitchers over power hitters. I was mildly surprised to find that Bernie Williams has better offensive numbers than any of the other candidates for the Dogs at this position. Perhaps I was surprised because he didn't stand

out as much in the Yankees lineup as he would have on another team. It may also be that he prefers not to call attention to himself. He just doesn't get the ink. He is, for example, a better hitter than Reggie Jackson. Williams was also a great center fielder. With Jim and Bernie, the Dogs wouldn't concede any defense at all to My Team. They would, however, fall short of Mays and Mantle with the bat.

4. CLEMENTE/KALINE. It would be hard to know who to start in right field with these two guys. Kaline looks to be slightly better with the bat, but that could be offset by the league he played in. It seemed like the National League was stronger then, just as the American League seems stronger now. Either way, the Dogs have a great right fielder. Both of these guys were perennial Gold Glove winners. I saw Clemente a lot and didn't see Kaline as much, but it is hard to imagine anyone playing right field better than Clemente. Offensively, I think Hank Aaron and Ken Griffey Jr. are significantly better. I may be losing a little defense in the deal but Griffey and Aaron could do a good job in right field. Of course, Clemente and Kaline would drive in a lot of runs, too, particularly out of the clean-up spot. I really didn't intend to have either of these guys hit clean-up because they were not primarily home-run hitters, but they are right-handed hitters. I originally had them hitting sixth, but if I had used them that way, I would have had Carew, Edmonds, McCovey, and Mathews, all left-handed hitters, hitting in a row. That would present a problem against a tough left-handed pitcher. The other advantage of having Clemente and Kaline in front of Mathews and McCovey is that they could run a little faster, which would make it easier to drive them in.

5. EDDIE MATHEWS/CHIPPER JONES. Captain Eddie was hell bent for leather all the time. He didn't have a fire burning in him; he had a blaze. Eddie's run production wasn't quite as good as Mike Schmidt's, but it was a little better than My Team's backup,

George Brett. His fielding was good, but not as good as Brett's. I think I have an advantage in overall baseball skills at third base. Mathews wasn't as athletic as Schmidt or Brett. On the other hand, Chipper Jones is as athletic as any of them. Chipper wasn't a dangerous right-handed hitter when he first came up, but he is now. He still has more power, however, hitting left-handed. He would be a good pinch hitter and could also come in for defense. In fact, he could also play shortstop, left or right field, and probably first and second base. I don't want to think about this too much because I want George Brett on My Team.

Before I studied Chipper's numbers, I thought about complementing Mathews with a right-handed hitter like Brooks Robinson or Ron Santo. Brooks would be better than anyone in the field except perhaps Schmidt. But Santo was pretty good, too, and he was a better power hitter than Brooks. In the end, I couldn't resist Jones's versatility in the field and value as a pinch hitter. I don't think My Team has a big advantage but I'd still take my chances with Schmidt and Brett.

6. WILLIE McCOVEY/FRANK THOMAS. Picking McCovey over Thome at first base was the hardest decision I had to make. Jim Thome has been a more devastating hitter than McCovey, but if the two of them had played contemporaneously, I think they would have been about the same. Neither of them were Gold Glove fielders but both were adequate. McCovey didn't have better hitting stats than Frank Thomas either, but again, he played when it was more difficult to post the big numbers. Stretch also had a much better arm than the Big Hurt. On the other hand, Thomas wouldn't have nearly as tough a time with the great left-handed pitchers as McCovey. But, in the second half of his career, Thomas has had so much trouble throwing that I might have to bring in McCovey for defense, which seems absurd. It is tempting to hit Thomas further up in the lineup because of his great OBA, but he could become a base clogger. If I were managing

the Dogs, I would probably give Chipper Jones more fielding practice at first base and use him for late-inning defense instead of big Stretch. With McCovey and Thomas, the Dogs would not be as good in the field as My Team's first basemen, Jeff Bagwell and Willie Stargell. They would, however, be good enough at the plate to give my pitchers trouble. At first base, I think I have a great combination with Bagwell and Stargell. Over the course of the long season, I would win a few more games with them than the Dogs would with McCovey and Thomas.

7. YOUNT/SANDBERG. If I played Pudge Rodriguez four of every five days, I would hit him eighth because Yount was a more productive hitter. If, however, I started Ozzie Smith, I would hit him second and move the other hitters down one slot. Rodriguez would still hit eighth and on the days when Steve Carlton pitched to Mc-Carver, I would hit Yount seventh and McCarver eighth.

8. I. RODRIGUEZ/MCCARVER. If Sandberg played instead of Carew, Ryne would hit seventh and Pudge or McCarver eighth, and Ozzie Smith would hit second. Actually McCarver was a lot better offensive catcher than many people think. He had midrange power and was fast enough that if the pitcher had to bunt him over to second or third, he wouldn't have to lay down a perfect bunt to do it. Toward the end of his career, he didn't throw very well, but at that time he was only catching Carlton, and the base stealers had trouble getting on base. If they did get on, Carlton might pick them off because he had a really good pickoff move. In his role on the Dogs team, Tim's throwing problem would not be a serious disadvantage. This sounds very complicated but it is not. What it would amount to is several routine lineup changes that everyone on the team would understand in short order.

I have more options with My Team because I have a slightly better lineup and a better bench. Putting Griffey Jr. in right field re-

ally tips the scales. It not only gives me a better left-handed hitting option, but it also denies the Dogs that option. Let's see how
the Dogs and My Team look side by side for the first five games.

GAME 1

1. Willie Mays CF	1. Rickey Henderson LF
2. Joe Morgan 2B	2. Rod Carew 2B
3. Barry Bonds LF	3. Jim Edmonds CF
4. Hank Aaron RF	4. Roberto Clemente RF
5. Alex Rodriguez SS	5. Eddie Mathews 3B
6. Mike Schmidt 3B	6. Willie McCovey 1B
7. Jeff Bagwell 1B	7. Robin Yount SS
8. Johnny Bench C	8. Ivan Rodriguez C
9. Roger Clemens P	9. Pedro Martinez P

Bench Players

RHH	RHH
Mike Piazza	Frank Thomas
Craig Biggio	Ryne Sandberg
Derek Jeter	Al Kaline
Frank Robinson	
LHH	**LHH**
Willie Stargell	Tim McCarver
George Brett	
Ken Griffey Jr.	
SWITCH	**SWITCH**
Mickey Mantle	Chipper Jones
	Ozzie Smith
	Tim Raines
	Bernie Williams

Bullpen

Smoltz	Fingers
Eckersley	Niekro
Rivera	Smith
Hoffman	Wagner

Lineups

Mike Schmidt might have trouble with Pedro Martinez. If so, George Brett would play the next time through the rotation. Because Pedro allows so few hits and walks, I would be aggressive on the bases, stealing and taking the extra base on a hit. I would not hit and run against him because he throws so many pitches that are hard to put into play. If Edmonds had trouble with Clemens, I would try Bernie Williams the next time. Clemens is tough to steal against, but you can be patient at the plate, run his pitch count up, and wear him down.

GAME 2

1. Mantle CF	1. Henderson LF
2. Morgan 2B	2. O. Smith SS
3. Bonds LF	3. Bernie Williams CF
4. Aaron RF	4. Kaline RF
5. Rodriguez SS	5. Thomas 1B
6. Schmidt 3B	6. Sandberg 2B
7. Bagwell 1B	7. Jones 3B
8. Bench C	8. Rodriguez C
9. Johnson P	9. Ryan P

Bench Players

RHH	RHH
Piazza	Yount
Biggio	Clemente
Jeter	
Robinson	
Mays	
LHH	**LHH**
Brett	McCovey
Stargell	Carew
Griffey Jr.	Mathews
	Edmonds
	McCarver
	SWITCH
	Raines

Bullpens are the same.

Everyone but Bench and Johnson would have the green light to run on Ryan. My lineup would feature top OBA hitters for walks. They would try to run the pitch count up. Don't hit and run—same as Martinez. First four Dogs batters plus Sandberg and Jones run on Johnson. Clemente in front of Thomas for speed. Brett would be the first pinch hitter against Ryan, and Yount would be the first pinch hitter against Johnson. Jeter and Biggio would be pinch runners and Raines would pinch-run for Dogs.

GAME 3

1. Mays CF	1. Henderson LF
2. Biggio 2B	2. Carew 2B
3. Rodriguez SS	3. Edmonds CF
4. Aaron RF	4. McCovey 1B
5. Robinson LF	5. Clemente RF
6. Schmidt 3B	6. Mathews 3B
7. Bench C	7. Yount SS
8. Bagwell 1B	8. McCarver C
9. Seaver P	9. Carlton P

Bench Players

RHH	RHH
Jeter	Sandberg
Piazza	Thomas
	Kaline
	Rodriguez

LHH	
Morgan	
Griffey Jr.	
Bonds	
Brett	
Stargell	

SWITCH	SWITCH
Mantle	Williams
	Raines
	Jones
	Smith

Bullpens are the same.

Day off for Bonds. A-Rod moves up with Frank Robinson playing. Flip-flop Bench and Bagwell because of Bench's ability to hit Carlton. (Note: I know Bench hit Carlton well. I have not considered match-up information in formulating these lineups, but would do that before each game. I would play back-up players when they had good success against the Dog's starter, but would leave hot hitters in, even when they normally had trouble with that day's pitcher. Match-up information would be available for hitters and pitchers who were in the same league at the same time. Many players will not have faced the opposing pitcher, in which case, I would have to guess and adjust the lineup as I saw tendencies develop.) Jeter and Morgan would be my pinch runners. I would have plenty of pinch hitters against the Dogs right-handed relievers. If Wagner were pitching for the Dogs, I would use Mantle against him first, and then Piazza. Clemente is hitting in front of Mathews for speed on the bases. McCarver is catching Carlton. Williams and Jones would hit for McCarver and Carlton. At first, beware of Carlton's pick-off move. If he is on his game, start trying to run on McCarver's arm. Same with Seaver. Be mindful of Bench's arm early. If Seaver is sharp, start running mid-game.

GAME 4

1. Mays CF	1. Raines LF
2. Morgan 2B	2. Carew 2B
3. Bonds LF	3. Williams CF
4. Griffey RF	4. McCovey 1B
5. Rodriguez SS	5. Clemente RF
6. Brett 3B	6. Mathews 3B
7. Stargell 1B	7. Yount SS
8. Piazza C	8. Rodriguez C
9. Maddux P	9. Palmer P

Bench Players

RHH	RHH
Biggio	Henderson
Robinson	Sandberg
Aaron	Thomas
Jeter	Kaline
Schmidt	
Bagwell	
Bench	
	LHH
	McCarver
	Edmonds
SWITCH	**SWITCH**
Mantle	Jones
	Smith

Bullpens are the same.

Day off for Aaron unless he pinch-hits against Wagner. Bagwell may come in for defense. Piazza catches Maddux. First three batters steal against Maddux. If Yount has trouble, play Smith the next time, as he could steal against Maddux. Edmonds and Jones would pinch-hit against Palmer and right-handed relievers. Thomas could also pinch-hit against Wagner. Smith and Sandberg would be pinch runners.

GAME 5

1. Mays CF	1. Raines LF
2. Morgan 2B	2. Carew 2B
3. Bonds LF	3. Williams CF
4. Aaron RF	4. Mathews 3B
5. Rodriguez SS	5. McCovey 1B
6. Schmidt 3B	6. Kaline RF
7. Stargell 1B	7. Yount SS
8. Bench C	8. Rodriguez C
9. Gibson P	9. Marichal P

Bench Players

RHH	RHH
Biggio	Henderson
Robinson	Sandberg
Jeter	Thomas
Bagwell	Clemente
Piazza	
LHH	**LHH**
Brett	McCarver
Griffey Jr.	Edmonds
SWITCH	**SWITCH**
Mantle	Jones
	Smith

Bullpens are the same

If Marichal is in a groove, start trying to steal mid-game. Pinch runners are Biggio and Jeter. Robinson would be the first pinch hitter against Wagner. Brett would pinch-hit against right-handed pitchers and start next time around if Schmidt has trouble with Marichal. Dogs would try to step out of the box against Gibson to break his tempo. They would have to watch out for a brushback pitch when they got back in. Jones and Edmonds would be the primary pinch hitters. Henderson and Sandberg would pinch-run and try to steal.

You may have noticed that Robin Yount is playing in all situations, except when facing a nasty right-handed pitcher. Because they would be hitting against right-handers Roger Clemens, Greg Maddux, Tom Seaver, and Bob Gibson, Ozzie would get ample playing time. If Ozzie were playing and hitting second in place of Carew, the Dogs could play Sandberg and hit him seventh to take advantage of his power. Clemente and Kaline are virtually interchangeable. If one had much better numbers against the other team's starting pitcher, he would start. McCarver might start occasionally when Carlton wasn't pitching, especially if Pudge was in a slump or had trouble with

My Team's starter. One advantage the Dogs have in most lineup configurations is that they would have at least one, and sometimes two, players on the bench who could pinch-run and steal a base. They also have more switch hitters.

The versatility of the Dogs is evident in the lineup, on the bench, and in the bullpen. Phil Niekro gives the bullpen a guy who can pitch virtually every day and can start a game as well. Rollie Fingers can pitch long or short. Lee Smith saved more games than any pitcher in the history of the sport. And Billy Wagner throws harder than any pitcher on either team, except Nolan Ryan. And Ryan is a Dog, too!

As far as starting pitchers go, the Dogs are probably equal to My Team. I just couldn't find enough difference among these ten guys to make an irrefutable case for or against any of them. My Team is supposed to be better, so I will say it is, but I will also say that any pitcher on the Dogs can beat a My Team pitcher almost half the time—perhaps four times out of ten. The Dogs can also create a variety of styles that would make it very challenging for me to draw up a lineup card. I hated to leave Sutton off the list because he won more games than most of the guys who are on it. I also agonized over cutting Gaylord Perry because I admire his ornery disposition and his incredible durability.

The pitchers who are on the Dogs roster are not dogs, underdogs, or any other breed of dog. They are Hall of Fame pitchers. This is the way I would line them up: I would come out on opening day with Pedro Martinez, because of his success in the postseason and his overwhelming arsenal. He would go against Clemens on opening day. The second game would pit Nolan Ryan against Randy Johnson. My Team would have to face the same type of stuff in the second game. This matchup would likely produce the most strikeouts. I would follow Nolan with Steve Carlton. With Lefty and Tom Terrific, the strikeout theme would continue. Both of them have pitched nine-inning games with 19 strikeouts. Seaver's ERA was a little lower, but

Carlton could beat him on any given day. Jim Palmer would go against Greg Maddux in Game 4. Palmer's stats are so good that I had him on My Team at first, before finally switching to Bob Gibson. Anyone who could shutout Sandy Koufax in the World Series at the age of 20 has to have what it takes to beat an All-Star team. He made the American League All-Star team six times and won the Cy Young Award three times. His control of the strike zone was excellent; his poise, like still water, ran deep— deep enough to hide his competitive fire. There would be ample poise and competitive fire with Palmer and Maddux on the mound. Finally, I would send Juan Marichal out against Bob Gibson in Game 5. This matchup would feature two of the best all-around athletes ever to have toed the rubber. It would be power against finesse and would provide the most dramatic contrast of styles. Although this is Game 5, it would be every bit as good as any of the other matchups.

As I think about these pitching matchups, I realize that if My Team played a full season against the Dogs, at least half the games would be relatively low scoring, even with all the Hall of Fame hitters in both lineups.

Skippers

One thing that jumps off the pages of the Dogs and lineup chapters is that I seem to be managing against myself. It wouldn't be fair to take the best players and leave the almost-as-good players to another manager. Of course, there would be plenty of good managers who would prefer some of the Dogs to some of the players on My Team. I think My Team is better than the Dogs, but I know there are managers who would take the Dogs and expect to beat me. Because I have chosen the Dogs players, I feel obligated to choose a Dogs manager, too.

There would be no better manager for any team, in the short term, than Billy Martin. In fact, a manager who was even more successful than Martin, Earl Weaver, said that he thought

Billy was the best he had ever seen at taking the assets of a group of players and forming a winning team. If he had speed, he would play little ball; if he had power, he wouldn't run so much. If he had good starting pitchers, as he did in Oakland, he would push them to the limit. Billy almost always won during the first few years of his tenure with various ball clubs, but Billy had a lot of trouble managing his own life. He was so combative that he often came to blows, whether on the field with the other team or in the clubhouse or dugout of his own team, even in a bar. Though he was a brilliant tactician, he had a short life everywhere he went. Billy could improve a team in a hurry, but he was not diplomatic. I am reminded that Branch Rickey once said that Leo Durocher "had the infinite capacity for taking a bad situation and immediately making it worse." When I first transcribed this quote, I mistakenly wrote "infantile capacity." My mistake may have suited Durocher, too, but it most certainly described Martin. His lifetime winning percentage was .553, but he was 1.000 in wearing out his welcome.

I didn't see very many Orioles games when Weaver was managing. I did see some and I did read his book *It's What You Learn After You Know It All That Counts*. I think I have a pretty good fix on him, yet I have seen Bobby Cox in action a lot more. Both of them had good teams throughout their careers and lasted a long time in one city. Bobby has spent 20 of his 24 seasons with the Braves and Earl spent all of his 17 years with the Orioles. Although Earl has a slightly higher winning percentage (.583), he did not face the challenge of adapting his managerial style to different teams in different ways. He almost always had good starting pitchers and a lot of powerful hitters. He kept matchup statistics before they became as readily available as they are now, and, like Cox, he was hell on umpires.

Like Earl, Bobby has had good starting pitchers. And he has had powerful teams, too. But, from year to year, he has, like Martin, had different types of offensive ball clubs. In the beginning of his second tenure in Atlanta, he had great pitching and fielding with only average hitting. Later, he had some great offensive teams. Like Martin, he would play little ball, stealing, hitting and running, and bunting and squeezing when he had to. And when he had more power, he would, like Weaver, wait for two walks and a three-run homer. It has all added up to a career winning percentage of .566 heading into the 2006 season.

Tony La Russa has been flexible, too, but his winning percentage (.537) is much lower than those of Cox and Weaver. Joe Torre has been as good as any of them lately, but he had some inferior teams when he managed the Mets and Braves and only an average team in St. Louis. As a result, his winning percentage is only .534. Whitey Herzog is another manager who should be included among the candidates. The White Rat has a winning percentage of .532 and won championships with both the Royals and Cardinals. He did not do so well, however, in Arlington and Anaheim. Leo Durocher has a .540 winning percentage and won enough championships to make the Hall of Fame, but he is the worst manager I ever played for. He was a good strategist, but his personality, like Martin's, rubbed a lot of people the wrong way, especially his own players. Herzog was popular with his players, the media, the fans, and his own general managers. I could say the same of Jim Leyland. Leyland won three division championships with the low-budget Pirates. And he won the World Series with the 1997 Marlins. He did not, however, have many good teams, and his lifetime winning percentage going into the 2006 season was .486. Tommy Lasorda finished first eight times, and he had a winning percentage of .526.

I hesitate to rank managers based on winning percentage, but the only way to judge them better is physically impossible: Rating the potential their teams in spring training, then watching them all year long. That way, you can rate them on the basis of how much they got from the talent they had and how well they did when they had to adjust for injuries. For instance,

I found Gene Lamont to be a very difficult opponent when he was managing the Pirates. Gene won the A.L. Central twice with the White Sox, but he had lousy teams in Pittsburgh. His winning percentage is only .496, but I know he was a good manager. Casey Stengel was a lot like Joe Torre. Casey was a terrible manager with the Dodgers, Braves, and Mets, but brilliant with the Yankees. The reason is obvious. He had much better players with the Yanks. When you put the good together with the bad, his success rate was only .508.

If I had to pit My Team against the Dogs, I would probably be more challenged to beat a Billy Martin managed team for the first two years. But since this is all hypothetical, I must assume that my players and the Dogs would be forever young and capable of playing many years. This being the case, I would rather face anyone than Bobby Cox. During my five years, we had pretty good luck against the Braves during the season, but they killed us three times in the playoffs—each time with a slightly different cast of characters. I admire the Braves for actively trying to improve on winning teams by making changes each winter, but I also admire Bobby for taking reconstructed lineups and winning the division every year.

If I had to go against Bobby in this hypothetical playoff, I would like my chances because I have a better team. Still, I would not be overly confident. If he had My Team and I had the Dogs, I wouldn't like my chances. As I have said several times, the Dogs could probably beat My Team 40 percent of the time. If I were managing them, and Bobby had My Team, I would expect to win at least 40 percent of the games.

When you look at the lineups chapter and see how little difference changing the batting order makes, you realize how difficult it is to get a strategic advantage over a team with better players and a decent manager. I think I have the best players, given the format of two players at each position with five starting pitchers and four relievers. If you switch to fourteen position players and add two relievers, as most modern managers would, you have a totally different book. I can't say that my format is the best. If a scenario like this actually played out, I might find the need for an extra pitcher or two. I do, however, feel that my starting pitchers (and the Dogs') could average seven innings per start, even against another all-star team. I know the pitchers' ERA would be higher facing all the top hitters, but I doubt they would have an ERA above 4.00. With My Team, I would allow them to keep pitching even if they gave up two or three runs early in the game.

By the way, I had some good teams and no really bad teams in Houston. I ended up with a winning percentage of .556 and I think I could take My Team and beat any of these great skippers.

So now we are back where we began, at the hot stove, on the rotisserie, at a SABR meeting, or simply in front of a computer. The players are all in place and the managers have their lineup cards ready. Gentlemen, you may brandish your SABRs. Let the cutting and slashing begin now.

Acknowledgments

I WOULD LIKE to thank the following baseball men for their insights: Joe Torre, Steve Rogers, Jerry Narron, Jack Billingham, Tony La Russa, Tom Paciorek, Phil Garner, Rick Dempsey, Jack Hiatt, Jim Kaat, Charlie Manuel, Dave Giusti, Don Baylor, Larry Bowa, Jamie Quirk, Ron Santo, Robin Yount, Eddie Kasko, Tony Kubek, Leo Mazzone, Don Zimmer, Mike Cubbage, Roger Clemens, Willie Randolph, Bruce Bochy, and Bill Greif.

In addition, I got some useful feedback from family members, including my wife, Judy; my brother, Rick; my niece, Katie; and her husband, Ben.

I would also like to thank Jim Brady and Kathleen Rizzo for their exhaustive review of the statistics that appear throughout the book and on the website www.SimonSays.com.

Index

Page numbers in *italics* refer to charts.

Aaron, Henry "Hank," 2, 11, 41, 91,
   113, 115, 125, 133, 135, *135,*
   136, 137–41, 142, 199, 219,
   220, 225, 247
   role in My Team lineups of,
      232–33, 236, 250, 251, 252,
      254
Adams, Franklin Pierce, 85
Aguilera, Rick, *186,* 198
Allen, Richie "Dick," 68–69
All-Star teams, 9, 36, 38, 124, 139,
   192, 201, 207, 223, 240, 257
Alomar, Roberto, 50, 63, 64, *65,* 67,
   68–70, 133, 205–7, 208, *208*
Alou, Jesus, 10, *10*
Alou, Matty, 168
American League, 4–5, 36, 92, 96,
   109, 113, 136, 142, 174, 187,
   191, 207, 221, 229, 247, 257,
   260
   Championship Series of, 98
   designated hitter in, 17, 22, 23,
      50, 59, 148
Anderson, Sparky, 97
androstenedione, 44
Aparicio, Luis, 89, 110
Arizona Diamondbacks, 180, 218
Ashburn, Richie, 117–18, 126, 177
Aspromonte, Bob, 123
Astrodome, 50, 59, 67, 90, 119, 120,
   123, 124, 136, 139, 154, 188,
   205, 220, 234, 240
Atlanta Braves, 15, 80, 82, 104–5,
   133, 139–40, 154, 155, 168,
   187–88, 258–59, 260
   see also Milwaukee Braves
Ausmus, Brad, 28–29, 30, 87, 202

Bagwell, Jeff, 43, *44,* 47, 48–49, 50,
   52, 53, 55, 56, 59, 83, 96, 131,
   199, 204, *204,* 205, 225, 237,
   238, 249

   role in My Team lineups of,
      230–31, 234, 236, 250, 251,
      252, 253, 254, 255
Baker, Dusty, 112, 140, 142
Bako, Paul, 29, 39
ballparks, 16–17, 23, 148, 246
   see also specific ballparks
Baltimore Orioles, 16, 23, 58, 65, 66,
   75, 95, 114, 115, 135, 147, 149,
   173, 174, 206, 208, 258
Banks, Ernie, 9, 43, 58, 88, 89–91,
   89, 94, 97, 98, 210, 212, 213,
   214
Bannister, Alan, 207
Baseball Encyclopedia (Palmer and
   Gillette), 14
"Baseball's Sad Lexicon" (Adams), 85
base-stealing statistics, 8–9, 17–18,
   31, 44, 65, 76, 89, 107, 108,
   127, 135
Bateman, John, 177
batting orders, 260
   on My Team, 231–40, 250–56
   theories on creating, 11–12,
      227–31, 240
   on Underdogs, 245–57
Bavasi, Buzzie, 201
Baylor, Don, 65–66, 72, 75–76,
   78–79, 114–15, 172, 173, 174
Beck, Rod, *186,* 198
Belanger, Mark, 95, 174
Bell, Buddy, 74, 75, 211
Bell, Cool Papa, 126–27
Bell, Derek, 237–39
Bell, Jay, 239
Bench, Johnny, 10, 30, *31,* 32, 33,
   34–35, 36, 38, 40, 53, 57, 67,
   163, 170, 199, 202–3, *203,* 224,
   225
   role in My Team lineups of,
      230–31, 234, 235, 236, 250,
      251, 252, 253, 254

265

Berkman, Lance, 103, 104, 105, 131
Berra, Yogi, 27, 30, *31,* 39, 143
Biggio, Craig, 9, 20, 63, 64, *65,*
    67–68, 69, 70, 96, 97, 199, 206,
    207, 208, 225, 237, 238
  role in My Team lineups of, 232,
    236, 246, 250, 251, 252, 254,
    255
Big Red Machine, 10, 12, 32, 38, 69,
    97
  see also Cincinnati Reds
Billingham, Jack, 34, 38, 68
Blanchard, Johnny, 122
Blyleven, Bert, 144, 150
Bochy, Bruce, 194–95
Bogar, Tim, 87
Boggs, Wade, 74, 75, 76, *76,* 209,
    211, *211,* 220
Bonds, Barry, 4, 19, 22, 51, 99,
    102, 104–5, 106–7, *107,*
    111–14, 115, 118, 125, 134,
    139, 141, 142, 199, 201, 216,
    225, 226, 233, 234, 235, 239,
    246
  role in My Team lineups of, 232,
    236, 250, 251, 252, 253, 254
Boston Braves, 260
  see also Atlanta Braves; Milwau-
    kee Braves
Boston Red Sox, 98, 106, 164, 178,
    185, 190
Bowa, Larry, 15, 77, 78
Boyer, Ken, 75
Bresnahan, Roger, 26
Bressler, Rube, 37
Brett, George, 74, 75, 76, *76,* 79–83,
    196, 199, 209, 248
  role in My Team lineups of, 233,
    234, 235, 236, 250, 251, 252,
    253, 255
Brock, Lou, 97, 101–2, 106, 110–11,
    215, 216, 217, 245
Brooklyn Dodgers, 39, 118–19, 260
  see also Los Angeles Dodgers
Broun, Heywood, 128
Brown, Kevin, 166, 180
Bunning, Jim, 150, 235
Burdette, Lew, 139
Burroughs, Jeff, 101, 104–5, 118

California Angels, 66, 155, 156, 201,
    207, 259
Caminiti, Ken, 72, 74, 75
Campanella, Roy, 39–40
Campaneris, Bert, 88, 188
Candaele, Casey, 20, 57, 72, 73
Candelaria, John, 157, 236
Candlestick Park, 113, 123–24, 159,
    222
Carew, Rod, 64, *65,* 67, 69, 206, 207,
    208, *208,* 209, 226
  role in Underdogs lineups of,
    245–46, 247, 249, 250, 251,
    252, 253, 254, 255
Carlton, Steve "Lefty," 4, 23, 38, 40,
    145, 146, *147,* 149, 156, 159,
    176–79, 203, 222, 223, 224,
    225, 226, 236, 252, 253,
    255–57
Carter, Gary "Kid," 30, *31,* 32–34, 40,
    203
Cash, Norm, 157
catchers, 15, 25–40, 86
  arm strength of, 32, 33, 35, 38
  calling of games by, 27–28,
    29–30, 32, 33, 34–35, 36–37,
    172, 202
  equipment of, 26–27
  offensive statistics of, 30–31, *31,*
    203
  old-timers as, 30, 39–40
  pitchers' relationship with, 28–30,
    36–37, 163
  on Underdogs, 202–3
  see also specific players
center fielders, 15, 117–28, 137–38
  as base runners, 119, 126, *127*
  defensive requirements of,
    117–18, 122, 127, 137–38
  offensive statistics of, 125–28,
    127, 217
  old-timers as, 126–27
  range of ground covered by, 118,
    122, 127
  team chemistry and, 122, 124–25,
    217–19
  on Underdogs, 217–19
  see also specific players
Cepeda, Orlando, 43, *44,* 49, 52–53,

Index

55, 58
Chance, Frank, 85
Charleston, Oscar, 127
chemistry, team, 19–20
    center fielders and, 122, 124–25
    first basemen and, 55–59
    left fielders and, 108, 109,
        110–12, 113, 114–15, 217–18
    relief pitchers and, 185, 189, 195
    right fielders and, 133, 142
    second basemen and, 68–69,
        208–9
    shortstops and, 94, 96–97
    starting pitchers and, 162–63,
        173–74
    third basemen and, 79–80, 81, 82
Chicago Cubs, 17, 69, 85, 86, 89–90,
    134, 154, 167, 197, 210, 243
Chicago White Sox, 46, 81, 197, 260
Christenson, Larry, 54–55
Cincinnati Reds, 10, 12, 32, 38, 68,
    69, 97, 102, 114, 121, 142, 170,
    230
Clemens, Roger, 7, 98, 144, 145, 146,
    147, 148, 149, 156, 159, 167,
    171, 173, 174–76, 179, 180,
    181, 182, 190, 192, 199, 218,
    222, 244, 250, 251, 255
Clemente, Roberto, 53, 130, 132,
    133, 135–37, 135, 141, 141,
    142, 219, 220, 220, 221, 226
    role in Underdogs lineups of,
        246, 247, 250, 251, 252, 253,
        255
Cleveland Indians, 106, 206, 208
closing pitchers see relief pitchers
Cobb, Ty, 3, 6, 21, 127
Cochrane, Mickey, 39
Coleman, Vince, 101–2
Collins, Eddie "Cocky," 62, 64
Concepcion, Dave, 10, 88, 95–96
conditioning, of players, 21–22, 140,
    175, 176, 179
Cook, Earnshaw, 228–29, 231, 238
Coors Field, 135
Cox, Bobby, 39, 155, 188, 258–59,
    260
Craig, Roger, 197, 198
Creamer, Robert, 124

Cruz, Jose, 130
Cubbage, Mike, 98, 189
Cy Young Awards, 7, 145, 146, 148,
    149, 155, 156, 157, 168, 173,
    174, 177, 178, 179, 180, 187,
    244, 257

Dark, Alvin, 222
Darwin, Danny, 193
Dawson, Andre, 130, 132–33, 135,
    136, 137, 221
Dean, Dizzy, 5
Dempsey, Rick, 53, 58, 75, 95, 172
designated hitter (DH), 17, 22, 23,
    46, 50, 55, 59, 148, 223
Detroit Tigers, 17, 32, 34, 39, 97,
    157, 164, 197, 213
Dickey, Bill, 39
Dihigo, Martin, 62
DiMaggio, Joe, 17, 121, 122, 126,
    127, 127, 128
Dodger Stadium, 30, 157
Doerr, Bobby, 62, 64
Doran, Bill, 13–14
Driessen, Dan, 10, 12
Drysdale, Don, 160, 176, 235
Durocher, Leo, 138, 167–68, 258, 259

Eckersley, Dennis, 184, 185–87, 186,
    189, 190, 197, 199, 224, 242,
    244, 250
Edmonds, Jim, 126, 217–18, 217,
    219, 226
    role in Underdogs lineups of,
        245, 246, 247, 250, 251, 252,
        254, 255
Edwards, Johnny, 28
Enron Field, 240
Erstad, Darin, 192
ESPN, 36
Eusebio, Tony, 29
Everett, Carl, 20
Evers, Johnny, 85–86

Farrell, Turk, 119
Fenway Park, 106, 109, 115
Fernandez, Tony, 88, 212–13
fielding statistics, evaluating of,
    13–16

Fingers, Rollie, 184, *186,* 188–90,
    197, 224, 225, 226, 250, 256
first basemen, 41–59, 86
    as base runners, *44,* 49
    defensive requirements of, 41–43,
        46–49, 62–63
    lob tosses of, 47–48
    offensive statistics of, *44,* 50–55,
        204, 205
    old-timers as, 43–44
    team chemistry and, 55–59
    on Underdogs, 204–5
    see also specific players
Fisk, Carlton, 6, 30, *31,* 36, 37, 40,
    203
Florida Marlins, 133, 259
Forbes Field, 51, 135
Forsch, Ken, 243
Franco, John, 183–84, *186,* 190, 191,
    192, 195, 224–25, 242
Franks, Herman, 151
Fregosi, Jim, 66
Frisch, Frankie, 62, 64
Fulton County Stadium, 138, 140

Gaetti, Gary, 73
Gaines, Joe, 102–3
Galante, Matt, 196
Galarraga, Andres "Big Cat," 43, *44,*
    46, 47, 48, 49, 53–54, 55
Gamble, Oscar, 157
Garciaparra, Nomar, 88, 212
Garner, Phil, 16, 52, 56–58, 189
Garvey, Steve, 13
Gehrig, Lou, 43–44, *44,* 83
Gehringer, Charlie, 62, 64
Gibson, Bob, 1, 4, 13, 23, 52–53,
    144, 145, *147,* 148, 149,
    160–64, 165, 171, 173, 174,
    176, 178, 179, 181, 182, 199,
    223, 235, 244, 254, 255, 257
Gibson, Josh, 39–40
Gillette, Gary, 14, 228
Giusti, Dave, 57, 219
Glory of Their Times, The (Ritter), 37,
    73
Gold Gloves, 9, 13–14, 36, 47, 49,
    63, 64, 66, 72, 74, 77, 80, 88,
    90, 94, 105, 106, 112, 125, 132,
    136, 140, 142, 164, 207, 213,
    246, 247
Gonzalez, Luis, 20
Gossage, Rich "Goose," 184, *186,*
    193, 196–97, 226
Grace, Mark, 49
Graham, Wayne, 103
Great American Ballpark, 127
Grich, Bobby, 64–66, *65,* 69, 174,
    207
Griffey, Ken, Jr., 3, 125–26, *127,* 128,
    141–42, *141,* 199, 219, 220,
    224, 225, 236, 247
    role in My Team lineups of, 232,
        233, 235, 249–50, 251, 252,
        253, 255
Griffey, Ken, Sr., 10, 12
Grote, Jerry, 163, 170
Guerrero, Pedro, 157
Guerrero, Vladimir, 130
Gutierrez, Ricky, 87
Guzman, Juan, 46
Gwynn, Tony, 132, *135,* 207, 220,
    220, 245

Hagen, Walter, 212
Hardin, Jim, 173
Harrah, Toby, 23
Henderson, Rickey, 4, 8, 101–2,
    105–6, *107,* 108, 110–11, 112,
    201, 215, 216, 217, 226
    role in Underdogs lineups of,
        245, 250, 251, 252, 254, 255
Henke, Tom, *186,* 198, 226
Henrich, Tommy, 215
Hernandez, Keith, 43, *44,* 47, 48, 49,
    54–55, 58–59, 204
Hernandez, Roberto, 81, *186,* 198
Hernandez, Xavier, 113
Herzog, Whitey, 58, 81, 183, 259
Hiatt, Jack, 55, 123, 124–25, 151–52,
    159
Hidalgo, Richard, 102
Hidden Game of Baseball, The
    (Thorn and Palmer), 228–29
Hirschbeck, John, 206
Hoefling, Gus, 176
Hoffman, Trevor, 166, 185, *186,*
    193–95, 196, 199, 242, 250

Index

Hofheinz, Roy, 177
Hooton, Burt, 7, 137
Hornsby, Rogers, 62, *65*
"hot-stove league," 1–2, 5
Houk, Ralph, 119, 121
Houston Astros, 2, 3, 10, 12, 16, 20,
    28–29, 37, 56, 68, 72, 74, 81,
    86, 87, 89, 96, 97, 102, 103–4,
    113, 114, 120–21, 123, 131,
    151, 156, 158, 166, 170, 174,
    175, 177, 180, 191, 193, 195,
    205, 210, 216, 217, 229, 230,
    231, 233, 237, 240, 241, 243,
    261
Hubbard, Glenn, 15
Huggins, Miller, 229
Hunsicker, Gerry, 87, 240–41
Hunter, Catfish, 144, 150, 188

*It's What You Learn After You Know It
    All That Counts* (Weaver), 258

Jackson, Reggie, 137, 157, 174, 188,
    220–21, 247
Jacobs Field, 50
Jansen, Larry, 151
Jenkins, Ferguson "Fergie," 4, 146,
    147, 149, 167–68, 170, 172,
    222
Jeter, Derek, 14, 15, 88, *89,* 91, 92,
    94, 97–99, 199, 212
    role in My Team lineups of, 232,
    234, 236, 250, 251, 252, 253,
    254, 255
John, Tommy, 144, 167
Johnson, Cliff, 37
Johnson, Judy, 71, 127
Johnson, Randy, 144, 145, 146, *147,*
    148, 149, 157, 166, 171, 173,
    176, 179–82, 199, 222, 244,
    251, 252, 256
Johnson, Walter, 155, 159
Jones, Chipper, 74, 75, 76, *76,* 79,
    80, 82–83, 209–11, *211,* 226
    role in Underdogs lineups of,
    247, 248, 249, 250, 251, 252,
    253, 254, 255

Kaat, Jim, 55, 144

Kaline, Al, 130, 132, 133, 135–36,
    135, 141, *141,* 219, 220, *220,*
    221, 226
    role in Underdogs lineups of,
    246, 247, 250, 252, 254, 255
Kansas City Royals, 150, 259
Kasko, Eddie, 109–10
Kent, Jeff, 62, 63, 64, *65,* 69, 206–7,
    208, *208,* 213
Killebrew, Harmon "Killer," 8, 43,
    44, 46, 49, 52, 55, 124
Kingdome, 127
Kison, Bruce, 165
Knowles, Darold, 57
Koufax, Sandy, 4, 5, 22, 124, 159,
    160, 162, 166, 173, 174, 176,
    178, 222, 236, 255
Kubek, Tony, 119, 121–23

Lajoie, Nap "Larry," 62, 64
Lamont, Gene, 260
Larkin, Barry, 88, *89,* 94, 95, 98, 99,
    212, 213, 217
La Russa, Tony, 45, 111, 187, 213,
    217–18, 230, 239, 259
Lasorda, Tommy, 30–31, 259
Lau, Charlie, 80–81
Lazzeri, Tony "Poosh 'em up," 62, 64
Leach, Tommy, 73–74
left fielders, 101–15
    as base runners, *107,* 108, 110–11
    charging of balls by, 101–4, 108,
    109–10
    defensive requirements of, 62–63,
    101–6, 108
    misjudging hit balls by, 102–4
    offensive statistics of, 106–8, *107,*
    216
    old-timers as, 106, 107, 113
    team chemistry and, 108, 109,
    110–12, 113, 114–15
    on Underdogs, 215–17
    see also specific players
Leyland, Jim, 239, 259
lineups, 227–61
    batting orders in, 11–12, 227–40,
    245–57, 260
    managers for, 257–61
    players' roles in, 237–41

lineups *(cont.)*
relieving pitchers' roles in,
240–41, 242, 256
right-handed vs. left-handed hitters in, 241–42
starting rotations in, 243–44,
256–57
lob tosses, 47–48
Lofton, Kenny, 50, 121
Lolich, Mickey, 150, 164
Lopes, Davey, 216
Los Angeles Dodgers, 7, 13, 16, 17,
30–32, 53, 114, 118, 124, 133,
137, 158, 160
see also Brooklyn Dodgers
Los Angeles Times, 114
Lyle, Sparky, 67, 155–56, *156,* 184,
196, 225–26, 242

McCarver, Tim, 30, *31,* 38, 40,
162–63, 176, 177–78, 179, 199,
203, 226
role in Underdogs lineups of,
249, 250, 251, 252, 253, 254,
255–56
McCovey, Willie "Stretch," 2, 43, *44,*
46, 49, 51, 55, 59, 113, 124,
204, *204,* 205, 226
role in Underdogs lineups of,
247, 248–49, 250, 251, 252,
253, 254
McGraw, Tug, 184, 224, 226, 242
McGriff, Fred, 43
McGwire, Mark, 44–45, 134, 239
McKay, Dave, 45
McLain, Denny, 164
Maddux, Greg, 13, 32, 38–39, 40,
144, 145, 146, *147,* 148, 149,
152–55, 159, 171, 173, 176,
179, 181, 182, 199, 203, 235,
236, 244, 253, 254, 255, 257
Magnante, Mike, 191
managers, 257–61
Mansolino, Doug, 81
Mantle, Mickey, 22, 39, 41, 117,
118–23, 124, 125, 126, 127–28,
127, 138, 140, 141, 142, 199,
217, 225, 246
role in My Team lineups of, 231,

232, 235, 236, 245, 250, 251,
252, 253, 254, 255
Manuel, Charlie, 56
Marichal, Juan, 4, 55, 124, 145, 146,
147, 148, 149, 150, 159–60,
173–74, 176, 222–23, 226, 254,
255, 257
Maris, Roger, 16, 121, 123, 134, 221
Martin, Billy, 257–58, 259, 260
Martinez, Edgar, 192
Martinez, Pedro, 1, 23, 98, 144, 145,
146, *147,* 148, 149, 164–67,
171, 173, 174, 181, 221, 223,
226, 250, 251, 252, 256
Matheny, Mike, 202
Mathews, Eddie, 74, 75, 76, *76,*
79–80, 82, 83, 209, 210, 211,
211, 226
role in Underdogs lineups of,
247–48, 250, 251, 252, 253,
254
Mathewson, Christy, 6, 21
Mattingly, Don, 5, 43, *44,* 47, 48, 49
Mays, Willie, 2, 3, 6, 20, 49, 55, 91,
113, 115, 117, 118–19, 122,
123–25, 126, 127–28, *127,* 137,
138, 140, 141, 142, 199, 216,
217, *217,* 222–23, 225, 246
role in My Team lineups of,
231–32, 235, 236, 245, 250,
251, 252, 253, 254
Mazeroski, Bill, 66, 68
Mazzone, Leo, 155, 188
Meluskey, Mitch, 29–30
Mesa, Jose, 198
Metzger, Roger, 86
Millan, Felix, 97
Milner, John, 163
Milwaukee Braves, 80, 122, 138
Milwaukee Brewers, 96, 133, 189
Minnesota Twins, 188, 207
Minute Maid Park, 105, 194
Molitor, Paul, 22
Montreal Expos, 33, 106, 110, 177,
180
Morgan, Joe, 10, 12, 38, 63, 64, *65,*
67–68, 69, 70, 114, 199, 206,
207–8, 225, 233, 246, 251
role in My Team lineups of, 232,

234, 236, 246, 250, 251, 252,
253, 254
Morris, Jack, 188
Murphy, Dale, 217, 221
Murray, Eddie, 43, 44, 46, 49, 53, 58,
174, 204, 205
Murray, Jim, 114
MVP awards, 39, 43, 51, 54, 75, 77,
90, 94, 107, 187, 188, 207, 208,
221, 233
Myers, Randy, 186, 198, 226
My Team, 3–5, 201, 204, 205, 219,
221, 240
batting orders for, 11–12, 231–40,
250–56
criteria for, 5–6, 22, 183–85
defense as important factor on,
12–16, 43, 46, 62, 83, 94,
95–96, 101–2, 114, 132
intangibles and chemistry as consideration for, 17–20, 55–59,
68–69, 76, 79–80, 81–82, 94,
96–97, 98, 108–12, 113,
114–15, 122, 124–25, 126, 133,
142, 162–63, 173–74
left-handed vs. right-handed hitters on, 19, 141–42, 235–36,
241–42
old-timers and, 3, 20–22
platoon strategy in, 16, 49, 59
statistics considered for, 6–19,
22–23
see also specific positions

Narron, Jerry, 35, 92, 142
National Baseball Hall of Fame, 4,
34, 36, 40, 55, 62, 66, 68, 73,
76, 77, 85, 88, 91, 92, 96, 108,
110, 117, 118, 125, 127, 136,
144, 169, 173, 177, 179, 181,
198, 207, 210, 212, 214, 215,
219, 257, 259
National League, 4–5, 7, 22, 29, 33,
54, 73, 75, 86, 88, 90, 107, 113,
136, 138, 142, 145, 174, 191,
192, 206, 221, 223, 226, 247
Championship Series of, 58–59,
188
Negro Leagues, 39, 62, 71, 126–27

Nen, Robb, 186, 198
Nettles, Graig, 74, 75, 211
New York Giants, 26, 86
see also San Francisco Giants
New York Mets, 16, 23, 31, 53,
58–59, 98, 156, 163, 164, 166,
208, 210, 259, 260
New York Yankees, 7, 14, 39, 79, 97,
98, 119, 121, 133, 155, 182,
192, 193, 201, 215, 229, 232,
247, 260
Niekro, Joe, 243
Niekro, Phil, 4, 147, 149, 168–69,
184, 190, 222, 224, 226, 243,
244, 250, 256

Oakland Athletics, 45, 66, 187, 188,
210, 258
offensive statistics, 7–8, 9–12
of catchers, 30–31, 31, 203
of center fielders, 125–28, 127, 217
of first basemen, 44, 50–55, 204,
205
of left fielders, 106–8, 107, 216
of right fielders, 134–36, 135,
138, 141, 220, 220
of second basemen, 64–67, 65,
206–8, 208
of shortstops, 89, 90–91, 93–94,
95–97, 214
of third basemen, 74–79, 76,
80–81, 82, 211
Oliver, Al, 215
Orosco, Jesse, 196, 225–26

Paciorek, Tom, 46
Palmeiro, Rafael, 13, 46
Palmer, Jim, 4, 23, 144, 146–47, 147,
148, 149, 171–74, 178, 223,
226, 253, 254, 257
Palmer, Pete, 14, 228–29, 231, 238
Parker, Wes, 48
Parrish, Lance, 30, 31, 32, 34, 203
Pelekoudas, Chris, 139
Pendleton, Terry, 74, 75
Percentage Baseball (Cook), 228–29
Perry, Gaylord, 4, 55, 146, 147, 148,
149, 150–52, 153, 154, 155,
222, 256

Peters, Gary, 110
Philadelphia Phillies, 23, 56, 77, 117,
    167, 176, 177, 178, 233
Piazza, Mike, 16, 30–31, *31,* 35, 36,
    39, 40, 67, 179, 199, 202, 236
    role in My Team lineups of, 234,
        235, 236, 250, 251, 252, 253,
        254, 255
Piersall, Jimmy, 122
pine-tar game, 79, 80, 196
pitchers *see* relief pitchers; starting
    pitchers
Pittsburgh Pirates, 56, 73, 105, 111,
    136, 168, 197, 239, 259, 260
platoon strategy, 16, 49, 59
Pujols, Albert, 139

Quirk, Jamie, 80, 81–82

Rader, Doug, 74, 75
Raines, Tim, 102, 106, *107,* 110, 215,
    216, *216,* 217, 226
    role in Underdogs lineups of,
        245, 250, 251, 252, 253, 254
Ramirez, Manny, 50, 102, 106, 114,
    134, 216
Ramirez, Rafael, 15
Randolph, Willie, 64, 98, 99, 218–19
Reardon, Jeff, *186,* 198, 226
relief pitchers, 22–23, 115, 155,
    183–99, 250, 261
    criteria for selecting, 183–85
    knuckleballers as, 224
    roles of, 240–41, 242
    statistics on, 6–7, *156,* 185, *186,*
        187, 188, 189, 191, 193, 224,
        225
    team chemistry and, 185, 189,
        195
    on Underdogs, 224–26, 244, 256
    see also specific players
Rettenmund, Merv, 163
Reuschel, Rick, 194, 235
Rice University, 103
Richard, J. R., 157, 158, 243
Rickey, Branch, 20, 126, 258
right fielders, 129–42
    arm strength of, 130–31, 133, 137,
        140

defensive requirements of, 62–63,
    129–33, 137, 140
offensive statistics of, 134–36,
    135, 138, *141,* 220, *220*
old-timers as, 133
team chemistry and, 133, 142
on Underdogs, 219–21
see also specific players
Ripken, Cal, Jr., 88, *89,* 92, 94–95,
    96, 98, 99, 174, 212, 213, 214,
    214
Ritter, Lawrence, 37, 73
Rivera, Mariano, 23, 185, *186,*
    192–93, 195, 196, 197, 242,
    250
Roberts, Robin, 7
Robinson, Brooks, 9, 65, 72, 74, 75,
    76, 78–79, 93, 174, 209, 210,
    211, *211,* 248
Robinson, Frank, 4, 65, 105, 107–8,
    107, 109, 114–15, 134, 141,
    142, 174, 199, 201, 216, 220,
    225
    role in My Team lineups of, 232,
        233, 234, 235–36, 250, 251,
        252, 253, 254, 255
Robinson, Jackie, 21, 39
Rodriguez, Alex "A-Rod," 3, 14, 15,
    88, *89,* 91–92, 93, 94, 95, 97,
    98–99, 199, 211–12, 225, 236
    role in My Team lineups of, 232,
        233, 234, 250, 251, 252, 253,
        254
Rodriguez, Ivan "Pudge," 30, *31,*
    34–35, 38, 40, 202–3, *203,* 226
    role in Underdogs lineups of,
        249, 250, 251, 252, 253, 254,
        256
Rogers, Steve, 33–34
Rookie of the Year Award, 36, 38, 170
Rose, Pete, 2, 9, *9,* 10, 12, 20, 38, 49,
    67, 97, 111, 159, 162
Roseboro, Johnny, 124, 160, 174
Rotisserie League, 1–2, 5, 261
Royal, Darrell, 66
Ruhle, Vern, 243
Ruth, Babe, 15, 16, 39, 62, 91, 95,
    107, 121, 133, 135, *135,* 137,
    138, 140, 229

Index

Ryan, Nolan, 4, 7, 68, 113, 145, 147, *147,* 148, 155–57, *156,* 160, 163, 175, 176, 178, 181, 221–22, 223, 226, 243, 251, 252, 256

sabermetricians, 1, 5, 148
SABR (The Society for American Baseball Research), 1, 18, 261
St. Louis Cardinals, 7, 17, 39, 48, 52, 54, 57, 58, 120, 154, 162, 164, 176, 177, 178, 210, 217, 239, 259
Sandberg, Ryne, 13–14, 62, 64, *65,* 66, 67, 69–70, 206, 208, *208,* 209, 226
   role in Underdogs lineups of, 246, 249, 250, 251, 252, 254, 255
San Diego Padres, 74, 133, 166, 180, 189, 194, 205, 206, 208, 210
San Francisco Giants, 55, 114, 124, 150, 151–52, 174, 222
   see also New York Giants
Santo, Ron, 74, 75, 76, *76,* 90, 110, 167, 209–11, *211,* 248
Schmidt, Mike, 15, 74, 75, *76,* 77–78, 79, 80, 82, 83, 93, 166, 199, 209, 211, 225, 247, 248
   role in My Team lineups of, 233–34, 236, 250, 251, 252, 254, 255
Schoendienst, Red, 122, 164
Scott, Mike, 59
Scott, Tony, 34, 131
Scully, Vin, 137, 161
Seattle Mariners, 95, 125, 142
Seaver, Tom, 4, 6, 23, 144, 145, 146, *147,* 148, 149, 158, 163–64, 169–71, 173, 178, 181, 182, 199, 244, 252, 253, 255, 256–57
second basemen, 42, 61–70
   as base runners, *65,* 67, 69
   defensive requirements of, 61, 62–63, 67–68, 71, 205–6
   offensive statistics of, 64–67, *65,* 206–8, *208*
   old-timers as, 63–64

team chemistry and, 68–69, 208–9
   on Underdogs, 205–9
   see also specific players
Shannon, Mike, 162
Shea Stadium, 23, 166, 170, 238
Sheffield, Gary, 133–34, *135*
Sherry, Norm, 33
shortstops, 15, 85–99, 117
   as base runners, *89,* 91, 93–94
   defensive requirements of, 63, 71, 86, 91–93, 94, 95–96, 213
   in double-play combinations, 85–86, 96
   offensive statistics of, *89,* 90–91, 93–94, 95–97, *214*
   old-timers as, 88–89
   range of, 86, 91
   team chemistry and, 94, 96–97
   on Underdogs, 211–15
Simmons, Curt, 139
Slusarski, Joe, 240
Smith, Lee, *186,* 190–91, 193, 225, 226, 250, 256
Smith, Ozzie, 15, 88, *89,* 92–94, 95–96, 99, 207, 212, 213, 214–15, *214,* 226
   role in Underdogs lineups of, 245, 246, 249, 250, 251, 252, 254, 255
Smith, Red, 22, 117
Smoltz, John, 184, 185, *186,* 187–88, 189, 190, 193, 197, 199, 224, 244, 250
Snider, Duke, 117, 118–19, 125, 126
Snow, J. T., 49
Sosa, Sammy, 22, 91, 133, 134–35
Spahn, Warren, 124, 159, 179, 222–23
Spiers, Bill, 238
Stargell, Willie, 22, 43, *44,* 46, 49, 51–52, 54, 56–58, 59, 67, 113, 199, 204, *204,* 205, 219, 249
   role in My Team lineups of, 234, 235, 236, 250, 251, 252, 253, 254
starting pitchers, 4, 7, 22, 115, 143–82
   as aggressive and mentally tough,

starting pitchers (cont.)
150, 151–52, 153–55, 157, 160, 161, 162, 163–65, 166, 172, 174–75, 176–77, 181
arm angles and release points of, 158–60, 165–66, 171–72, 176, 180
batters hit by, 157, 163–65
catchers' relationship with, 28–30, 36–37, 163
innings per start by, 146, 149, 153, 154–55, 168, 175–76, 181, 221
knuckleballers as, 168–69, 224
old-timers as, 144–46
recent power surge and, 143–45, 148
rotations of, 243–44, 251, 252, 253, 256–57
statistics on, 7, 22–23, 144, 145–49, 147, 156, 159, 160, 164, 166, 168–70, 172–73, 175, 177, 178–79, 180, 181, 222, 223
team chemistry and, 162–63, 173–74
on Underdogs, 221–23, 256–57
see also specific players
statistics, 6–19
base-stealing, 8–9, 18, 108
evaluating fielding, 13–16
margin for error in, 16–17, 23
offensive see offensive statistics
on relief pitchers, 6–7, 156, 185, 186, 187, 188, 189, 191, 193, 224, 225
on starting pitchers, 144, 145–49, 147, 156, 159, 160, 164, 166, 168–70, 171, 172–73, 175, 177, 178–79, 180, 181, 222, 223
Staub, Rusty, 180
Steinbrenner, George, 99
Stengel, Casey, 119, 260
steroids, 44–46, 106–7, 134–35
Sutter, Bruce, 186, 197–98, 226
Sutton, Don, 4, 145, 147, 148, 158–59, 160, 171, 172, 222, 256

Tejada, Miguel, 14, 88, 212
Tekulve, Kent, 57
Tenace, Gene, 210
Texas Rangers, 35, 91, 92, 157, 193, 259
Texas Tech University, 103
third basemen, 71–83
defensive requirements of, 62–63, 71–74
offensive statistics of, 74–79, 76, 80–81, 82, 211
old-timers as, 83
quick reactions of, 71–73, 74
team chemistry and, 79–80, 81, 82
on Underdogs, 209–11
see also specific players
This Ain't Brain Surgery (Dierker), 3
Thomas, Frank, 43, 44, 46, 49, 50, 59, 204, 204, 205, 226
role in Underdogs lineups of, 248–49, 250, 251, 252, 254, 255
Thome, Jim, 43, 44, 46, 49, 50, 56, 204, 205, 248
Thorn, John, 228–29
Three Rivers Stadium, 135
Tiant, Luis, 124, 150
Tiger Stadium, 135
Tinker, Joe, 85–86, 88–89
Torborg, Jeff, 25
Toronto Blue Jays, 46, 206, 208
Torre, Joe, 14, 15, 91, 99, 139, 192, 259, 260
Trammell, Alan, 88, 89, 96, 98, 213–14, 214
Traynor, Pie, 71, 76
Tudor, John, 7

umpires, 28, 29, 56
Underdogs, 4, 48, 70, 99, 128, 167, 182, 190, 196, 198, 199, 201–26, 233, 235, 236
batting orders for, 245–56
intangibles and chemistry as consideration for, 208–9, 216, 217–19
possible managers for, 257–61
statistics and, 6–19
see also specific positions

Index

Van Slyke, Andy, 105, 217, 239
Virdon, Bill, 111–12, 119–20, 237–38
Vizcaino, Jose, 105

Wagner, Al, 73
Wagner, Billy, *186*, 195–96, 226, 240,
    250, 253, 254, 255, 256
Wagner, Honus, 3, 73–74, 77, 88, *89*,
    94, 209, 212
Walker, Larry, 133, 135
Wall, Donne, 154
Weaver, Earl, 16, 65, 78, 149, 172,
    258, 259
Wetteland, John, *186*, 192, 193, 226
Whitaker, Lou, 64, 96
White, Frank, 64, 207
Wilhelm, Hoyt, 184, 190, 224, 243,
    244
Williams, Bernie, 22, 98, 126, 217,
    217, 218–19
    role in Underdogs lineups of,
    245, 246–47, 250, 251, 252,
    253, 254
Williams, Billy, 4, 106, *107*, 108–9,
    110, 112, 215, *216*, 245
Williams, Matt, 50, 74, 75

Williams, Ted, 15, 95, 106, 107, *107*,
    113, 232
Wills, Maury, 97
Winfield, Dave, 130, 132, 133, *135*,
    136, 137, 215, 221
World Series, 39, 56, 74, 121, 137,
    164, 173, 188, 192, 218, 257,
    259
Worrell, Todd, 198
Wrigley Field, 17, 90, 109, 110, 167
Wynn, Jimmy, 125

Yankee Stadium, 16–17, 39, 44, 78,
    126, 128
Yastrzemski, Carl, 106, *107*, 108,
    109–10, 113, 215, 216, *216*,
    245
Yount, Robin, 5, 9, 88, *89*, 94, 95,
    96–97, 98, 99, 189, 212, 213,
    214, *214*, 215, 226
    role in Underdogs lineups of,
    246, 249, 250, 251, 252, 253,
    254, 255

Zimmer, Don, 185